A Thousand Ways to Die

My family, in better times, in a portrait that loomed large in my childhood. From left to right (top row): Curtis Worthington, Cossette Worthington, Clifford Worthington, Elisabeth Brown, and Gary Worthington; (bottom row): Horace Worthington Jr., Wanda Taylor, Ida Mae Worthington-Dyitt, Horace Worthington Sr., and Patricia Hollimon. *(Courtesy of Lee Family)*

A Thousand Ways to Die

THE TRUE COST OF
VIOLENCE ON BLACK
LIFE IN AMERICA

TRYMAINE LEE

ST. MARTIN'S
PRESS

First published in the United States by St. Martin's Press, an imprint of St. Martin's Publishing Group

EU Representative: Macmillan Publishers Ireland Ltd, 1st Floor, The Liffey Trust Centre, 117–126 Sheriff Street Upper, Dublin 1, DO1 YC43

A THOUSAND WAYS TO DIE. Copyright © 2025 by Trymaine Lee. All rights reserved. Printed in the United States of America. For information, address St. Martin's Publishing Group, 120 Broadway, New York, NY 10271.

www.stmartins.com

The Library of Congress Cataloging-in-Publication Data is available upon request.

ISBN 978-1-250-09801-6 (hardcover)
ISBN 978-1-250-09802-3 (ebook)

The publisher of this book does not authorize the use or reproduction of any part of this book in any manner for the purpose of training artificial intelligence technologies or systems. The publisher of this book expressly reserves this book from the Text and Data Mining exception in accordance with Article 4(3) of the European Union Digital Single Market Directive 2019/790.

Our books may be purchased in bulk for specialty retail/wholesale, literacy, corporate/premium, educational, and subscription box use. Please contact MacmillanSpecialMarkets@macmillan.com.

First Edition: 2025

10 9 8 7 6 5 4 3 2

*To those we've loved and lost,
my grandfather Horace Worthington,
my great-uncles Cornelius and MacClinton Woods,
and to my grandmother Ida Mae Worthington-Dyitt,
whose faith was beyond measure*

Contents

	Introduction: Blood Clots and Bullets	1
1.	Cornelius	11
2.	Our American Life (and Death)	45
3.	Catharsis	66
4.	(G)un-Civil Rights	99
5.	Trouble Man	128
6.	The Way of the Gun	152
7.	Gigglebox	180
8.	"Let the Water Heal Our People"	215
	Postscript: A Thousand Ways to Die	234
	Epilogue	243
	Acknowledgments	*253*

How long, LORD, must I call for help,
but you do not listen?
Or cry out to you, "Violence!"
but you do not save?
Why do you make me look at injustice?
Why do you tolerate wrongdoing?
Destruction and violence are before me;
there is strife, and conflict abounds.
Therefore the law is paralyzed,
and justice never prevails.
The wicked hem in the righteous,
so that justice is perverted.
—**Habakkuk 1:2–4**

This is the story of a gun, so it can't be a happy one. If time were taken someday by someone to trace the life history of a gun, he would reveal a story of tragedy, terror, grief and, more than likely, crime.
—*The Chicago Defender*, **December 16, 1950**

In America, it is traditional to destroy the Black body—it is heritage.
—**Ta-Nehisi Coates**

A Thousand Ways to Die

Introduction

BLOOD CLOTS AND BULLETS

Being Black in America offers inexhaustible ways to die. I almost met my death one night in the summer of 2017 when I was awakened by a crushing pressure in my chest. It felt like someone had jammed a beach ball inside of me, pumped it to the verge of exploding, and then pumped it some more. I was nauseated, dizzy, and washed in cold sweat.

I looked up and found my wife standing in the doorway of our bedroom, her eyes filled with fear and wider than I'd ever seen them. This startled me because she has the kind of smallish-almond eyes that narrow to quarter slots when she laughs. She's most beautiful when she's like that, so filled with joy that her eyes nearly get lost in her face. Yet what I saw staring back at me were doughy white orbs wet with worry. I had a sinking feeling that at any moment our then five-year-old daughter would be roused from bed by all the commotion and materialize on her mother's hip with the very same doughy-eyed look. But she was sound asleep, comfortably twisted like origami in her favorite Doc McStuffins sheets. For just a moment, I felt at peace. Baby girl wouldn't have to see me like this. Her Superman dad rocked to his knees by some sort of kryptonite.

What was crushing down on me that night was death. At the age of thirty-eight, I suffered the type of heart attack that kills its victims so often that it has its own ominous nickname: the widow-maker. A blood clot lodged in one of my heart's major coronary arteries was starving my heart of life-sustaining blood and oxygen. With each minute, the clot grew larger, and death's grip grew tighter. Prior to that night, I hadn't thought much about how the human heart worked, but now I can picture the long snaking line down the left side of the model heart I'd stared at in high school biology class—my tortured artery—all jammed up. Statistically, nearly half of all heart attack deaths come within the first hour. I barely survived the night. The paramedics, who arrived twenty minutes after that ball nearly blew through my chest, took my blood pressure, asked a few questions, and then said I seemed okay, but they would take me to the hospital if I wanted. I chose not to go.

My wife was scheduled to go on an out-of-town work trip that next morning, and my little Nola was starting camp later that day. I figured I'd tough it out until my family was taken care of. That decision almost cost me everything. I tossed and turned through the night, unknowingly inching toward my end. My wife canceled her trip, and we dropped Nola off at camp. I hobbled doubled over into an urgent care center, and they pointed to the door and told me to get to an emergency room immediately. The cardiologist who later helped save my life by inserting two stents to clear the clot said that if I hadn't gotten to the hospital when I did, I likely wouldn't have lived.

None of this made sense to me. I'm a former high school and college athlete. I don't smoke or have high cholesterol, high blood pressure, diabetes, or a family history of heart disease or early death. Yearly checkups with my doctor never included any mention of heart disease. Yet there I was, fighting for my life.

I'm one of the lucky ones. I survived. But survival was just the beginning. For a long time after my heart attack, there wasn't a single hour of the day when I didn't fixate on my own death. Death was there in the morning when I woke up, alongside me when I dropped my daughter off at school, peering over my shoulder as I told my wife to have a good day at work. It was there during my workday, at home or on the road, a constant presence. And almost always, without fail, before I closed my eyes at night, I wondered if that would be the night that I finally closed them for good. I was losing sleep thinking about all the class trips and science experiments that I'd miss. The family vacations that would never be booked. The weddings and anniversaries that would go uncelebrated. Thoughts of all the beautiful, mundane, familiar things that make life so sweet had turned sour in my ominous fortune-telling. I ached at the idea of my wife, Gabrielle, becoming a widow and my little Nola growing up without her father.

Although I have been physically healthy most of my life, my heart and spirit have taken on tremendous psychic burdens. I've spent more than twenty years as a journalist reporting on stories that led me to people who had just missed death, or others who were withering from the weight of someone else's. I've chronicled the tragedy of lives taken too soon, most often with guns. I have traced the path of bullets ricocheting from person to person, wreaking physical and emotional havoc long after victims are laid to rest or their scars keloid over.

Upon reflection, I probably came to this work because of the intergenerational suffering guns have rendered in my own family. A century ago, a Deep South murder catapulted my ancestors into the waves of the Great Migration, and decade by decade in the North, gun violence would threaten to drown us. Generations of loss would affect us in different ways, the trauma yanking us back and pushing us forward in a dizzying time warp.

So it's preternatural that I've made a career as a griot of sorts, telling the tales of Black death and survival. In that way, I'm bilingual, translating the pain of others into something palatable, something that might stick in the guts of anyone willing to listen. But evidently these stories have stuck with me, too, achingly knotted into the threads holding my heart together.

A blood clot and a bullet are very different things. But both have the ability to take and twist a life. The trauma of my own near-death experience puts questions of death and survival into stark relief. As I healed physically and emotionally, these questions took on a new sense of urgency. Not only in trying to understand the big picture of human mortality, fragility, and finding meaning in survival but more personally as a husband, father, son, and brother. As a man. As a Black man.

My precious Nola is in middle school now. A self-assured big girl who has long since shed her Doc McStuffins blanket. But I still can't shake those post–almost dying days when my little girl was still little and grew more curious by the day. In those early days, Nola's bath time routine became peppered with questions. Why are we here? Why did God make us? What happens when we die? I tried to satisfy her flowering mind the best that I could. I told her that we're here to do good, that I have no idea why God made us, and that some people believe that when you die, your spirit leaves your body and goes to heaven or hell depending on how good you were. "What do you believe, Daddy?" she asked. I struggled to give her a good answer.

For a long time when she asked me about what happened to my heart, I tried to explain that a clot got stuck in my artery the way a drain gets clogged with gunk, and not enough blood was getting through.

"But why did it happen?" she asked.

"It just happened," I told her. "Some plaque broke off, and

the clot filled its place." Her face scrunched up. She sensed there was more to it than that. And so did I.

She's asked many of the same tough-to-answer questions with news of the latest police killing of an unarmed Black person, the umpteenth mass shooting, or the garden-variety murders that fill the daily news. I struggle to answer why things are the way that they are, especially when it comes to Black folks like us. I haven't found adequate words to explain to my daughter how death falls uniquely on us, let alone how death nearly fell on me. But I do believe the two are inseparable.

Throughout our history, the gun has been a cudgel, beating us back into place if we dare to ever live too fully or too freely. Few, including me, have escaped its reach.

The gun was used to capture the first enslaved Africans, dragged from home with flintlock rifles at their backs, and then lifted to their faces like flagpoles for a bloody greeting in the hell of the Atlantic World. It was the weapon of choice for white slave patrols, the predecessors to the modern American police, who stood between Black folks and freedom. During the Civil War, guns left a bloody trail that led finally to emancipation. Through Reconstruction, guns in Black hands fended off armed and masked Klansmen, and helped Black people build nascent political power and the infrastructure of citizenship. By the close of Reconstruction, guns in white hands ushered in a century of political violence, so-called Redemption, pushing the formerly enslaved as far back into slavery as possible, through widespread lynching, mass shootings, and the social and legislative violence of Jim Crow. Thousands of Black families fled the South during the Great Migration, an exodus toward the promised land of the North, where they believed they'd find good jobs, less hate, and something like solace. In the North, they found crowded slums and a kind of "up South" racism that felt eerily similar to down South racism; here were more armed and angry white men, just with different accents. Those who remained in the South during the brutal fight for Civil Rights saw leaders and laypeople assassinated by white supremacists with long-range rifles, beaten by the butts of shotguns during marches, or shot with pistols at close range.

In the Black Power years, colored folks became BLACK and lifted fists and firearms, shedding the politics of respectable "good" Negroes, and then felt the full militaristic heft of state surveillance and violence; through the eras of trickle-down economics (that never trickled down), mass incarceration, and crack when the government helped send South American cocaine and American guns into Black slums, where illegal Black gangs and legal police gangs waged a bloody war that left Black America trapped in a vicious cycle of sanctioned and unsanctioned violence and incarceration, pushing this country to record highs in gun homicides; to today, with everyday gun violence, suicides, police-involved shootings, mass shootings at churches and schools and supermarkets and birthday parties, and shootings for knocking on the wrong door or turning into the wrong driveway. Yet the gun industry continues to manufacture millions of new guns a year, and conservative right-wing lawmakers continue to pledge allegiance to guns and not to their constituents who are being slaughtered with them.

Gun violence is an American problem, not just a Black American problem. But Black people are thirteen times more likely to be shot and killed by police and seven times more likely to be shot dead by another civilian with a gun. Even eight years of the first Black president in the late aughts couldn't spare us the deep and public welts. Barack Obama's hometown of Chicago became the poster child for the scourge of urban gun violence in America. But not just in the most obvious ways the progun advocates have spun so gleefully. Deeply segregated Chicago, fed by a pipeline of guns from faraway states and nearby counties where guns are plentiful and easy to get, with an entrenched gang culture and consistently corrupt police force, reveals the many ways in which structural violence begets gun violence.

Black people in America have always had to contend with these lines of demarcation, reinforced and maintained by white men, and those deputized by them—with guns. That notion was made plain with the killing of Trayvon Martin in 2012 in Sanford, Florida. Armed with a can of AriZona iced tea and a bag of Skittles, he was shot down in his father's suburban apartment complex by a white-identified Hispanic man patrolling for people he thought didn't belong there. Trayvon fit the bill, criminalized because of his hoodie and brown skin. Trayvon's killing was a callback to the earliest days of Black struggle and freedom, a reminder of the unfinished business of Reconstruction. Our freedom has always been fleeting, fragile. Its limits are sketched out by lines we can barely see, and boundaries we cross at our peril. Sometimes I wonder if we're free at all.

The policing of Black bodies with guns is as old as America itself. Congress passed its first Fugitive Slave Act in 1793, which George Washington signed into law. A second was passed in 1850 as part of a compromise to keep the union together. The 1850 version mandated that the federal government actively help slave catchers track and apprehend people who'd escaped slavery. The act coerced everyone to take part in the policing of Black bodies; bystanders were threatened with fines and imprisonment if they didn't help catch runaways. Armed with the new law and guns, white kidnappers had carte blanche to snatch and enslave free Black people, too. This deep investment incentivized the larger white population, and segments of the Black population, to play an active role in policing Black people.

This racial vigilantism is deeply American. For all the hope of change promised during the Obama years, what would come next would be anything but hopeful. The shooting death of a seemingly endless list of unarmed Black people by police or vigilantes, protests and rebellions in their names, then the often-violent whitelash that followed, thrust this country into new territory when it comes to guns and political violence. Of the more lasting impacts would be the election of Donald Trump to the presidency and a surge of unabashed racial hate, violence, and animus. Trump fortified the federal bench and its highest court, the Supreme Court, with conservative justices with a barely veiled agenda that included reversing gains on gun control.

When Nola asked if I almost died from my heart attack, I hesitantly said yes. I made a promise to her when she was still in the womb that I'd always tell her the truth. My answer, that the heart attack almost killed me, left her silent for a long moment. "But how?" she asked. "How did you almost die?"

I wanted to tell her that for far too long, I'd taken all that I'd seen as a reporter and all the terrible things that came before me, before us, and buried it down deep until the weight became so great that my heart simply couldn't bear it. That it all began long before that day, with a really, really bad thing that happened to our family back down South. And in so many ways, long before that. But I'm still trying to figure out how much truth a little girl needs.

When my heart attack happened, I was writing a book on the many costs of gun violence. For years, I sat soul-deep in people's suffering. I traveled across the country talking with survivors of gun violence, trauma surgeons, therapists, activists, cops, and frontline workers in the trenches of the fight to save lives. I was searching for the untenable costs of gun violence in actual dollars, lost lives, and stolen dreams.

Yet I had little idea just how costly this work would be. The chapters of this book almost became the final chapters of my life—this book almost killed me. Just weeks after turning in an early rough draft, that blood clot near my heart stopped me cold in my tracks. For my whole career, I'd been witness to other people's pain while ignoring my own. At times, it felt as if I were single-handedly bearing the weight of every injustice, every police killing, every mother's or father's unbearable broken heart. I'd hide bits and pieces of that stuff wherever I could. But the residue would find its way into my sleepless nights.

I spent countless days on the road in a high-pressure journalism career that I loved, a career that I'd built from the ground up on pure hustle, passion, and compassion, but with no real guidance on how to manage the stuff I couldn't put words to. I found myself in a cycle of stress and insomnia, and sometimes I'd try to wash away both with long nights and liquor.

During my recovery from my heart attack, a certain kind of clarity set in. I almost died. But I didn't. While I can't change what happened yesterday, I still have today—or at least this moment—to live. Survival offered me a new vision on life, a second chance. No more burying the hardest, darkest parts. It was time to dig it all up, to lay it flat and handle it. Not just what I witnessed and chronicled as a journalist but the unseen forces and circumstances that shaped who I came to be. My heart attack offered a new perspective on all the life and death that I'd seen before it and all that I'd experience after. I was drawn even closer to the realities of what survivors face and what's truly lost in early death. What's lost in Black death.

This is why I wrote this book. To lay bare the cycle of American gun violence, the historic interplay of Black life and death and guns, as well as the avalanche of debt it creates. How the lives caught in its grind are forever changed. But I also sought to explore the other forms of violence that eat us up, the emotional, seeming birthright violence that comes with being Black in America. And what preserving Black joy and Black resistance looks and feels like. What freedom might mean for a people who have never truly been free.

The tally of American violence is deeply disturbing, or it should be, were it not such a routine part of everyday life. And anti-Black racism and violence are even more entrenched, potent enough to erode the most strident of American dreams. My own family hasn't been spared in any of this. Our American dreams are as stripped and weathered as any other Black family's.

Until now, there has always been an implicit and unspoken rule in my family. We never talk about family business outside of the family. We buried the killings deep, yet the truth was always there, gnawing at us, moving in ways that we couldn't fully understand.

I've decided that this rule will end with me. I'll have to explain our history to Nola. That Black boys and girls her age are sometimes snatched away in ways her white friends typically are not. I'll tell her how our family fled north. I'll tell her that in spite of the painful ripples caused by so much death, we've been gifted with lives meant to be lived. That our stories are still being written, one chapter at a time. This is who we were and who we are. And that it's up to her to help guide us to who we will become. We have the power and responsibility to thread our own narratives. This is her story as much as it is mine.

1

Cornelius

Ida Mae was the baby of the family then, born in Dodge County, Georgia, a chocolate wisp of a thing with fingers and toes long and skinny like wire grass. Her father, William, was a serious man, an illiterate tenant farmer who grew corn and cotton. The enslaved were prohibited by law from learning to read and write, keeping their hands calloused and occupied with labor and not books. Enslavers believed that uneducated Black people were less likely to rebel. Slavery was over by the time William was born in 1873, but the illiteracy rate for African Americans was still nearly 79 percent. Despite the limitations of the world around him, William valued family over everything. He and his wife, Bessie, had four children: Ida Mae; Rose, age three; Cornelius, twelve; and Willie, the eldest at fourteen.

It was a couple of days after Christmas, settlement time, the annual tally of debts and balances owed to white landlords by poor Black farmers like William who dredged a meager living off land they'd never own. Everyone in the family was expected to carry their weight around the house and with the farmwork, especially leading up to settlement. That included Cornelius, who that day was sent off on horseback to run errands. It was the last time anyone in the family would see him alive.

Later that night, word got back that he'd been shot dead. William had an idea who'd done it, some white men who'd threatened the family over some petty grievance, but there was little they could do. There wasn't a lawman anywhere east of

The death certificate for Cornelius Woods, my great-uncle, who was twelve when he was shot and killed in a sundown town in Georgia.

the Ocmulgee River—or west, for that matter—who would've wasted a bead of sweat on a dead Black boy. That's not the way the law worked in Jim Crow land.

It was 1923 and not uncommon for Black life to be snatched at the end of a noose or a bullet. Even his death certificate was striking in its mundanity. *Age: 12. Cause of death: gunshot wound.* The killing may have ripped a hole in the family, but the stretch of south-central Georgia where they lived was known for lawlessness, against Blacks mostly but sometimes among its whites, too. Countless broken Black bodies were buried all over the county, from the farmlands to the woodlands, in shallow graves and old slave cemeteries, some never to be found at all.

They belonged to dead men like Eli Cooper, who was lynched in 1919, Samuel Bland and William Steward, who met the same fate in 1915, Frank Mack in 1911, John King in 1909, Henry White in 1908, Jesse Williams in 1892, and Jesse Polk in 1890, all murdered either by organized or spontaneous acts of racial terror. Lynchings were often public spectacles, family events that would draw massive crowds. The Bland and Steward killings drew an audience of "several hundred persons, including a number of women, [who] had visited during the day the spot where they hung to a tree," read an Associated Press report beneath the headline NO INVESTIGATION OF LYNCHING OF NEGROES.

In another violent episode in Dodge County in 1918, a white plantation overseer demanded that a Black man who lived and worked on the farm with his wife and children help remove some fencing from the property. The Black man refused and went into town to object to the plantation's owner, the president of a local bank. The owner wasn't at his office. And when the Black man returned to his cabin, he found his wife dead, half her body blistered with shotgun pellets. In the backyard, he found his seventeen-year-old son "shot into shreds with buckshot." The man's nine other small children witnessed the killings. Soon after, a mob of white men in cars grabbed the Black man and dragged him to the local jail to "protect" him. The next day, a friend bailed him out of jail so that he could attend the double funeral for his wife and son. After the burial, the sheriff ordered the Black man to return to the plantation to work, "under strict orders that he would be held with his life as a pawn for the future safety" of the white man who murdered his family. The white overseer was never questioned or charged.

The town of Fitzgerald, where Cornelius was killed, in neighboring Ben Hill County, was a bona fide sundown town, a place where Black folks were warned to be gone by sunset. Or else.

Fitzgerald was established in 1896, and its earliest residents were a mix of former Union and Confederate soldiers who'd come together in equanimity in the postwar decades. They held joint memorial parades, named their streets after both Union and Confederate heroes, and rallied around another shared principle: white supremacy. A *Washington Post* article published the year of the town's founding detailed a meeting attended by three hundred white men who unanimously passed a resolution to ban Black people from the Colony of Fitzgerald. Ahead of the meeting, townsmen posted notices adorned with skulls and crossbones that read: "Laborers—There will be a meeting of the laboring class and mechanics of the city of Fitzgerald tonight at 7:30 o'clock in the Fitzgerald block for the purpose of excluding all colored labor from the colony. If this is to be a white man's colony, let's have it white; if not, let the niggers have it.—By order of the committee." In another report, a correspondent with the *Wilmington Star* was wowed by how efficiently the white folks of Fitzgerald "had taken the bull by the horns and settled the negro question by excluding them from the town and town affairs." He marveled that "there are but three or four negro voters within the town limits . . . There is probably no town in the South that can compare with this place for good order and sobriety. An arrest for any cause is the greatest rarity and a lady without escort may walk the streets at night in perfect safety"—as if the only threat to white women was Black men. These proclamations of white purity weren't rhetorical. They were punctuated by violence and bloodshed.

As I pored over decades of newspaper articles and other accounts from that swath of Georgia counties, littered with brutal violence, one particularly galling case from the summer of 1903 stood out. A headline from *The New York Times* lamented, LYNCHED THE WRONG NEGRO—MAN GEORGIA MOB THOUGHT THEY HAD KILLED STILL LIVES.

Some days ago a negro was shot to pieces by a mob in Dodge County for attacking Miss Susie Johnson, a young teacher. It now develops that the negro who was lynched never saw Miss Johnson, and was, therefore, innocent of the crime. The members of the mob thought they were lynching Ed Claus, the real assailant of Miss Johnson, and it is said that the young woman identified the lynched negro as her assailant. The negro told the mob that he was innocent, and begged for time to secure witnesses to his statement, but the mob was merciless and shot him to death. The lynching occurred after the supposed criminal had been chased across seven counties. After the lynching an investigation was begun by officers with the result that they have located Ed Claus, and a posse passed through here this afternoon to arrest him. Gov. Terrell has taken cognizance of the fact that the wrong negro was lynched by offering a reward of $300 for the apprehension of Ed Claus.

Reading these accounts, I recall Ahmaud Arbery jogging through a white neighborhood in Georgia, and the whip of violence that lashed at him.

Soon after Cornelius's death, the Woodses fled Georgia. They were not alone.

Black folks like my family began leaving the South en masse around 1915, often with violence biting at their heels. They headed to cities in the industrial and urban North mostly, in search of safety and security that was in short supply in the hostile, rural South. Between 1915 and the mid-1970s, about six million Southern Black people would make a similar journey in what historians call the Great Migration. For six decades, African Americans left in droves for Chicago, Detroit, Philadelphia, and St. Louis. They escaped the backwoods of Louisiana and the Carolinas for Los Angeles and smaller cities like Baltimore, Maryland, and Syracuse, New York. Before the migration, nine out of ten Black Americans lived in the South, mostly in rural areas, with Georgia, Mississippi, and Alabama having the largest Black populations in the United States. By the 1970s, the Black population had shifted dramatically, with the majority of Blacks then living in California, Illinois, and New York.

What they were running *from* was just as important as what they were running *toward*. Even during the hopeful post–Civil War period known as Reconstruction, some 2,000 Black Southerners were lynched. By the early 1930s, the number of Black lynching victims across the country had risen to nearly 4,000. The states with the highest out-migration around the turn of the century were those that experienced the most racial violence and lynching, including Georgia, whose brutal treatment of Blacks rivaled that of notoriously vicious Mississippi and South Carolina. Between 1920 and 1930, 260,000 African Americans left Georgia, more than Alabama and Mississippi combined.

"In some counties the Negro is being driven out as though he were a wild beast. In others he is being held as a slave. In others, no Negroes remain," Georgia governor Hugh M. Dorsey said in a 1921 address in Atlanta on "The Negro in Georgia," which outlined the vast extent of peonage, acts of individual cruelty and lynching that white people were heaping onto Black people in his state. The violence had become a social and legal crisis.

Dorsey recalled more than one hundred examples of recent white violence aimed at Black people in counties across the state. In one case, a Black man sentenced to thirty days in the Fulton County chain gang for vagrancy was bonded out by a local farmer's son for five dollars. He was taken back to the family's farm with ten other Black men, where they were overseen by armed guards by day and locked up at night. The men endured months of forced labor. When he and another man tried to escape, they were caught, whipped, and sent back to work. One begged for death, and the white owner obliged, shooting him. The farmer then tied a weight to his body and dumped it in a pond.

"To me it seems that we stand indicted as a people before the world," Dorsey said. "If the conditions indicated by these charges should continue, both God and man would justly condemn Georgia."

Governor Dorsey's condemnation of racial violence was a striking stance for a Southern Democrat of that era, when the party was still staunchly segregationist. But Georgia was at a crossroads. The surging exodus of Black labor was creating an economic crisis, and national attention on Southern racial horrors deterred Northern investment. Dorsey's past may have also shaped his evolving views. In 1913, as a prosecuting attorney, Dorsey secured the conviction of Leo Frank, a Jewish factory superintendent accused of murdering thirteen-year-old factory worker Mary Phagan. Dorsey's popularity soared. But when Frank's death sentence was commuted to life in prison, a mob dragged him out of prison and lynched him in Mary Phagan's hometown. This was the Woodses' America, their Georgia, where my family line on both sides stretched down through slavery and into neighboring counties, including Irwin County, where Cornelius was born and where just forty-five years earlier Confederate president Jefferson Davis was captured by Union troops. On the day they fled, Bessie drew her babies, Ida Mae and Rose, close and hastily prepared them for the journey north. Grabbing what they could of their belongings, the Woodses followed a path similar to those taken by enslaved people who, under the cloak of night, followed the stars north in search of freedom.

In the coming years, the Woods family would find little solace in the so-called promised land of the North, with its de facto segregation, crowded conditions, and more sophisticated forms of second-class citizenship. They'd work hard to make a way where there was none, building community with folks just like them, who fled the only home most of them had ever known.

My grandmother Ida Mae Woods was a year old when her older brother was killed. Recollections of his death have been handed down, drawn out piecemeal as my family put more distance between them and what happened in that forsaken little town in Ben Hill County, Georgia. The family eventually settled in southern New Jersey, not far from Philadelphia. They hoped that fleeing the racial violence of the Jim Crow South would spare their descendants a similar fate. But murder, police killings, and violent feuds would chase them every step of the way.

The Guns-for-Slaves Cycle

Theirs was a violent birth, as a new people in a new nation through kidnapping, war, and bondage. And in the centuries since their shackled feet first touched the Western World, the shadow of violence has clung to their lineage. The gun has been central to that violence. If you trace the history, you'll find an uncleavable relationship between the trade of humans and the trade of guns, a devil's deal that has haunted us from the so-called Slave Coast of West Africa into the bowels of the white man's slave ships. For centuries, the curse held, reaching across the Atlantic Ocean and into labor camps in the Caribbean and the Americas, sinking generations of Black people in an abyss of physical and spiritual bondage. Though guns have also served as defense from those bent on our breaking, mostly, they've been used to destroy us.

The transatlantic slave trade was not only fueled by the economic exploitation of slave labor but by the trade in guns. In fact, the two are inextricably linked. Even before the first enslaved Africans were dragged into the hell of the Atlantic World, guns had sealed their fate. Tens of millions of Africans were snatched from their homelands, their labor used to colonize the West. And there's little doubt that the psychic residue of what our ancestors suffered, by way of the gun, continues to stain us today.

The guns-for-slaves cycle, a pact between European and Euro-American slavers and their coconspiring African chiefs and rulers, might be the most important and yet overlooked aspect of the transatlantic slave trade, from which much of America's massive economy and wealth was built. Advancements in firearm efficiency, quality, and production made the gun the most significant technological innovation introduced to West Africa by white colonizers. In the hands of West African enslavers, guns helped to rapidly expand the trade, making firearms a critical commodity in building white Western power.

The mass importation of guns for captives changed the way war was conducted in Africa and shifted the regional balance of power, creating what economist Warren Whatley describes as "a vicious cycle, a raid or be raided arms race." Guns not only offered devastating firepower and incentivized intra-African wars and raids, but they were used as a form of currency for trade with African rulers who were willing to swap their prisoners of war for game-changing weapons. They were also used to barter with kidnappers all too eager to raid neighboring villages, armed to the teeth with the white man's guns. Firearms became the staple cargo aboard ships headed from Europe to the west coast of Africa, where kidnapped Africans, criminals, and the human spoils of regional wars were sold off. Though the ships transported various tradable goods, including rum, textiles, iron, and copper, it was guns and gunpowder that proved most valuable.

The Dutch were major early players in the guns-for-slaves market. As Protestants, they weren't bound by the Catholic Church's prohibition on selling guns to non-Christians. These early Protestant gun dealers carved out an entirely new market in Africa. The English followed suit as they entered the global slave economy in earnest. In the coming decades, Europe shipped a half million guns a year and an endless supply of gunpowder to West Africa.

By the mid-eighteenth century, when the slave trade reached its peak, guns became the most traded commodity for captives. In some instances, Europeans would only trade guns. In others, kingdom and tribal leaders would demand payment exclusively in firearms for their Black captives. The world's burgeoning firearms industry—and the new global economy itself—was in no small way fueled by these multinational arms and human-trafficking rings.

A long-held myth claims that slave traders simply traded people who had already been captives of war. But "it was not the war which was the cause of the Slave Trade, but the Slave Trade which was the cause of the war," wrote Thomas Clarkson, a leader of the British abolition movement, in 1839. The result of these manufactured conflicts was an endless and unscrupulous expansion of the human trade, enslaving farmers and craftsmen, fathers and mothers, sons and daughters. Hundreds of years later, in classrooms across America, Black people's history begins with us as slaves on Southern plantations. In fact, African people did not drop from the clouds or sprout from the ground as some sort of slave species; they were made, molded, and modified in the white colonial imagination.

Century by century, the white world fed on slaves and guns, growing fat and powerful. The Black world would be torn asunder by hunger, trapped in a cycle of slavery, depletion, dependence, and trauma. This deadly trade left Africa and Africans, both in America and on the continent, economically and psychologically wounded. Those wounds still ache in ways few could ever have imagined.

The Return

The remnants of this colonial past and that damned devil's deal still loom over much of West Africa. All along the coast, old colonial fortresses still overlook the ocean that carried African captives away to alien lands. These slave fortresses have been given new names, reimagined as castles and repurposed as historical tour stops. Today, you can walk their dark and jagged halls and buy locally crafted jewelry and art, T-shirts, and trinkets. But the veneer of modernity has done little to wipe clean the stench of this awful history.

These foreboding structures, once topped with cannons like crowns cocked toward the sea, were warehouses and transfer stations for incoming and outgoing cargo. There were special chambers for precious metals and foodstuff. There were quarters for guns and munitions. And dungeons for human cargo, Black bodies, bodies that would be defiled here, packed and loaded like livestock.

In the summer of 2019, nearly four hundred years to the day that the first "20 and odd Negroes" from Angola landed ashore in Jamestown, Virginia, aboard the Portuguese ship the *White Lion*, my family and I made a pilgrimage to West Africa to commemorate the anniversary.

For two weeks, we trekked across the west African country of Ghana with dozens of other African Americans on a reverse trip to the motherland. By bus, we made our way from Accra to Kumasi to Cape Coast. We visited villages where we were greeted by tribal council members and chiefs. We were feted in dirt lot celebrations honoring our return with elders who blessed us with hands on our cheeks. Young men beat on calfskin drums, and it felt like they were beating to the rhythm of our souls. Young women danced to the same beat, the beat of those drums and our hearts. Over and again, we were told, "Welcome home." We bought art and custom-made outfits from local tailors and enough kente cloth to Afro-centrize the entire borough of Brooklyn. There were moments of ethereal joy, a kind of spiritual familiarity that would've been hard to conjure even with the most contrived Pan-African vision quest to find home, in a place we'd never known, some five thousand miles away from our own. But I also felt a deep, unvarnished sorrow like nothing I'd ever experienced in my life.

We walked barefoot in the "Last Bath River" in Assin Manso, where countless African captives were forced to bathe for the last time before being marched to the coast and to those castles, and eventually into slave ships. The Cape Coast Castle is among Ghana's most infamous coastal dungeons. On our tour, we stumbled into a dark, dank room where male captives would've been held. There were no windows and just a trace of light. The air was suffocating and still. Our guide told us that this particular dungeon was beneath a church erected by Christian enslavers, placed intentionally above the enslaved Africans so they could hear their European captors praying to their god, as their own African spirits were being ripped away. Those who survived the march to the coast, many from the interior of western Africa, would languish in these crowded, godless cells until the slave ships arrived.

For a long moment, I stood there, in that place, and inhaled deeply, swallowing mouthfuls of last breaths and salty tears. And I almost choked. My wife waited just outside of the entrance, refusing to step any farther into the place. But Nola, my brave girl, grabbed my hand. Together, we walked into the cavernous dungeon. Her hand was still so little in mine back then. And as we lost ourselves in what I have no doubt was a hell, I could taste every bead of sweat and pain and blood and loss that had ever been spilled there. I ran my fingers across the jagged stone walls and felt the ancestors' bowed spines breaking my skin. Their scarred flesh was now mine. The wetness in my eyes became a wrenching in my gut, a heaving in my chest. I wanted to bend and weep and purge everything that I didn't even know was trapped inside of me. Their anguish and mine. I was angry at the white men who saw so little of our humanity, or their own. But I was also angry at their African conspirators, even the unwitting ones.

At that very moment, I heard a man's voice, just above a hush.

"Wipe your tears."

I looked over my shoulder through blurry eyes and saw no one.

"Wipe your tears."

Then I looked down at Nola, who was in a trance of her own.

"Wipe your tears."

We were alone.

Again and again, "Wipe your tears." I dried my eyes with the back of my hand. I lifted my chin and tugged at Nola. The muted light leading away from the dungeon pulled us up a set of steps and toward a door with an old sign bolted over it. The sign read, "Door of No Return." I pushed through the heavy wooden door, and a blast of light and life washed over our faces. Through squinted eyes, I saw a long row of small fishing boats. They were weather-beaten but brightly painted, staggered along the beach, where local boys the color of night tended to the guilt or benevolence of tourists like us.

I took one deliberate step after another until I was at the bottom of those ancient stone steps, standing in the sand with those boys and those boats, where our ancestors' feet last touched the continent. I took a fistful of that hot African sand and turned my face to the sun. I exhaled.

We did what our ancestors never could. We returned.

Later that night, the African moon sat high and bright, sending streaks of white light jetting across the crashing waves outside of our beachfront hotel in Elmina. We gathered with other Black Americans who'd made the pilgrimage back to the continent. Collectively, we rejoiced. We let our naked toes sink into the sand, and we smiled as the cold ocean water lapped over our ankles. Nola and I let the tide chase us up the shore. And we laughed louder than we had in as long as I could remember. We laughed so loud and for so long that I know the ancestors could hear our freedom. At least I hope they could.

It was August 20, 2019. Scholars believe August 20, 1619, was likely the day that those first enslaved Africans landed in Virginia on the *White Lion*. Exactly four hundred years later, my family commemorated those ancestors, and with them the birth of a new people, our people, African Americans. And we did so on African soil.

That day, August 20, is also Nola's birthday.

To the Atlantic World, with Guns at Their Backs

It was the gun at the backs of millions of kidnapped Africans that forced them from their homeland through doors of no return. Millions would perish during the Middle Passage, the monthslong journey across the Atlantic Ocean between Africa, the Caribbean, and the Americas. They were packed in the bowels of ships with names like *Henrietta Marie*, *Isabella*, *King David*, and *Lord Ligonier*. Some of the captives would leap to their watery graves rather than face the sure cruelty of life in bondage. But many others, stacked and chained, would die of "suffocation, maimings, stranglings, starvation, and cold-blooded murders." To survive meant facing a different kind of death and horror—a lifetime of enslavement and violence.

The inherent violence of the transatlantic slave trade was just the beginning. From the insanity of slave ships, they'd experience the depravity of America's slave labor camps—the ones some refer to rather romantically today as *plantations*. The first Africans enslaved in America and their descendants who'd follow would come to know lives bound by the white man's laws, their violence, and their guns.

That early racialized gun violence was part of a much broader effort to dominate North America and subdue its original inhabitants. European colonizers waged a centuries-long campaign to wipe out Indigenous people, systematically robbing them of their lives, their land, and their freedom. Perhaps the most American thing of all is that Crispus Attucks, a Black man of African and Indigenous ancestors, would become the first casualty of the American Revolution. He was gunned down in Boston on March 5, 1770.

As firearm technology continued to develop into the early nineteenth century, guns helped snuff the fuming threat of rebellion and insurrection that was constant in the South as the enslaved population swelled and grew more restless for freedom. But as the gun in the hands of white supremacists kept freedom out of Black ones, Black people with guns of their own represented white slave society's greatest fears.

Lawmakers did everything they could to keep Black people unarmed. An early Georgia law in the mid-1700s required all plantation owners and white men employed by them to join the Georgia militia. Members of the militia were required to make monthly inspections of all slave quarters in the state. The patrollers were ordered to search "all Negro Houses for offensive Weapons and Ammunition" and to stay vigilant against the prospect of uprisings and escapes. They were also required by law to catch and give twenty lashes to any enslaved people who strayed from plantation grounds. Lethal force was almost always considered a reasonable response to an uncontrollable slave.

Gunning for Freedom

The Civil War delivered freedom through musket fire. Tens of thousands of insurgent Black people took up arms alongside white Northern Union troops, ultimately helping to untether America from its "peculiar institution." But even before the war, abolitionists, enslaved Black people, and freedmen increasingly turned guns on slave society, adopting a more militant posture, calling on blood for freedom. Perhaps the most famous among those revolutionary abolitionists was John Brown, a white man who believed he was called by God to violently overthrow the institution of slavery.

In 1859, Brown led a group of about twenty men, white and Black, including three of his sons, on a raid of the federal armory at Harper's Ferry, Virginia. The plan was to seize as many as possible of the one hundred thousand weapons stocked inside, which Brown and his comrades would then turn over to enslaved would-be revolutionaries who'd deliver freedom to their people and a violent death knell to slavery.

The night of October 16 was damp and chilly as Brown and his men made their way down a dark, five-mile country road headed toward Harper's Ferry. They marched two abreast, led by two men with rifles. Along the way, they were joined by a handful of enslaved men who couldn't resist their chance at freedom. They moved in silence, "as solemnly as a funeral procession." In some ways, it was just that.

Brown's name has stretched through the annals of American history. He's become a singular shorthand for the revolutionary spirit of abolition by any and all means. And no doubt, he was the ultimate ally and coconspirator in the pursuit of Black liberation. But he did not fight alone and was certainly no more committed than the five Black men who rebelled alongside him. Four of the five were free people. The contributions of Osborne Perry Anderson, John Anthony Copeland, Shields Green, Lewis Sheridan Leary, and Dangerfield Newby have been largely lost to history, obscured in the shadow of their great white ally, relegated as nameless Black footnotes. But they were always so much more.

The best known of the five, Lewis Sheridan Leary, was a free Black man from a saddle-making family from North Carolina. As a young man, he made his way to relatively progressive Oberlin, Ohio, in search of better opportunities. Leary enrolled in Oberlin College, which anomalously in the mid-nineteenth century admitted Black people and women. There, he was drawn into the abolitionist movement and joined the local American

Anti-Slavery Society. Through this network, he met John Brown. Leary needed little convincing to join the would-be revolutionary. At Oberlin, Leary met John Anthony Copeland Jr., another free Black man from North Carolina. Copeland's father was manumitted in his enslaver's will, and his mother was born free.

Almost a year before joining Brown, Leary and Copeland had been leaders in another daring freedom effort. On September 13, 1858, they along with other abolitionists stormed the jail in Wellington, Ohio, where an escaped enslaved man was being held. John Price had fled Kentucky but was captured by slave catchers in Oberlin. The Fugitive Slave Act of 1850 required all citizens to assist in the capture and return of runaway slaves. But many abolitionists had committed themselves to not just opposing the law but breaking it on behalf of any enslaved person who sought sanctuary in free states. Copeland and the other abolitionists were able to help Price escape to Canada. But his freedom came with a cost. The slave catchers were outraged by the rescue and demanded that the abolitionists be arrested and tried for violating the Fugitive Slave Act. A federal grand jury indicted thirty-seven people in connection with Price's rescue, including twelve free Blacks, among them Leary and Copeland. Both men were released from jail and joined Brown's men before they ever made it to trial.

The Oberlin-Wellington Rescue proved to be a pivotal, emboldening moment in the abolitionist movement.

Shields Green, another Oberlin-Wellington veteran to join John Brown, escaped slavery in South Carolina through the Underground Railroad north to Rochester, New York. In Rochester, he met Frederick Douglass, who reportedly housed Green for nearly two years. Douglass introduced Green to his more radical abolitionist friends. During a trip to Chambersburg, Pennsylvania, they met with Brown, who was trying to convince Douglass to join his planned raid on Harper's Ferry. Douglass saw the move as dangerous, futile, and unnecessary. But Green took up Brown's invitation to go to war against white supremacy.

Dangerfield Newby was a blacksmith by trade. Born enslaved in Virginia, he was the eldest son of Henry Newby, a white farmer, and Elsey Pollard, an enslaved Black woman. His mother was owned by another white man, but Pollard's enslaver allowed her to live with Newby as husband and wife. The couple had eleven children, and with the enslaver's permission, the family moved to Ohio so the family could live together in freedom. As a young adult, Newby worked as a blacksmith in Ashtabula County, in the far-flung northeastern part of the state. That's where he first met John Brown, whose son John Brown Jr. lived nearby. By then, Newby had seven children with an enslaved woman named Harriet. Harriet's enslaver, a doctor, was having financial troubles, so he planned on selling her and the couple's seven children to a cotton plantation in Louisiana. Newby tried to buy Harriet and the children's freedom. When those negotiations fell through, he decided to join Brown's fight as a last resort to liberate his family. In 1859, over the spring and summer months, Newby's wife wrote him a series of letters, addressing each to her "Dear Husband" and signing them "Your affectionate wife."

"I want you to buy me as soon as possible, for if you do not get me somebody else will . . . their has ben [sic] one bright hope to cheer me in all my troubles that is to be with you," she wrote in her final letter to him.

The fifth of Brown's Black compatriots was Osborne Perry Anderson. Born free in West Fallow Field, Pennsylvania, Anderson also attended Oberlin College. He then moved to Canada, where he worked as a printer for an abolitionist newspaper, the *Provincial Freeman*, and joined the Chatham Vigilance Committee, dedicated to helping escaped formerly enslaved people. It was through this network that Anderson learned of Brown's planned revolution, and just a year before the raid, the two men finally met.

By 10:00 p.m. on that damp fall evening, the men had taken the armory and arsenal. Past midnight, they took control of a bridge into town and, with the morning light, nearly a half dozen armory employees as hostages. Townspeople started firing on the raiders, and by around 10:00 a.m., a local militia had mustered and taken position surrounding the armory.

Newby was the first to die. A sniper from a nearby building fired a six-inch spike into his neck. White townspeople reportedly cut his ears and genitals off as souvenirs and left his mutilated body in the street for several days. Nearly half of Brown's freedom fighters would be killed during the siege. Those who survived were captured by the militia and turned over to US troops. Copeland and Green were hanged by authorities on December 16, 1859. "If I am dying for freedom, I could not die for a better cause. I had rather die than be a slave," Copeland reportedly said on his way to the gallows.

John Brown survived and was quickly tried for treason, murder, and inciting a slave insurrection. He was found guilty on all charges and was executed by hanging on December 2, 1859. He was the first person in US history to be executed for treason. His final words were passed in a handwritten note: "I John Brown am now quite certain that the crimes of this guilty land will never be purged away, but with Blood. I had . . . vainly flattered myself that without very much bloodshed, it might be done."

Of the five Black men who joined Brown at Harper's Ferry, Anderson was the only one to survive the raid. He somehow managed to flee, and along with Albert Hazlett, another of

Brown's men, holed up in a stretch of nearby mountains. Well concealed, they traded shots with their pursuers, killing a few of them, according to Anderson's account.

Once the soldiers gave up their hunt, Anderson and Hazlett made their way out of the mountains, finding an old boat tied up along the shore of the Potomac River, which they used to cross the river into Maryland. From there, Anderson traversed Pennsylvania, via the Underground Railroad, eventually making it back home to Canada. Years later, Anderson wrote *A Voice from Harper's Ferry*, the only first-person account of the raid. He wanted "to save from oblivion the facts connected with one of the most important movements of this age . . . the overthrow of American slavery."

When Anderson died in December 1872 of tuberculosis (known then as *consumption*) at the age of forty-two in Washington, DC, he was remembered in a small obituary that ran in a Chester County, Pennsylvania, newspaper as "an intelligent colored man" and "the last survivor of those with old John Brown in the celebrated raid on Harper's Ferry."

The raid on Harper's Ferry ratcheted up already seething tension over the slavery debate. The United States was on a collision course toward the Civil War.

At the onset, free Black men lined up to join the fight for freedom. The Lincoln administration had considered the idea of allowing Black men to join the Union cause, but initially opted against it, citing federal law established in 1792 that barred Black people from bearing arms for the US Army. Blocking Black participation in the fight was also politically convenient. The administration thought that allowing Black men to pick up arms would push border states to secede. But pressure by powerful abolitionists, mounting Union army losses, and a declining number of white volunteers forced a reconsideration. Among Lincoln's most persistent agitators was Frederick Douglass, who believed deeply that African Americans should have the right to fight for their own freedom. On several occasions, Douglass met with Lincoln to make the case. But he also waged a very loud public campaign, writing articles and delivering speeches advocating for the cause. It was the right, just, and moral thing to do. And allowing Black men to enlist would help undermine the Confederacy's claim that their war was solely for states' rights and not about slavery.

In July of 1862, Congress passed the Second Confiscation and Militia Act. The act freed people who were enslaved by supporters of the Confederacy and members of the Confederate army. Then, slavery was abolished altogether in all US territories. By late July of that year, a preliminary draft of the Emancipation Proclamation was drawn up by the Lincoln administration. Once it was formally instituted, recruiting Black soldiers became critical to the Union's war efforts.

In 1863, Frederick Douglass, by then one of the most famous men in America, Black or white, called on African Americans to take up arms in the name of freedom and defense of the Union. In an editorial, titled "Men of Color, To Arms!" Douglass wrote, "There is no time to delay . . . Liberty won by white men would lose half its luster."

> Better even die free, than to live slaves . . . This is our golden opportunity. Let us accept it, and forever wipe out the dark reproaches unsparingly hurled against us by our enemies. Let us win for ourselves the gratitude of our country, and the best blessings of our posterity through all time.

Douglass drew on his own experiences to motivate Black folks to stand up and stand strong in the name of freedom's war.

In *Narrative of the Life of Frederick Douglas, an American Slave*, he recounted a defining incident in his life. His then-master sent him to a "slave breaker" to wear down the young troublemaker. After months of torment, Douglass decided to fight back. After the man delivered one particularly violent blow, a kick to the ribs, Douglas leaped to his feet and threw his fists. The fight lasted hours, with Douglas at one point grabbing the man by the throat, ending in a draw.

> It was a glorious resurrection. . . . My long-crushed spirit rose, cowardice departed, bold defiance took its place; and I now resolved that, however long I might remain a slave in form, the day had passed forever when I could be a slave in fact. x

Ultimately, the Union army, including nearly two hundred thousand African American soldiers, won the war, defeating the South and legal slavery in the United States.

Reconstruction and Redemption

Emancipation delivered America's captive Black masses, some four million souls, freedom from their physical chains, but not their social or economic ones. Two years after the Civil War, famed abolitionist and journalist William Lloyd Garrison described the post-emancipation lot of Black folks as suffering a "homeless, houseless, landless, penniless freedom."

Between 1865 and 1870, the Thirteenth, Fourteenth, and Fifteenth Amendments were passed, abolishing slavery, establishing birthright citizenship, and giving Black men the right to vote. This period offered Black people great optimism; for the first time this multitude of formerly enslaved people were able to participate in this country's purported democracy as US citizens. With the right to vote came the first generation of Black politicians who filled local, state, and even federal seats, positions once held by enslavers. Citizenship brought the power to build homes and farms and businesses. Black towns sprouted up across the South on soil they'd worked for generations and could now call their own. Institutions like schools and churches were pillars for this new Black nation of freedmen and freedwomen, whose faith would carry them through the best and worst of times.

But where one war ended, another began. White Southern resentments would stew unchecked, not only fueled by the Union's so-called War of Northern Aggression but also a hatred for Black people who dared seek agency and freedom against their former masters.

The white South did everything it could to make emancipation a failure. Southern legislatures enacted sweeping Black Codes aimed at narrowing Black freedom even further. And they did so with the full-throated support of President Andrew Johnson.

Ascending to the presidency after Lincoln's assassination, Johnson was an avowed white supremacist who'd fought to preserve the Union but not to end slavery. Johnson, for a period, had been a slaveholder. As president, Johnson offered wide protections to former enslavers, proclaiming, "This is a country for white men, and by God, as long as I am president it shall be a government for white men." Johnson immediately reneged on many of the promises made to Black Americans, including General William Tecumseh Sherman's Special Field Order No. 15, which declared that confiscated Confederate land "on the coastline from South Carolina to Florida be given to newly freed Black families." The order came after Sherman's scorched-earth march to the sea where he led sixty thousand soldiers on a 285-mile march from Atlanta to Savannah, Georgia, confiscating Confederate land, livestock, and supplies. Once in Savannah, Sherman called a meeting of twenty local Black pastors who said they wanted land for their people. Sherman offered each family forty acres that they could take over and farm for themselves along with surplus army mules to help them work the land, cementing the promise of "40 acres and a mule" in the Black American canon.

Tens of thousands of Black families had made "Sherman land" productive, but soon after Johnson took office, he ordered federal troops to evict many of these families. Some Black people fought off returning white people with guns. About two thousand Black landowners kept the land they'd been given at the close of the war. But the majority of those who stayed did so on land they'd never own. They stayed on as sharecroppers.

The end of the war and beginning of Black freedom would shift American society and the culture of the South in other ways, too. The South was awash in surplus military weapons, and armed white-supremacist organizations like the Ku Klux Klan were rising to prominence. At the same time, elites and what was left of the Southern aristocracy began pushing rhetoric that the Reconstruction governments would not "protect the interests of white southerners from newly freed and politically-empowered Black people."

Critical to the restoration of white power after the Civil War was the gun. Southern states launched a flurry of tyrannical laws against the freed people. Strict vagrancy laws were passed that carried with them the penalty of arrest, fines, or being leased to private labor to pay those fines. Black people couldn't testify against white assailants in courts. And Black people, Black citizens, couldn't own or bear firearms. Between 1865 and 1866, state lawmakers in Alabama, Arkansas, Florida,

Georgia, Louisiana, Mississippi, North Carolina, South Carolina, Tennessee, Texas, and Virginia all passed Black Codes to ensure Black Southerners were put back in their place, all but ensuring a return to white political and economic domination.

Whites lived in fear of a free Black mass who might attack, especially where whites were outnumbered. Members of the armed Ku Klux Klan took to marauding at night to terrorize Black families. Other groups sprang up alongside the Klan, including violent local white supremacist leagues and other terror organizations. In 1867, Douglass urged Black folks to again take up arms against white supremacists: "A man's rights rest in three boxes," Douglass said. "The ballot box, the jury box, and the cartridge box."

In response, Black folks started forming their own militias. One of the most notable examples was the Louisiana Native Guard, founded in 1862 to fight for the Union. Many of its members had escaped slavery. After the war, the Louisiana Native Guard was reorganized as a state militia and played a key role in protecting newly enfranchised African American voters from violence and intimidation during elections.

In the end, the gains of Reconstruction would be undone by white fear, violence, and weaponized politics. The presidential race of 1876 between liberal Rutherford B. Hayes and conservative Samuel Tilden would end in a contested election. With the Compromise of 1877, Hayes, a Republican, could have the presidency if he agreed to remove federal troops that had served as a buffer between newly emancipated Black folks and the whites who despised them.

After the protections of Reconstruction crumbled, African Americans were routinely killed for having the gall to speak up, being so uppity as to want their own land, schools, and businesses. Or for wanting to vote. One practice that became common was for Black folks to march to the polls together, armed. Decades after emancipation, as this racist war of redemption was being waged, the famed Black journalist and anti-lynching crusader Ida B. Wells-Barnett wrote: "A Winchester rifle should have a place of honor in every black home, and it should be used for that protection which the law refuses to give."

Jim Crow's Guns

Between 1877, the most recognized end of Reconstruction, and 1950, at least four thousand people were killed in documented lynchings. The true number of Blacks shot down, hanged, beaten to death, or otherwise killed in racist attacks during that period may never be known.

Violence sent many folks hurtling northward in hopes of finding peace, or at least something closer to freedom. The mass exodus of Black labor out of the South left the region economically hobbled.

Killings like my great-uncle Cornelius's, at the hands of white power, fueled the engine of this new kind of railroad headed to the North. But hope isn't the only thing they carried north. All their hurt and pain, the trauma and psychic toll they experienced in their old Southern lives would manifest in new ways in the so-called promised land. And the burden of it all would be handed from one generation to the next, bending our backs in ways we're just now getting straight.

In the summer of 2018, I toured the South in search of a connection between the symbols of the old Confederacy and the so-called New South. It's one thing to tear down a monument made of brick or marble. How do you tear down what's in the hearts of men?

The trip took me (and my friend and colleague *The New York Times*'s John Eligon) from Virginia, through Kentucky, Mississippi, and finally to Alabama, one of the citadels of Southern violence aimed at Black people. In Montgomery, I visited the National Memorial for Peace and Justice, a stunning outdoor homage erected "for those abandoned by the rule of law." It's a solemn place, acres filled with places to reflect and remember, art installations that track the Black American journey in realism and abstraction. At the heart of the memorial are rows of weather-beaten steel columns. As you walk by them, the floor begins to descend, slowly, and the columns begin to rise until you are standing beneath them as they dangle above. On each of the eight hundred steel pillars is the name of an American county and the names of Black men and women who were lynched there. Standing below, there's no shrugging off the weight that each carries. One pillar was marked *Dodge County*, my family's home until Cornelius was murdered.

"We want people to understand that the violence that African Americans experienced was a direct consequence of two centuries of enslavement because that ideology of white supremacy that was shaped, and developed, and nurtured, and crafted during slavery is what gave rise to the lynching history," Bryan Stevenson, lawyer, historian, and director of the Equal Justice Initiative, the organization that runs the museum, told me as we walked the memorial grounds. "This is terrorism . . . It does something to everybody's consciousness about what justice means."

I stood there racked with a sense of deep loss, seeing the names of Black folks like Cornelius's etched in rusted steel.

"We've had people come, some of whom live in Chicago and Detroit and Cleveland, but they know their people are from Florence County, South Carolina . . . and all of a sudden they just start to have this intensely emotional response to seeing a name, and I think for me, that was what is so powerful, is these names have never been spoken," Stevenson said that day. "Just naming the unnamed victims of this violence and terrorism has its own kind of power."

I couldn't help but think of all the kinfolk we've lost whose names will never be known outside of their families and communities. The people never given proper respect in life or in death, whose names never made the public memorials, let alone contemporary records.

The price of white fear and Black suffering in the American South is still being paid. Recently published research led by Dr. Nicholas Buttrick of University of Wisconsin–Madison has found that the more enslaved people a US county had in 1860, the more guns its residents have today.

"The extent to which people feel unsafe only predicts gun ownership in counties in the South, where the more unsafe people feel, the more likely they are to own a gun," says Professor Buttrick. The South today leads the way in both guns in the hands of its residents and the rates of people killed by them.

From slavery to Jim Crow segregation, violence and subjugation were the ties that bound Blacks to a semipermanent state of mourning in this country.

Migration as Escape

My great-uncle Cornelius was just a boy back in 1923 when we believe a white man shot him dead in rural Georgia. But he was a Black boy. And in America, then as now, the life of Black boys has been rendered cheap. No amount of bloodshed has been enough to repay the seeming birthright debt that Black families owe.

To say it plain, our dying has always been as segregated as our living, be it by lynch mob, police bullets, or the kind of communal violence that grows in response to deep hunger, economic instability, social isolation, and segregation. Through the everyday tragedy of modern gun violence that festers in still-segregated cities and towns across the country, it has been the gun and bullet that has haunted Black life most.

Cornelius's death wouldn't be the last time that my family would pay on this violent debt. In that, we're no different from many Black families who fled the American South, an exodus of millions that would redefine America. There were hopes of better days and better opportunities. The big manufacturing plants making cars and processing meat and piecing together all the trappings of modern American life had jobs to fill, and the Black labor class offered a viable supply of workers. When America shifted to a war economy with the onset of World War II, those Northern factories drew Southern Blacks like a magnet. But what many found in the North, while less explicitly hostile, was more of the same with a different accent. The South preached segregation and practiced it. The North preached equality but practiced widespread de facto segregation through racial housing covenants, redlining, and other forms of systemic segregation and subjugation.

My great-grandparents William and Bessie and their children first landed in Philadelphia, where William found work at a sugar refinery. In the decade before they arrived, the Black population in the city exploded, from 84,000 in 1910 to 134,000 in 1920. And by 1930, there were 219,000 African American residents. Nearly half of them came from just four Southern states: Georgia, Maryland, South Carolina, and Virginia. Black men found jobs working in steel mills, shipyards, and munitions plants in the wider Philadelphia metropolitan area, and at the docks and wharves at the sugar mills and oil refineries that dotted the Delaware River, including Camden, New Jersey, adjacent to Philadelphia. Black women mostly found jobs as domestics, doing the cooking, cleaning, and childcare for white families. Eventually, the Woodses settled across the Delaware River in Camden County, New Jersey, and moved to East Berlin, an all-Black settlement filled with other native Georgians.

William wanted his own and would work hard to get it. Great-Granddaddy soon got a horse and a buggy and claimed a patch of land where he grew vegetables, which he'd ferry over to nearby Philadelphia to sell at market. Later, he took a job as a laborer with the municipal parks department. Bessie was a homemaker. As his children made their way through school, William learned to read and write alongside them. They saved up enough money to buy a modest house. And the family continued to grow. In the coming years, William and Bessie had six more children: Simon, Nathaniel, Shelley, David, MacClinton, and Bernard. Two other children, Samuel and Curtis, didn't survive their first year. Young William Jr. grew into a man. He married and had children of his own. Grandmom Ida Mae and her sister Rose, the next oldest behind William Jr., were blossoming into beautiful young women.

Clint and the Cop

Ida Mae was twenty-eight when her second brother was shot and killed. It was after midnight on Mother's Day 1951. And MacClinton, the second youngest of the Woods children, was lingering around the gas station where he worked. Clint, as family and familiar folks called him, was seventeen years old and in love with cars. He'd tinker with them, take them apart, and put them back together again. He enjoyed cars so much that he got a job with THAT local gas station, where he'd pump gas and do the occasional oil change for customers.

To this day, it's unclear exactly what Clint was doing at the gas station that night, long after closing time. But at some point, Clint caught the attention of a passerby, a young white man not too much older than he was. There's no way Clint would've known it then, but the fresh-faced stranger coming toward him from the shadows was a rookie cop. State trooper Emil J. Bock, twenty-four, had recently been assigned to the area after a bunch of late-night break-ins. He was walking his new beat in plainclothes. Bock took Clint for a burglar or a car thief and confronted him and then placed him under arrest. Bock was on foot and had no way of driving Clint back to the police station. When Clint told him that his car was parked nearby, Bock demanded that Clint drive them to the station. Somewhere along the way, something went terribly wrong. Bock told his commanders that instead of turning the direction of the police station, Clint turned onto a secondary road and sped in the opposite direction. He said Clint ignored commands to stop the car, so he drew his service revolver. Just then, the car careened off of the road and crashed into a tree. Clint and Bock were tossed from the car. Bock said that he'd lost his grip on his pistol and that it landed on the street between him and Clint. Bock said they both lunged for the gun. As they struggled over the weapon, Clint crumbled to the ground with a shot to his chest.

The shooting happened in West Berlin, the white side of the town. Like a spark, word quickly spread to East Berlin's Black community, inflaming long-simmering racial tension. There were only two witnesses to the shooting, and one of them was dead. The following day, a headline in the *Courier-Post* read,

TROOPER'S GUN KILLS YOUTH IN STRUGGLE AFTER CRASH:
BOTH LUNGE TO RECOVER WEAPON.

William and Bessie collapsed under the weight of Clint's death. Another of their boys shot by a white man with a gun. The ripples from Clint's death spread wide, enraging an entire community. Neighbors streamed to the Woodses' front porch to offer William and Bessie their condolences. When asked what anyone could do to help, William said over and again, "God will take care of it in his own way."

During an evening prayer vigil later that week at the tiny Green Grove Baptist Church, where my people have worshipped for generations, mourners crammed into the pews and wept alongside the family. The sound of sobbing beat through the walls and out into the night, as those who couldn't squeeze inside of the church gathered outside to pray under the stars.

William, a founding member of Green Grove, sat silently with tears welling in his eyes. A stoic man of few words, he rarely showed much emotion. But with every bit of them tumbling down his cheeks, he lifted his head toward the heavens and cried out in anguish, pleading to God for justice. He'd been denied justice some thirty years earlier in the killing of Cornelius; he couldn't take another round of the same.

Two weeks later, Bock was dead, killed on his motorcycle during a high-speed chase and crash. Justice, as far as anyone in Black Berlin could tell, was served.

On a fall afternoon not long ago, I sat in a circle of relatives, uncles and aunts old enough to remember when Clint was killed. They told me the story best they could recall. Most were just six or seven years old at the time of his death.

My aunt Liz, the eldest of my mother's sisters, pulled out an old tape recorder. And when she hit Play, I could hear my grandmother Ida Mae's voice, just as I'd always remembered it. She had this lilt in her voice that made everything she said sound a bit like a question. A melodic inquisition in every breath.

The officer "died a horrible death," Grandmom Ida said, recalling the incident decades later. "And in that case, I felt that justice reigned. Clint wasn't the kind of boy that would get into hassles and that sort of thing with a policeman. But at that time, I guess Black was not beautiful, and whatever transpired between them, he was shot."

2

Our American Life (and Death)

While Clint's death was a cruel reminder of the most vicious limitations America placed on us, my family continued to grow. In the North, the seeds that William and Bessie planted in New Jersey would blossom into marriages and births. But again and again, their lives would collide with guns and the other forces that rush us to early death.

A Time Before and Again (Horace)

There's this old portrait that's been in my family longer than I have. For decades, it hung on the wall of my grandmother's home in West Berlin, New Jersey, where she ran a boardinghouse. As a little boy, I'd sit at her knee in front of her fireplace, warmed by the wood burning in the hearth and carried away by the sweet smell of her perfume. Grandmom Ida has been gone for some time now, but so many of my memories of her still float on that fragrance—something like a vanilla bean dipped in Bible study—the most beautiful scent you could ever imagine. As a child, I'd sit at her feet and stare up at that big, sepia-toned family portrait hanging on the wall and get lost in its details. There she was with my grandfather Horace Worthington, surrounded by their eight children. My aunts and uncles with Afros and polyester suits and shirt collars as big as their heads. My mother and her sisters had wide pearly smiles. Her brothers, one wearing a freshly pressed military uniform, held their chins high and their spines stiff. Grandmom Ida looked so regal, the way her warm smile complemented her bulbous green-beaded necklace, which popped against her bright burgundy turtleneck as much as her smile did. Grandpop Horace is sitting to her left on the arm of a beige leather chair, looking every bit the proud patriarch. His gorgeous head of salt-and-pepper hair, his mustache, and his crisp seersucker suit, pink shirt, and burgundy tie give the kind of Black man cool you'd expect in a 1970-something cognac ad. From everything I've heard about Grandpop, he was equal parts mischief and masculinity, stoic with his chiseled face and bushy, arching eyebrows that we all claim as our own.

The story of Ida Mae and Horace's courtship and eventual nuptials have become the stuff of family lore, recounted in the mouths of a generation, now slipping away, as an illustration of simpler times. While my grandmother found her way to New Jersey from Georgia, my grandfather's paternal side had made their way to Jersey from Delaware. In 1870, his great-grandmother Comfort Worthington showed up on the census rolls, having been born in Delaware in 1802. Both of his maternal grandparents were born in New Jersey in the early 1850s.

The way I've always heard the story is that Grandmom Ida and Grandpop Horace met in a bean field. Throughout the harvesting seasons, the big white farmers would send buses out to Black communities in the area to pick up day laborers to harvest whatever crop was in season. Black folks would be dropped off on farms and in fields all across South Jersey to handpick beans, berries, and other crops. On one of these harvesting days, during bean season, the two of them caught each other's eyes under the hot summer sun. Ida Mae was pretty and skinny and just seventeen. Horace was hazel eyed and handsome with wavy hair, a number of years her senior. They'd sneak off to flirt out of earshot of others. Soon, flirting became more, and sometime later, Ida Mae became pregnant. When Ida's father, William, a tough, Bible-believing Georgian, found out, he was furious. He threatened to have the twenty-five-year-old Horace arrested, or worse, if he didn't marry Ida Mae. In August of 1939, Horace and Ida Mae got married in a shotgun wedding. Their family would grow larger by the year. There'd be Horace Jr., Gary, Elizabeth, then Clifford, Patricia, and the twins Curtis and Cosette, and then the baby of the family, my mother, Wanda.

Grandpop Horace landed a job at a pipe insulation factory, where he worked for decades. Grandmom was a homemaker, a mortician student, a part-time model, and an occasional nurse. They eventually bought a house in West Berlin, the white side of town. And in the years to come as their children grew older and started having children of their own, many of the siblings moved within a few blocks of their parents. By the time I was about six and spending my after-school hours at Grandmom's place, half the time I'd be sprinting from house to house, grabbing sugar or flour from my uncle Gary's or taking some mail to my aunt Pat's place, where on the way I'd run into my uncle Curtis hanging out and drinking under the tree in another relative's yard across the street. This was our neighborhood, a Black enclave in an otherwise white world.

My grandmother's house was also the family business. Many in my family, including Grandmom Ida, ran boardinghouses out of their homes. They provided food and shelter for all sorts of folks: old hard-luck veterans, the mentally ill, the old or infirm. Nearly all these clients, as the family called them, suffered from some form of physical, mental, or emotional limitation. They were well taken care of by my grandmother.

I grew up eating lunch elbow to elbow with this menagerie

of mutes and misanthropes, the kind of people society often throws away. For many of them, even the white ones, the large extended Worthington family was more family to them than their own flesh and blood. I have fond memories of a couple of them, who until their dying days remembered Little Trymaine even as I grew big and moved away. My mother worked at my grandmother's boardinghouse. I'd head straight there after school each afternoon. I'd run up the steps with an armful of books and she'd be busy making beds or cleaning bathrooms or getting dinner ready. There'd be trays stacked with plates loaded with sliced potatoes or vegetables and chicken. My grandmother would be on the phone taking care of her business or laughing with relatives far and near.

I'd spent countless hours of my young life in that house, absorbing the constant flow of life in and out of the place. My mother standing at the screen door at the back of the house calling the guys in for lunch. The trays of soup and sandwiches. The rough-hewn tweed couches. The television stuck on what seemed like an endless loop of *M*A*S*H*, *Bewitched*, *Hogan's Heroes*, and *The Andy Griffith Show*. The smell of mothballs and cigarette-washed men and women and the sound of constant chatter and vacuums and doors knocking and bells ringing and people yelling out for this one or that one. It was an ecosystem fed by family and a revolving cast of clients, who one of my uncles referred to cynically as *the light bill*, *the car note*, or *the mortgage*, because each resident client came with guaranteed income supplemented by the state or by well-off relatives.

But what I remember most and what I've always been drawn back to was that family portrait hanging not far from the fireplace. If there was ever an object correlative in little Trymaine's life, it was that portrait. It had a way of grounding me in who we were and who I was before I had a true sense of either. But I felt it. The image of my family, my big, beautiful, Black family dressed to the nines, would be a constant wallpaper in my early formative years. It's a glimpse into a time in my family that I never knew but a time that would shape and reshape our lives in unimaginable ways. Those years, with the gravitational force of my grandparents keeping everyone else in orbit, have been mythologized in the stories I heard growing up. We heard about our grandparents' bitter breakups and hard-fought makeups. The family trips to Ohio. Of Grandpop Horace as Big Daddy to his CB radio buddies. And my grandmother trying to find her way as a mother and then a grandmother after a spin at modeling didn't pan out. This was most clearly a time before. A time a few years before I was born, yes. But also, a time before it happened again. One of the last times my family was whole.

A Bullet, then a Splash of Sirens

My mother, Wanda, remembers the highway opening up in a splash of red lights and sirens, a dizzying kaleidoscope pitched against a bleak night sky. It was the wee hours of a cold December morning just a few weeks before Christmas, and she was racing down the White Horse Pike toward the hospital in Berlin. The police cars and ambulances and the shrill of their sirens filled every fiber of her body with dread. She prayed that the writhing in her chest and that soul-knowing feeling rushing up from her gut was a lie. Pulling up to the hospital, she found herself in the thick of a swarm of police officers pushing in and out of the ER. Amid the chaos, she made out a familiar figure in the back of one of the police cars parked by the entrance. It was Horace Jr., one of her older brothers. She looked past the police car and saw another of her brothers, Gary, being dragged out of the hospital in handcuffs. She ran inside and found a group of white nurses huddled and cowering as a pair of police officers restrained another of her brothers, a wild-eyed Clifford. Through the chaos, she could hear her eldest sister, Elizabeth, wailing from down the crowded hallway. She followed her sister's screams, pushing through a gauntlet of nurses and patients and police until, finally, she saw her mother, Ida Mae, broken to her knees.

"My God! My God! My God!" Ida Mae cried out to Wanda. It happened again.

Hours earlier, Grandpop Horace had come home from his late-night shift at the pipe insulation factory where he'd worked for twenty-seven years, many of them spent on the night shift. As weary as he'd grown from years in that factory, he was looking forward to retiring in a couple of months. He was sixty-one and could taste freedom just around the corner, savoring the idea of spending lazy days doing whatever he pleased, which most certainly would've included more fishing and time on his CB radio with his trucking buddies who passed the time shuttling up and down the interstates shooting the shit on their radios. They called him Big Daddy, a fitting handle given his towering frame and barrel chest. "Breaker, breaker. Boys, this is Big Daddy comin' at you," he'd say, hunched over his radio. Night after night, it was the same thing, his buttery, baritone voice calling out to his buddies rolling down the proverbial byways and highways and through the industrial ether.

It was a little after midnight, and Horace had finally sat down at the kitchen table to eat dinner—a plate of liver, rice, and gravy that Grandmom Ida had cooked earlier and left in the oven to keep warm. She was in bed by then. So was one of their older boys, Clifford, who'd been having a tough time ever since he returned from Vietnam. Horace had taken just a few bites when he heard a knock at the door.

The first blast came as he twisted the doorknob. Then came another and another. One bullet tore into his jaw. The second struck him in the gut. The third bullet ricocheted off the doorknob as Horace slammed the door shut.

Ida Mae was yanked awake by her husband's desperate screams.

"Ida, Ida, I've been shot!" he called out, blood streaming from his face and pooling through his work shirt.

As she ran from their bedroom, he collapsed in her arms, gasping in pain.

"I've been shot in the stomach, and I tried to run," Horace yelled, "and he shot me in the mouth."

Ida Mae could hear the pain and fear in her husband's voice. She took a step back and with wide eyes pawed at the blood smeared across her nightgown. Horace stumbled toward the telephone and called the ambulance himself.

One by one, the children got the phone call that Daddy had been shot. They rushed to the hospital where Horace had been taken. His three sons tore through the place like a firestorm, only stopped by cops and cold reality. The doctors said that he was in extremely critical condition and braced them for the worst. Trauma surgeons worked for five hours trying to remove the bullets.

The family took turns sitting vigil by his side, cycling between the ER and home to catch a couple of hours of sleep when they could. But there would be no rest. Later the next evening, Horace's condition worsened, and nurses warned that anyone not at the hospital should get there as soon as possible. But even as Grandpop lay dying in a hospital room, his shooter was still on the loose.

Through the haze of madness, Ida Mae managed to utter a name to police: Cecil Wright.

A Dying, Segregated City

Ida Mae and Horace owned a small rental apartment in Camden, about fifteen miles from their home in West Berlin. Situated on the Delaware River directly across from Philadelphia, Camden had once been a regional draw for a diverse workforce looking for good-paying industrial jobs. That included a wave of Black migrants. Several weeks before the shooting, a Black man named Cecil Wright had come to look at my grandparents' apartment. He liked what he saw and put down a $160 deposit on the unit. But after the deposit, Wright went missing. No calls. No visits. Nothing. About ten weeks later, Wright resurfaced, saying he was ready to move in. But by then, my grandparents had rented the apartment to another tenant. Wright demanded his money back, but they refused, reminding Wright that the deposit was nonrefundable. Horace told Wright that he could fight for his money in court. A hearing in Camden municipal court was scheduled for late December.

By the time Cecil Wright came looking to rent an apartment from my grandparents in the mid-1970s, quality housing in Camden was hard to come by, especially for Black folks. Years of redlining, segregation, and white and economic flight had squeezed Black residents into a handful of mostly hardscrabble neighborhoods.

Camden had once benefited from its prime geographic location along the Delaware River, ideal for manufacturers making and moving goods up and down the East Coast and west through neighboring Pennsylvania. In its heyday, the city was home to the Campbell Soup Company, the New York Shipbuilding Corporation, RCA Victor Company, and other major shipping and manufacturing companies. While the city had a small but relatively diverse population heading into the early twentieth century, made up mostly of working-class ethnic whites and a small minority of African Americans, Black people started arriving en masse in the post–World War II years. Yet when it came to housing, most Black folks were hemmed in by restrictive racial housing covenants, strict segregation, and crowded public housing projects.

In the early 1960s, the state of New Jersey launched an expansive, federally subsidized, so-called urban renewal program in Camden that would not only exacerbate the city's housing crisis but also dealt a crippling blow to Camden's Black community. Construction of the I-676 "North-South Freeway" tore downtown Camden in half, displacing nearly 1,300 families, of which an estimated 85 percent were Black or other people of color. Other nearby projects razed much of Camden's commercial corridor along Broadway. Going back to the 1930s, downtown Camden had been redlined, deemed too Black to be worth investing in or properly valuing. In an undated government record from the era, downtown was described as "the heart of the city" with solidly built old brick homes, but also that there was an "infiltration of questionable residents"—namely, that 50 percent of the people who lived there were identified as "negro" and another 50 percent as "foreign born." In short order, property values collapsed, and municipal services were curtailed.

Through the 1960s, in the tailwinds of white flight, hundreds of homes and dozens of blocks in Camden were demolished to make way for other public works projects that would further squeeze Black life. Approximately three thousand units of low-income housing were demolished in downtown Camden between 1963 and 1968. The confluence of white flight, segregation, a diminished tax base, economic divestment, and straight-up neglect created slum conditions in Camden that bred Black angst and hopelessness. The city was hungry. Crime and violence were increasing.

In 1969, rumors spread that a young Black girl was beaten by a white police officer. As night fell, hundreds of protestors marched to Cooper University Hospital. The protests would smolder into rebellion. At dusk, gunshots rang out. An officer and a civilian wound up dead. The city exploded in shattered glass and arson. Two years later, in August 1971, police fatally beat a Puerto Rican motorist, and the city once again erupted. In a single night of unrest, three people were shot, eighty-seven were injured, and more than a dozen fires were set.

These events hastened the complete economic death of this poor and increasingly segregated city. Camden lost a third of its white population in the 1960s. In 1972, just a few years before my grandparents would meet Cecil Wright, there were only a few census tracts in South Jersey outside of Camden with a sizable Black population. There was historically Black Lawnside, famously a stop on the Underground Railroad and later a hub of Black cultural and political life in South Jersey; Chesilhurst, where I grew up, a Black enclave carved out of the mouth of the Pine Barrens; and suburban Berlin Township, where my grandparents lived.

As the years went by, the industrial jobs that lured hundreds of thousands of Black folks to Camden dried up or went overseas. Most of the ultra-segregated and redlined neighborhoods grew increasingly volatile and violent. The children and grandchildren of Black people who had weathered the racial strictures of the Old South and all its violent underpinnings were left with the unchecked baggage of racism, disinvestment, and poverty. Black tenants and homebuyers were left to fend for themselves. In spite of these terrible conditions, many, like my grandparents, were industrious and entrepreneurial, with enough gumption to try to make a way where there was none. Yet gumption alone could not keep them safe.

St. Louis Cecil

Back in 1960, as Camden was beginning to be carved up in the name of progress at the expense of her Black residents, the nascent civil rights movement, which had been slowly percolating for decades, finally began to boil over. Black folks in big and small ways put increasing pressure on the system of laws that kept America separate and unequal. The spirit of organized rebellion was sweeping across the nation.

Many years before my grandparents crossed paths with Cecil Wright, Wright was a teenager in St. Louis, Missouri, another city bound by segregation and a creeping post-industrialization. In the years before the civil rights movement culminated in the signing of the Civil Rights Act of 1964, which banned discrimination based on race, color, religion, sex, or national origin, and a year later, the Voting Rights Act of 1965, which guaranteed access to the polls, Black youth all across the country, particularly in the South and Midwest, began staging sit-ins at segregated lunch counters. Cecil Wright was one of them. For weeks in October of 1960, Wright and a group of teenagers in St. Louis waged a campaign aimed at the city's downtown restaurants, hotels, and five-and-dimes—businesses that refused to serve Black customers or served them in "Colored Only" sections. With each sit-in the teens staged, they'd be arrested and then released. And each time, they'd be at it again. The first sit-in was sparked after the group were refused service at Pope's Cafeteria. They followed that up with a sit-in the next day at a local Howard Johnson's. Their protest made the local and national news, with their names and photos stretching across the pages of Black newspapers throughout the country, including *The Chicago Defender* and *Baltimore Afro-American*. The movement was a success. Just a month after the protests began, six major downtown St. Louis cafeterias announced that they would begin serving Black customers, and the City of St. Louis Board of Aldermen introduced a bill that would prohibit discrimination based on race or religion in places of public accommodation. These were hard-fought victories in one of the country's most segregated cities. Those fights changed that city and the young people like Wright that made a difference.

Fighting in Vietnam would also forever change Cecil Wright. He joined the air force during the war. After he returned, he married a young lady he'd known back home in St. Louis and eventually moved to Philadelphia in search of new opportunities and a fresh start. They'd have children, but something had changed in Wright. He had become an abusive womanizer. Eventually, he and his wife split for good, and Wright became "a once-a-year kind of father" limited to making brief appearances during the major holidays.

Hard on his luck and estranged from his family, Cecil struck out on his own, looking for a steady job and a place to stay. That's when he came across the listing for the Worthingtons' apartment.

Cecil's Got a Gun

On December 8, 1976, Cecil Wright showed up at my grandparents' place around 8:00 p.m. looking for Grandpop Horace. My uncle Clifford, another scarred Vietnam vet, answered the door and told him again what his father had said just days earlier. The deposit was gone. Harsh words were exchanged. The war left Clifford with an ongoing battlefield in his mind, and a perpetual hair trigger. Wright showing up on the family's doorstep must've felt like another ambush. Clifford, in a huff, told Wright that his father was working late and wouldn't be home for hours. Wright drove to a nearby diner and waited for Horace to clock out. Not long after midnight, Wright returned to the house armed with a .32-caliber semiautomatic pistol. He knocked on the door, and as my grandfather got close, he opened fire. Then Wright fled, hiding out for days as the New Jersey State Police put out a multistate bulletin for his capture. He finally turned himself in, confessed to the shooting, and said that he was angry that Horace had reneged on a deal to rent him the apartment. Wright was charged with murder and carrying a deadly weapon.

Wright's trial was held later that summer. And my mother, Wanda, and other family members attended each day, choking back tears as prosecutors presented crime scene and autopsy photos showing the damage Wright's bullets had done to their father's body. Wright was convicted and sentenced to twenty-five to thirty years in prison for the murder. At his sentencing, Judge I. V. DiMartino said he felt Wright's crime "required a severe custodial sentence."

"When someone leaves his home with a gun, the inevitable occurs," the judge said. "Someone is hurt or killed. It cannot be his intent to talk while armed. He must, as the jury found, intend injury."

Our Family, Our Fate

The story of Grandpop's murder is one of my earliest memories. For much of my childhood, I spent almost every day in the house where that man took his life. I came and went through the doorway where he was mortally wounded. I ate peanut butter and jelly sandwiches at the same table where Grandpop ate his last meal. And I've walked the path of his final footsteps more times than I can count, from the kitchen to the back bedroom, where he collapsed in my grandmother's arms and left her with a crimson stroke of blood across the front of her nightgown.

From the moment of Grandpop's death, our family would be broken into a million little pieces. Even those yet born would be handed a gaping hole that we've had no idea how to fill. "You never really return to normal. Whatever normal is," my mother says. "You just function the best you can, knowing that they're never coming back."

More than forty years have passed since the day my grandfather was killed, but the hurt today is as thick as it was the day his life was stolen from his family. The mere mention of his name, Horace Worthington, still pulls a weight over any room it's uttered in. Great sadness, resentment, guilt, and anger still consume my aunts and uncles. Some have carried a deep shame. My uncle Clifford, who earned a Purple Heart in Vietnam, blamed himself for what Wright did that night. Was it the way he barked at him when Wright came knocking? His life in the years after the shooting was turbulent, filled with struggles with substance abuse and bouts of homelessness. He carried that misplaced guilt with him until he died in 2010, found dead in his car parked inside of a storage unit. His prized Purple Heart has never been recovered. His brother Curtis struggled with alcoholism and many of the health issues that come with heavy self-medication, including cirrhosis of the liver, which took his life in 2003. There's also been various fractures among other siblings, fissures exacerbated by the deep emotional toll the murder heaped onto them. "You go through all the motions of it. You cry, you try to deal with the hurt, but a murder is different than just a death," my mother told me, sitting at her kitchen table just months ahead of the fortieth anniversary of her father's murder. "I don't want to say, 'just a death.' But it's a different kind of death."

My mother would never let us play with toy guns. On birthdays and other celebrations, she would grow anxious at the sight of balloons because they threatened to explode unexpectedly, like gunfire. Decades later, she is still racked by the memory of the images of her daddy's body on a gurney, on full display during the trial of the man who killed him. My mother told me that losing a loved one to murder is like losing a limb. "It's almost like cutting off a major part of your body; it's just like you have to learn to compensate and you can't really. Because it's gone and it's never coming back."

They did their best to cope but were reminded every moment that they had been disfigured. There's a deep unfairness in the pangs of this kind of death, of having a loved one snatched away so violently. But there's also the unfairness of a carceral system that doesn't have the capacity or desire to value Black life, let alone deliver justice to Black victims of violence, especially when the perpetrator is also Black.

One afternoon in the early 1980s, my uncle Gary was working as a postal worker with a route in Camden. On this particular day, he reached into his mailbag and came across a letter for Cecil Wright. Wright had been sentenced to as many as three decades in prison, but he was released after serving less than eight years. As Gary stood there on the corner of Haddon Avenue, just yards from where the man who killed his father now lived, a pulse of rage coursed through his body. Authorities gave no warning to my family that Wright was scheduled for release. For my aunts and uncles, it was as if their father had been murdered all over again. His murderer would walk quietly among them while their father lay in a grave at the old Black cemetery in East Berlin. What was their father's life worth? For Wright and the system, it was worth less than a decade behind bars, while my family has never been paroled from the heartache the murder caused.

My grandmother suffered most. She fell into a deep depression that would take years to shake, marked by bouts with alcohol abuse and a series of turbulent relationships. After my grandfather died, Grandmom Ida married a man named William Dyitt. They had a tumultuous and at times violent relationship. He was physically and verbally abusive with a mean, jealous streak. Once, during a breakup, he found my grandmother at a bar having a conversation with another man. He pressed up behind her and stabbed her in the back with a penknife. She spent weeks in the hospital. Police arrested him for attacking her, and he disappeared for a couple of years before resurfacing and finessing his way back into her life, much to the dismay of her adult children. They married in a small ceremony in Atlantic City in 1978. As the years wore on, their relationship grew less volatile, and my grandmom found a salve in deep religiosity. I grew up with a Jesus-loving grandmother who wore fancy church hats and an easy smile, who expected good manners, *yeses* instead of *yeahs* and who required Little Trymaine to be her travel buddy as she ran errands all around town. And even Mr. Bill, as I called him, evolved, mellowing into a grandfather figure who gave me a silver dollar or a piece of candy anytime I saw him. And despite my grandmother's churchgoing ways, she didn't take mess from anyone and taught me to speak up for myself. I got into a fight with a white kid down the street when I was seven or eight years old. And as I ran up the driveway to her house, I remember her standing at the front door saying, "He better look worse than you." Which he did. I got her message loud and clear. You'll have to fight in life, and you'd better fight hard. Her steady manner belied the violent turmoil that had enveloped so much of her life.

Back then, I had no idea the extent of what she'd been through. I only knew her as the prayerful grandmother who smelled like vanilla and loved a fancy hat and Jesus. And trust, she loved her some Jesus. Up until her last days, if you'd ask how she was doing, she'd say, "Blessed by the best." And I can still hear her voice singing a church song she'd written: "There's gonna be some rain in your life, sometimes. But get on your knees and pray, the Lord is gonna show you the way." My grandmother had a faith stronger than anything I could ever muster. There's been far too much rain for me to feel otherwise.

My generation grew up with a deep adoration for Grandpop Horace. His life became the stuff of family lore. He was bigger and badder than any man who'd ever walked the planet. He was handsome and debonair, a loving and committed father with a wife with her own sense of freedom and agency. I wish I could've laid eyes on him just once, to marvel at the spatter of freckles that march across our noses. Our thick, arching eyebrows and that Worthington mischief of ours. Until my early adult years, I'd never asked about the details of my grandfather's murder or the pain it caused our family. But as I've gotten older and become a father myself, I feel a hurt that I've never truly felt before.

Not too long ago, I took my wife's grandfather, who was strong and sharp at ninety-four then, out fishing on my favorite lake in upstate New York. From sunup to sundown, we cruised up and down the shoreline, catching bass and filling long pauses with fishing stories about the big ones caught and the big ones that got away. He taught me just the right way to string a float and the perfect *pop-pop* of the wrist to entice even the most finicky crappie—or sacalait, as they call them back in Louisiana, where he's from. It was the greatest day of fishing I'd ever had. Later that night, I sat alone with a glass of bourbon and melted in muffled tears. Chest heaving, snot running, tears. The day stirred in me what I could have had with my own grandfather. The lessons. The long silences. The laughs. The perfect knots and wrist-pops. It was the first time in my forty-plus years of life that I'd cried for my grandfather. It was the first time I truly felt the ache of his loss. More than anything, I just wanted my grandfather.

"A Shameful Thing, a Sad Thing"

Our family wasn't the only one torn apart by the shooting. No one in my family has ever had any direct contact with Wright or his family, but I couldn't help but wonder what ever happened to him. Was he still alive? Does he have any remorse? Why murder a man over $160? And what had his people been left to carry? So I went looking for them. I eventually found Wright's daughter, Dominica Branche. She was thirteen at the time of the shooting.

After a bit of back-and-forth via email, we arranged a call. I was nervous and a bit apprehensive. What did I actually hope to get out of this conversation, so many years later, with people who had no role in the killing? But the other part of me wanted and needed answers. I decided to keep the call a secret from my family. I wanted to have as clear-eyed and sober a conversation as I could. I went into reporter mode, carefully weighing my words and tone.

The first thing Dominica said was that her father had died back in 2014. "Through the grapevine, we heard that he shot a man. But it's one of those things you just don't discuss. You never speak on them, and that's part of the problem. I don't tell people my dad killed a man and was in prison; that's a shameful thing and a sad thing."

Dominica remembers her mother doing what she could to keep the news of her father's crime quiet. But over the years, the picture of what he'd done became much clearer. The first gun she saw was one her mother kept under her pillow, a tiny little thing with a pearl handle. It was a gift from her father. After her father was sent to prison, her mother fell further into despair. She carried a sadness deep in her soul. They lived poor, on welfare and from paycheck to paycheck from the jobs her mom would pick up at various factories in Philadelphia. Though Dominica described her father as mostly absent, in his later years, he maintained a peripheral kind of relationship with his children. It's hard to balance the young man he was before moving to Philadelphia and the man he was after. She grew up hearing stories from her mother and aunts about how back home Wright was a smart and athletic teenager who'd made a name for himself as a young civil rights activist who helped to desegregate the city's lunch counters. But something was broken in Wright in the fifteen or so years between then and the murder of Grandpop Horace. "The people with all the issues have all the guns," Dominica said.

The killing left an indelible gap in Wright's family. But in his later years, with his crime and prison long behind him, Wright worked to build a relationship with his grandchildren. For them, he was the grandfather who tried his best to make graduations and big moments.

For a couple of weeks, Dominica and I went back and forth on the phone and email. I sent her articles about the shooting and news clips I found about her father's time in the movement.

In our final phone conversation, Dominica said she'd no longer be talking with me.

But she offered what I'm certain no one in my family had ever received. An apology. "I'm sorry," she said. "A thousand sorrys couldn't change anything. But I'm sorry for all that your family has been through."

Black Death, Black Reporter

The more I dig into what happened back in '76, the more my personal and professional life today feels hinged to the past. For two decades, I've been a journalist, the kind that tells stories about the way Black folks have lived and died in America. The ugly and beautiful parts of our experiences here, the weight of bearing witness, the resilience no human should have to muster, the ache of death and the pure unadulterated Black joy of surviving America, our way, with all the rich irony of Black life here. For so long, I've wrestled other people's grief into stories. Yet all the while, I've kept my own family's story tucked away as if it were some secondary plot in my life. When in reality, in ways I can't fully explain but know to be true, the past, our past, has led me to this moment.

I have this folder in my office with old newspaper clippings from when Grandpop was killed. I pull them out every now and then. In one of the articles, the reporter describes my grandmother's testimony on the first day of Wright's trial. Grandmom Ida told the judge and jury how she was shaken awake by Grandpop's "desperate screams." I can feel the bite of each word.

"'Ida, I've been shot.'"

"'I tried to run and he shot me in the mouth.'"

"He must have grabbed me because there was blood on the front of my nightgown."

It's hard to read those lines. The worst, most private day of my family's life in newsprint for public consumption. But over the years, I've written hundreds of stories with similar lines about shootings and last breaths and smears of blood. And as routine as they have become, they never get any easier to write.

So many of us in this craft take a cynical, arm's-length approach to covering life and death in this country. Some reporters treat (Black) life, death, and American violence as some sort of cheap commodity. But it's always so much more, and it deserves care and compassion. We deserve care and compassion.

Grandpop Horace's murder marked a turning point in the kind of violence that Black folks would experience in the coming decades. Industrial cities like Baltimore, Camden, Chicago, and Philadelphia would convulse under the death of industry. Their swollen populations, bound by racial and economic segregation, along with a looming war on drugs—which was a proxy for a war on Black and poor people—would experience a destructive rise in police and community violence. The 1970s would give way to decades of hostile economic policies that would further fleece Black America of wealth and opportunity. Structural inequality, poverty, overpolicing, and easy access to guns created a toxic mix in the 1980s and 1990s.

Time and again, my family would be touched by the plague of gun violence. In 1996, a young woman put a bullet in the back of my stepbrother George Green's head. His body was found in the back seat of a car dumped in Camden. His death was among a record number of murders in the city of Camden that year, a record that would stand for seventeen years. In 2007, a cousin, Jeffrey Brown, eighteen, was among a trio of teenagers who shot and killed a man during a botched home invasion and robbery in Atlantic City. He was sentenced to twenty-two years in prison. The youngest in the group was just fourteen at the time of the killing. Just two years later, in 2009, Jeffrey's twenty-five-year-old brother, Marcus, was shot and killed. He bled out beneath the glow of Atlantic City streetlights. His grandmother, only a few blocks away at the time, had heard the shots from her bedroom window. To this day, gunfire fills her nightmares.

3

Catharsis

I grew up hearing the story of how gun violence took Grandpop Horace. I took it for granted. But years later, when I was a teenager, with my stepbrother George's killing, the grim notes struck a bit differently. While I'd never known my grandfather, for a stretch of years, my stepbrother George was a regular figure around the house on random weekends and over holiday breaks. We weren't close, but he was within reach. He was older by five or six years, and even then, I knew that he was trouble(d). Once, on Christmas morning when I was maybe ten, I was shaken awake from the top bunk in my bedroom by sparring whispers. I peeked over the railing and could see my stepfather pleading with his son, begging him to front him some crack cocaine. I never told anyone about what I saw or heard that morning. I've carried it with me for all these years. At that tender age, I witnessed a side of my stepfather and stepbrother that revealed their humanity in a way that forever altered the way I saw them—and the world.

Both father and son had lived lives strung in one way or another to drugs and violence. My stepfather lost his father when he was just a boy, stabbed to death in Harlem by a bunch of teenagers. After his father's death, he started using hard drugs in his teens and would spend the rest of his life battling addiction. He and my mother got married when I was seven. Not long after my stepfather moved in, I remember going into the hallway closet to grab my coat to go out and play. When I reached into the pocket of what I thought was my coat, my little fingers found their way around a hypodermic needle. I'll never forget the look on my mother's face when I handed it to her, like her world had been flipped upside down. Our family would spend the next fifteen years in a dizzying spiral of his drug binges, disappearing acts, and incarceration.

There were a surprising number of good times braided in with the bad. Pop, as we call him, no doubt loved me. Of my two siblings and three stepbrothers, my sister was the only girl. And of the brothers, I was the one most inclined to school rather than the proverbial streets. I always felt like Pop appreciated that about me. I got into a little trouble here and there, was never afraid to fight, and maybe a bit emotional, but I was a good student, likable, and probably the most athletic of the brothers. I marched to my own beat.

It was Pop who taught me how to properly catch and throw a baseball. He also taught me how to fish. We'd spend long summer days watching bobbers dipping in and out of our favorite little ponds. The first time I called him *Dad* was when he surprised me with my very own fishing pole. None of the others spent as much one-on-one time with Pop as I did. He was often good spirited and had great taste in music. He had an enormous record collection filled with records from the O'Jays, Earth, Wind & Fire, the Chi-Lites, and Marvin Gaye. And after he introduced me to the Last Poets, I'd never again hear the spoken word the same.

Pop had lots of skills, too. He worked hard as a brickmason. He could fix your car or your roof, or build you a deck all with his bare hands. Much later, in my teen years, it was Pop who would get his buddies at the auto mechanic's shop to let go of whatever junkers they had in the garage for a few hundred bucks that he'd then pass to me on a sweet repayment plan.

I loved Pop. But at the height of his addiction when I was the last of my siblings still living at home, I experienced the darkness of his drug abuse and drug-induced delusion in a way that no one else did. When he was in the throes of his addiction, calls from angry homeowners he'd ghosted mid-job would start pouring in. His juggling act had become too complicated, all the balls he had in the air—contract jobs, family, an expensive drug habit, lies, and disappointments—became too heavy and they'd land all at once with a thud. Then there was the emotional tumult. I never felt completely unsafe, but it did feel like I was watching the water rise slowly all around me. For some reason, I was able to anchor myself with my head partially above water, while those around me thrashed while drowning.

My mother worked a 3:00 p.m.–11:00 p.m. shift as an aide at the nearby Ancora Psychiatric Hospital. So I spent many evenings alone with Pop, who often would be holed up in our basement with the lights off, getting high and paranoid. He'd creep up the steps, push open the door just wide enough, and ask if I was hearing the voices, too. Other times, he'd just disappear for days on end. My mother would bore into the depths of Camden to pull him out of whatever hole or hovel he'd buried himself in.

While Pop was a generally good guy fighting off bad demons, after a while, it was hard to separate the good guy from the demons. Sometimes, after one of his binges, he'd stumble in looking and smelling like hell. I'd hear his footsteps on the living room floor above my head, marching toward his and my mom's bedroom. And then there'd be the inevitable sound of tussling or jostling and arguing. Once, in one of these homecomings, my mother took a shadeless lamp and jammed the hot bulb into his chest until it blistered and bled through his undershirt. Another time, I heard his lumbering footsteps, some shouting, and then a massive thud. I jumped from my bed and froze at the bottom of the steps leading to the kitchen, where the crash had come from. I stood there, paralyzed, and I didn't know why. Then I blinked and I was standing at the top of the steps in the doorway. Pop and my mother were wrestling on the kitchen floor. My mother's eyes were filled with rage, and his were dazed. I could always tell when he was high by the look in his eyes and the sound of his voice, which became oddly stilted when under the influence.

"Watch out, man, she got a .38!"

I looked down, and in between their trembling, pretzeled hands was a small black gun. My mother was straining to get her finger around its trigger. And Pop was doing his damnedest to keep that from happening. My mother always hated guns. But there she was, ready to put a bullet into her crack-addicted husband. I stood there, for what felt like an eternity, waiting for a bang to bring the whole house crashing down. That bang never came. I don't even remember what happened next. I don't remember being afraid, just exhausted and expecting the worst. I had been schooled early that it's not *if* bad things will happen, it's *when*. And when you mix drugs, guns, and betrayal, bad things are likely to happen sooner than later.

But it wasn't just that dangerous mixture. Both of them had been carrying around the trauma of violence in different ways. My mother, trapped in mourning her father's killing. My stepfather, turning his trauma into self-destruction. Later, when my stepbrother was murdered, Pop fell further into the abyss of addiction. A few years later, another of his sons died of cancer. He's lived his life ever since tormented by regret.

That none of us were killed that day is beyond me. But that moment did signal another kind of death. No matter how many times Pop would get clean, relapse, get clean again, and promise to get better and be better, I think that moment was the beginning of the end for us. His absences grew longer and more sporadic. A cloud of suspicion and anxiety settled over our house. I'd hear my mother crying alone behind her bedroom door. All I could do was turn inward, a space where I could find freedom if not peace.

I was starting to get into some trouble at school. Not with my grades. I was always an A/B student who was part of my elementary school's gifted and talented program. But I was quick to fight. I never liked bullies and took pride in my willingness to fight any of them anywhere. In sixth grade, I was suspended two or three times for fighting. The only thing that saved me was the benefit of the doubt that I'd earned in the classroom. The Trymaine who was landing in the principal's office for scrapping was the same Trymaine who was winning writing contests, loved reading poetry, and always got along with his teachers. By then, my older brother, Oliver—or Lil Man, as we called him—was finding his way to the streets. When he turned sixteen, he took himself out of school and spent most of his young adult life making ends meet his own way. (Funny story about that phrase, *making ends meet*. As kids, we'd sometimes go to the far end of the deli section at our local ACME to buy the days-old, sliced, chipped, and beat-up pieces of meat that the butcher would slap onto a Styrofoam tray, wrap in cellophane, and sell at bargain prices. Some folks call it "end meat" or "end cuts." I grew up thinking that "trying to make ends meet" meant you were down so bad you could barely afford to buy the deli *end meats*.)

When I was twelve and just starting to hang out at the basketball courts near my house, my mother made a life-changing decision. She sent me to Milton Hershey School, a tuition-free boarding school in Hershey, Pennsylvania, for poor and low-income students. With its $17 billion endowment, it's the wealthiest private school in the United States. Years earlier, my mother and an aunt tried to enroll my brother and a cousin at the school, but they refused to go. I was different. I saw an opportunity. I saw the videos and pamphlets featuring a diverse group of smiling kids and rolling green expanses. I gobbled up every note struck about scouting and canoeing and student homelife.

Soon after I enrolled and moved onto campus, I learned things weren't always as sweet.

The student homes were led by houseparents who were tasked with making sure we were safe and fed, followed the rules, and did our chores. They'd shuttle us back and forth to school or to events on and off campus. Some were mission-driven to help elevate us beyond our circumstances. Others, though, believed that we needed civilizing, the same way the government once saw Native American youth who they forced into distant boarding schools. To some of the most racist houseparents, we needed breaking.

While I was a well-liked student who dove headlong into writing, English, history, and social studies while also playing on the football, basketball, and track teams, I was a so-called problem child in the student home. I was raised to be Black and proud and could spot a racist a mile away. When the famously white supremacist book *The Bell Curve: Intelligence and Class Structure in American Life* was published, expounding on the supposed natural mental inferiority of Black people, I got into an argument with my then-housefather. He agreed with the book based on his experience in the military, where he claimed Black soldiers didn't occupy any leadership positions because they weren't smart enough to be promoted into them. Another time, I got into a fight with another houseparent who insisted on calling collard greens *colored greens*. In the six years I spent at Milton Hershey School, I was transferred from three different student homes because houseparents didn't know how to handle me. There were certainly good men and women who worked at the school and helped guide me through those turbulent teen years, including a host of teachers and coaches who saw in me what many others wouldn't or couldn't. But there were also pain points along the way.

From the seven-thousand-acre Milton Hershey School campus that stretched across bucolic farmland in the town that Hershey built, where the morning sun was often met with the sweet and pungent combination of wafting chocolate and cow manure, we sometimes struggled to pry ourselves from our worst experiences. The emotional strain of being away from everyone who loved us, back-home friends, and everything we'd known could be overwhelming. Some cracked under the pressure and left. Others would act out and were kicked out. Still others withered academically, socially, or emotionally. Many of my classmates had experienced some of what I had back home, often a much more extreme version. One friend's parents died in a murder-suicide. Others had parents who'd been shot dead or struggled with drugs, alcohol, or the pangs of poverty. A number had parents who were incarcerated.

Once, in tenth grade, I accidentally sparked a campus-wide gun scare that ended with multiple suspensions and an expulsion. On a trip to Walmart, I found these heavy, lifelike, silver toy handguns. They looked just like the real deal. I bought one and showed it to a friend. The Halloween dance was approaching, and I had a novel, albeit incredibly dangerous idea of rolling into the dance with our fake guns, black hoodies, and white hockey masks like the ones made popular by the sadistic killer Jason in the *Friday the 13th* horror movie franchise. But soon after those toy pistols were off the shelves, the trouble started. One kid used one of the alloy guns to rob someone in the bathroom. Others were caught goofing off with them in class and in the hallways by teachers and sent to the principal's office. One by one, kids were getting jammed up.

Things hit a crescendo just hours before a big football game against a rival in the nearby city of Harrisburg, the state capital. There was real concern by the administration that if one of us went to the game and flashed one of our fake guns, someone might get shot with a real one. School officials sent out a warning that anyone caught with one of the Walmart guns would face serious punishment. They began searching lockers and patting people down. I was in the locker room getting dressed for the game when I saw the principal, flanked by other administrators and coaches, moving through the rows of lockers like G-men. They went directly to where a good buddy was sitting, tying on his cleats, and grabbed him by his arm and whisked him away. I was frozen in shock. I still had my gun back at the student home under my mattress. I just knew this was it for me. Everything I'd worked so hard for all came down to a twelve-dollar toy gun from Walmart. But no one came for me. I finished getting dressed, boarded the bus, and played in the game.

When I finally got home, I ran to my room and lifted up my mattress. No gun. Then my roommate, Bernard, one of my best friends to this day, walked in and dapped me up. "I got you, man," he said with a smile. He'd tossed the gun out of our bedroom window and into the bushes before inspection. I later retrieved it, and two days later, on Sunday, during our requisite worship service at the massive Founders Hall auditorium, I dropped it in a bathroom trash can. I was in the clear. My teammate wasn't so lucky. He was suspended indefinitely.

Looking back, it's scary to think about how that cheap

toy gun could've upended my life. Almost twenty years to the day after that Halloween dance, twelve-year-old Tamir Rice was shot down by police in Cleveland with a toy pistol in his hands. He had been playing outside of a community center when someone called 911 saying a man was waving a gun at passersby. The police killed him within seconds, opening fire from a flung-open patrol car door before the car even came to a stop. After his death, I spent hours talking with the boy's grief-stricken mother and father. And when they pulled out old photos of the chubby-faced kid, I saw myself at twelve. Black boys have a way of looking like men to people who've never truly seen us. We're rarely given the privilege of childhood or the space for boys-will-be-boys high jinks.

The coming years at Milton Hershey would be filled with great highs and lows. I'd made the honor roll, was an explorer scout, played varsity sports, and wrote for the school yearbook. I also took advanced communications classes, where I spent many days roaming the halls with a camera in hand, taking photos or videos of my classmates before heading back to the photo lab to develop the pictures by hand. I had a close group of friends, still my brothers to this day, and a string of first loves and first everythings.

But there would be some incredible lows, too.

Latoya Lawton and I became friends our freshman year. We were in the same homeroom. Lawton. Lee. Any alphabetical roll call or seating put us next to each other. Toya had this beautiful brown skin and always wore baggy jeans and Timberland boots. She looked and sounded every bit of Brooklyn, where she was from. She laughed easily and loudly but was also tough. She never backed down from a fight, and she had a few. Ours was the most beautiful platonic relationship I've ever experienced. One night, during the summer between our junior and senior years, she called me, giddy about a party she was headed to at Rockaway Beach in Queens. We talked for about twenty minutes as she was ironing a pair of white jeans she was going to wear. We laughed a lot and talked about our upcoming senior year back on campus. And then we said goodbye. It would be our last.

The next morning, I got a call from my friend Bernard. He said Latoya was dead. She'd gone to the beach with her cousin, another friend of ours, and a couple of guys. Her cousin got caught in a rip current and was dragged away from the shore. Toya couldn't swim, but that night, she jumped in to save her.

When he said Latoya died, I heard the words, but I couldn't understand them. For a long moment after we hung up, I was numb. When my mom came home, I met her at the top of the steps in the kitchen, and when I repeated the words—*Latoya died*—I finally understood them. I collapsed into her arms, crying like I'd never cried before. I collapsed in her arms, crying like I'd never cried before. When I think of my sister Latoya, I'm brought back to the pain of that day. She was just seventeen.

Black folks not being able to swim, and drowning because of it, is one of those nasty little holdovers from Jim Crow when Black people were denied access to public pools. Still today, Black children face the highest risk of drowning, with just 36 percent knowing how to swim, compared to 60 percent of white children.

A year or two before I went off to Milton Hershey, Pop went off to prison. From what I understand, he got high one day and touched one of my cousins inappropriately. With his record and charges, he ended up spending several years behind bars. He went in when I was in sixth grade and didn't get out until after I graduated from high school.

During Pop's prison years, we'd visit him on weekends. My mom would cook and pack his favorite foods in Tupperware containers that she'd hand over to guards to stab through before they'd clear it for delivery. We'd sit in the huge visiting room and wait to see him stroll from behind a guard's desk, his slow steps as big as his smile. There was a playroom off to the side of the room. The playroom's floor was covered with blue wrestling mats, and there was a TV hoisted high up in the corner of the room, secured in what looked like a big old locked birdcage. There were dozens of us kids in that little room, the majority of us Black or Hispanic, with some poor whites sprinkled in, from all over New Jersey, all grappling in our own way with young lives bound by the precarity of the system.

In 1996, the year I graduated from the Milton Hershey School and as Pop was preparing for release, his son, my stepbrother George, was murdered. Five days before Christmas, neighbors in East Camden found his body in the back seat of a green Plymouth. He was shoeless and his head was wrapped in plastic bags. He was twenty-four years old. Weeks later, an eighteen-year-old woman named Alicia Jolly was arrested and charged with his murder. Her story was that she came home and found him dead, but the police and a witness said she was braiding George's hair when she pressed a gun to the back of his head and shot him twice. A man named Marvin Johnson said he was there when it happened. He even confessed to helping dump George's body. She was sentenced to twenty-seven years in prison. But she only ended up spending five and a half years behind bars.

Life After Death

Many years later, so much of what I experienced as a kid would be relived through my reporting. Through journalism, I would be born again, this time behind ribbons of yellow crime scene tape.

The cosmic connective tissue keeps revealing itself. When Grandpop Horace was shot and the trial of his killer got underway, a reporter named Renee Winkler covered the story for the *Courier-Post*. Twenty years later, she also covered George's murder. Winkler's stories were matter-of-fact, the straightforward who, what, when, where, and why style that journalists are taught from the beginning. I've written hundreds of stories just like that. They serve a straightforward aim of keeping the reporter—and, to some degree, their readers—at an emotional distance from those involved. No matter how wrought, how painful, or how disturbing a story is, the teller of the story is unflinchingly sober, and their journalistic integrity is unimpeached and uncompromised. There is certainly some value in that kind of reporting. Hyperbole and drama can cloud the basic facts, or at least distract from them. But reporting devoid of an emotional center often does more than just keep lines unblurred. It can unwittingly (sometimes wittingly) strip the subjects of such reporting, especially victims, of their humanity.

Gun Griot

In my early days as a street reporter, I'd often pull up to a crime scene even before the homicide detectives arrived. Too many times to count, I'd find a Black man my age or younger dead with a halo of blood or brain matter splashed on the pavement. It became routine. I'd count the shell casings—four, five, six—sprinkled around freshly fallen bodies. They'd be tossed like a constellation of stars hovering around dark moons. Drive-by shootings would leave long, rolling tails, like the handle on the Big Dipper. The more up close and personal, the tighter the orbit.

I'd trace the little numbered police cones marking where each spent shell had fallen, the way a fairy-tale character might follow a trail of breadcrumbs back home. But these victims never had such fortune. Murder led them astray. Some of them were killed over turf, some in revenge. Many were victims of the deadly grind of the drug trade. Others were killed by the police. A high number were innocent victims caught in the cross fire—too many of them children. Most often, these victims were poor and Black.

I learned to identify family members by their level of grief. Inconsolable wailing, unsteady feet, breathless delirium—a mother or sister. Angry with balled fists and tears—a brother or close cousin. Girlfriends often stumbled in after the scene was set, clawing dizzily at the police tape. The best friends and homeboys stayed close but not too close, trading whispers before floating away in groups of three or four people at a time, revenge bubbling up in their minds. The fathers always seemed stoic, either numbed by the pain or resigned to the way Black male life is so easily lost or stolen. They had been young and Black once; they knew the score. For years, I lived this kind of *Groundhog Day* existence, a highlight reel of murder and mayhem that never changed no matter how many times I popped my head up at crime scenes across the country. I'd watch the most miserable carnivals form around those fallen constellations of mothers and lovers, siblings and friends weeping over the young and the dead.

In their faces, I'd see the faces of my own family. I saw my own mother's tears and could imagine my older brother and cousins with guns tucked in their waistbands, ready to squeeze off shots had I been the one left with a bloody halo. I saw myself in many of them. Young and Black and just trying to find a way to survive forces bigger than we'll ever be.

Many times, the victims' families saw me as one of their own, too. They often shooed away other—white—reporters but shared with me the last intimate memories they had of their loved ones. They dug up old yearbook photos and reeled off their dead boy's—they were almost always boys—hopes and dreams. I like to tell myself that I've served as a conduit for the last whispers of lives lost too soon. That I am a griot passing down the stories of how we live and die and everything in between, a truth teller riffing on the tragic mundanity of American gun violence and the systemic, institutional, and structural racism that feeds it. But for those of us keeping tabs, especially on the impact of guns in Black and brown communities, there is no solace. This exhausting pas de deux between Black death and Black scribe is as much a performance in journalism as it is a perpetual act of purgation. For many of those who cheat death, the survivors, there often is no healing, no level of exorcism that can rid them of the emotional and spiritual, let alone physical, scars left by gun violence. Few things shatter a body, or a mind, like a bullet. Survival is sometimes uglier than death. Victims often lose limbs, their ability to walk or talk. Some lose control of their bowels, and some, their minds. In places where gun violence happens most, what's left are whole communities warped with seen and unseen scar tissue.

Each time I wrote of these last breaths or broken bodies, it was as if a piece of me was breaking, too. With each story, I was brought to the edge of death, on repeat. Their names and faces have piled up inside of me. I thought I ran out of room a long time ago, but the list has never stopped growing. There are also the tangible keepsakes I've held on to. The school and yearbook photos. The family pictures. The funeral programs. The newspaper clippings. The mini-biographies I wrote in chicken scratch in too many reporters' notepads to count, filled with ages and dates and the tortured poetry of the scenes where they'd fallen.

In life and death, but especially in death, I've done everything in my power to translate the pain of others into something digestible, something that might absorb in the guts of anyone willing to listen. Thinking about it now, it all seems so dark and morbid. But there have been beautiful moments, too. Knowing what I know now about the media in general, I'm not sure how forthcoming I'd be with some random reporter showing up on my doorstep on the worst day of my life. But even in folks' darkest hours and the worst days of their lives, so many have revealed extraordinary vulnerability, a kind of openness with me, a brother-stranger.

Kevin's Dream

The tenets of journalism include this idea of objectivity and never becoming part of the story. So we sometimes build artificial barriers between ourselves and the people we cover. I never quite bought into that notion, though I'd learn to go through the professional motions while still trying to be my authentic self. When I'd be invited closer, I'd cling to those moments, relishing the way it felt to have the veil falling between us. I'd be lying if I said I'd never shed tears with someone I was interviewing or shared knowing glances in admission of the hard truths we couldn't deny.

Many years ago, just months into my one and only reporting internship, I found myself in one of those veil-dropping moments. I was covering police and crime for the *Philadelphia Daily News*. My daily routine included keeping tabs on the chatter from the police scanner perched by my desk and calling police headquarters and various law enforcement sources to see what if any bloody news was being made out in the streets. One day, I got word that a couple of teenagers had been shot and left badly wounded. For the coming weeks, I kept checking in on the case. And finally, after weeks of sniffing around and countless calls to sources, I learned that the most badly injured of the two boys was recovering in a hospital not far from the *Daily News*. A stranger, I talked my way into the building and up to his room, and soon, I was silenced by what I saw.

After introducing myself, I stood there, watching a snarl of tubes and wires snake from his body. They coiled across his sunken chest and belly, tangling his lanky, limp brown frame. I stared down at him, studying every contour and groove of his narrow brown face, the way his eyes beamed through a haze of medication.

The incessant whoosh and beep of his breathing machine, a hulking contraption in the corner of the room, broke through the pregnant silence between us. His eyes grew wide as he labored to speak. His lips quivered.

"I have this dream," he says. "Every night, it's the same thing."

He's on a basketball court dribbling and passing, cutting through the lane. He pivots, spins left, steps right, catches the ball just inside of the three-point line, and as he jumps to shoot, he's rising, flying through the air like he has jet packs strapped to his legs. He can feel the heat melting the rubber soles off his high-top sneakers and singeing off his laces. And it feels good. Every sensation feels like it's his first time feeling anything and everything. Then he shoots, savoring the last kiss of the ball as it floats off his fingertips. With his shooting arm still raised in the air, he watches the ball as it hangs high above the rim before it crashes down into the net.

"It's like I'm really playing," he says, "because I can feel everything."

A toothy smile stretched across his face as he let out an airy, wheezy laugh. I smiled back and looked across his bed to where his mother stood, expecting her to smile, too. Instead, I found an ocean of tears welling in her eyes and her hands trembling, one clenched over her mouth and the other over her heart.

"I'm still paralyzed, but it doesn't stop me," he says as his mother looks away, hiding the inevitable flood of emotions. "It doesn't stop me. Nothing can stop me. God wouldn't give me anything I couldn't handle."

Silent tears tumbled down her cheeks.

"I'm going to try to live a regular life," he says.

For a long moment, his mother and I stared deep into each other, then down onto his scarred body.

By then, I was becoming accustomed to seeing the damage that bullets do to Black bodies. They leave them hollow and lifeless. In that tangle of tubes and wires was a young man doing everything he could to stay alive.

It was late July 2003 inside a small, dimly lit room at the Jefferson Moss-Magee Rehabilitation Hospital in downtown Philadelphia. Kevin Johnson was just nineteen. I wasn't too much older and nearing the end of my internship at the *Daily News*. A little more than a month earlier, a group of teens tried to rob Kevin for his $150 Allen Iverson basketball jersey. He and a cousin were waiting at a trolley stop in Southwest Philly when the other guys rolled up, pointed to the jersey, and told him to "give it up." When he refused, one of them pressed a gun to the back of Kevin's neck, just inches below his skull, and pulled the trigger. When his cousin turned to run, they shot him in the face. Both survived, but Kevin was instantly paralyzed.

All these years later, I still think about Kevin. He had such an amazing sense of optimism despite his world being torn down so violently. We were both so young back then with so much to look forward to that summer. He was working at McDonald's and hoping to get into college by the start of the next semester. I'd managed to finally finish my four-year degree in about six and a half years and was amazed that I was actually getting paid to write. But that one bullet changed everything. It knocked Kevin off his feet and into paralysis. I'd never be the same either. Something inside of me was left frozen, too. From his bedside to the writing of these words, my life and career have been tethered to his spirit and the shock of all that he'd lost.

It wasn't just Kevin's infectious buoyance. Or his courageous fight to stay alive. Both of those things have certainly stuck with me in deep, meaningful ways. But what I haven't been able to escape is the incalculability of the cost that he and his family would pay for the bullet lodged in his spine. He paid with his freedom, his mobility, and any future he and his family had ever hoped for. And for what? The robbers that shot him never even got the jersey they wanted so badly. The bloody rag had to be cut off Kevin's back by paramedics. But what they took was priceless. They robbed his mother of a loving son who was just finding his footing in the world, his siblings of an adoring brother who'd chase them up and down the block, and the world of whoever Kevin would've grown to become, unbound by a wheelchair.

But there were other costs, too. From the moment that bullet dug into Kevin's body, the tally began to tick. His medical bills mounted quickly. Before the rehab facility would discharge him, the family's bi-level row house would need to be renovated: a special outlet for his breathing machine needed to be installed, a wheelchair ramp would need to be erected, doorframes needed widening, and the bathrooms needed to be overhauled. All of that or they'd have to move out. Or the unthinkable: send Kevin to a nursing home. He would require twenty-four-hour care to keep him alive and a specially equipped van to transport him and his hulking new wheelchair. That was just to get him home. It was money they didn't have. Within months of the shooting, his family's meager savings were exhausted.

The shooting threw off the family's orbit in so many intangible ways. But the financial blow was a secondary injury that none of them had anticipated. In the coming years, the costs related to Kevin's medical condition would be staggering, in the millions. There were the big-ticket items like the several-thousand-dollar wheelchair ramp and his wheelchair, which cost $35,000. Some of his medications were a few hundred dollars a month. There were adult diapers and supplies needed to keep his tracheostomy and breathing tubes clean. The family scraped together what they could to pay some of these bills out of pocket. Kindhearted strangers helped a lot. But the bulk of the financial costs to keep Kevin alive were paid by taxpayers through public insurance. His mother, Janice, quit her job with her then-husband's restaurant cleaning business and took on the full-time job as Kevin's caregiver. As the family's debts skyrocketed, Kevin's health plummeted.

Just one bullet. The cascade of costs and consequences

sparked by a bullet, purchased for as little as twenty-five cents a round, started an avalanche of millions. Not just for families like Kevin's but for all of American society.

Million-Dollar Bullets

Economists Philip Cook and Jens Ludwig, who years ago did some of the most foundational work on the economic impact of gun violence, place the societal cost of a single gunshot injury at more than $1 million. Every gun death costs us more than $5 million. Consider the more than one hundred thousand people who are shot in the US in any given year and the price tag becomes staggering. The vast majority of gunshot victims will survive, but many, like Kevin, will suffer catastrophic injury requiring costly medical care and rehabilitation for the rest of their lives. Thanks to medical advancements, these victims are living longer lives, multiplying those costs. Ted Miller, an economist with the Pacific Institute for Research and Evaluation, says that in the aggregate of much broader direct and indirect societal costs, gun violence costs an astonishing $557 billion a year. Some conservative estimates put these costs at 2.6 percent of the US gross domestic product (GDP). These aren't monies that are satisfied with some IOU sent to zip codes that suffer the brunt of the bloodshed. American taxpayers from the burbs to the battle zones shoulder millions every single day to satisfy the myriad costs of bullets hitting flesh. Taxpayers, survivors, their families, and employers pay an average of $7.79 million in health care costs and another $30.16 million in police and criminal justice costs, according to Everytown for Gun Safety. Employers lose about $1.47 million a day in productivity, revenue, and costs to replace gun violence victims, and society writ large loses $1.34 billion daily in quality-of-life costs related to gunshots.

While these figures are mammoth, they obviously don't consider the many hard-to-account-for costs: lives lost or ruined, homes wrecked, communities divided, emotional trauma.

Of all the questions that I had standing there in Kevin's hospital room, listening to his mother running through the seemingly insurmountable costs of keeping Kevin alive, there is one that has begged itself from that moment to this one. How much are we willing to pay? I've spent much of my career asking that same question of police, politicians, victims, and perpetrators of violent crime. I've asked it in cities across the country. I rephrased it and reconsidered it as I grew from a cub reporter to a seasoned veteran. The question took on greater significance in the era of the Black Lives Matter movement, when the philosophical and rhetorical value of Black life was being debated in the streets and in the media in the wake of the shootings of unarmed Black men and women by police. In wrestling with these ideas, I think about Kevin's plight and the plight of so many other young Black people in poor and working-class communities, those who suffer a disproportionate number of daily shootings.

I think of Ralph Green. In 1993, Ralph, a sixteen-year-old gunshot victim from Brooklyn, was called before a congressional panel on gun violence. He testified that he'd grown up in a tough neighborhood where violence, guns, and shootings came in spades. Before the shooting, he was a promising athlete whose prowess earned him starting spots on the varsity football and basketball teams as a freshman in high school. Then one day, his life came crashing down—with a bullet. In the year between the shooting and being asked to testify in Washington, he underwent fourteen surgeries, including the amputation of his left leg. His hospital costs at that point had already climbed higher than $1 million.

"How many million-dollar bullets will it take before someone wakes up?" Ralph asked the panel. "Aren't these gunshots loud enough?"

The story I wrote about Kevin was one of my first front-page stories. The *Philadelphia Daily News*, with its tabloid format, published a full front-page photo of his smiling face. I'm not sure I've ever been so moved by a smile as I was that day. I knew then that the Kevins of the world meant way more than headlines and quotes.

The Debt

For years, I lost touch with Kevin and his family. In that time, he suffered many physical and emotional setbacks. He cycled in and out of the hospital to treat various medical complications related to his injury. But he fought for his life each step of the way. While his body struggled to heal, his big heart beat stronger than ever. When one of the young men who shot him, Michael Wittington, was released from prison, Kevin and Janice were able to meet him. Kevin not only forgave him for what he did, he befriended him. The two ate heaping plates of Janice's spaghetti together and played video games.

"He kept me strong. If he was mad, angry, I wouldn't have been able to wake up every morning and take care of him," Janice tells me. "He was very cheerful, always smiling. But I'd hear him crying at night . . . I could hear him through the baby monitor that I had set up. He would never let me see that. But I'd be there holding that monitor crying right along with him. He'd be downstairs crying and I'd be upstairs crying."

One day, Kevin's tears finally stopped. At the end of 2006, as I was preparing to leave *The Times-Picayune* in New Orleans for a job with *The New York Times*, I got a call from my mother. She saw on the local news that Kevin had died. I remember holding the phone in silence for what felt like a millennium as I played back that day at his bedside. A malfunction with his breathing machine left him brain-dead. It was a little more than a week before Thanksgiving, and his family made the hard decision to take him off of life support. The NBA star Allen Iverson, whose jersey Kevin was wearing when he was shot, covered the costs of his funeral.

Yet Kevin's family continues to pay an unpayable debt.

After Kevin's death, his mother pushed her husband away, blaming him for Kevin's death. Earlier on the night that he died, Janice decided to go to bed early, expecting her husband to be home from work within the hour. She woke to the chirping of the front door alarm and the emergency siren from Kevin's breathing machine going off. She rushed downstairs to find the machine powered off. Kevin wasn't breathing, and her husband was walking in the door an hour later than she'd expected.

Janice has struggled with anxiety, depression, sleeplessness, and memory loss since Kevin's death. Her doctors have diagnosed her with post-traumatic stress disorder, and she's on a cycle of antidepression drugs to keep her mentally and emotionally moored. Every Monday at noon, she sees her therapist, who has given her tools to cope, but nothing has addressed the root of her pain: her son is gone.

"It's getting worse. Ain't nothing getting better," she says. With each passing day, there's more shooting and killing in Philadelphia. The news reports trigger her anxiety. Fourth of July fireworks do the same thing. Each explosion. Each crackle and boom blow another hole in her chest.

When Kevin died, a little piece inside of everyone who loved him died, too. His mother is withering. His two sisters are struggling to find their way. His brother went and got a gun license and has grown almost irrationally protective of his family. Nafese, the cousin who was with him the night he was paralyzed, isn't the same either. He's "still respectful, still smart," but he has taken a darker path in life. He's turned his pain into self-destruction. He drinks and smokes weed and hangs out with thugs, Janice said. He's been in and out of jail and has been shot a second time. If the shooting that left the cousins wounded pushed Nafese to the edge, Kevin's death pushed him over it.

"If I could put a cost on my feelings, my emotions, it would be in the millions," Janice tells me, more than fifteen years after Kevin was shot. "Because I lost so much when Kevin passed away, and it feels like I'm losing more every single day."

Janice says that she wishes everyone would have had the chance to see Kevin's struggle, to see him rolling down the block in his wheelchair, sucking air through a ventilator tube by day, and by night hear his whispered tears.

Life, Loss, and Libations

On the corner of Thirteenth Street and Erie Avenue in Philly, on the broadside of a row house, there's a thirty-eight-foot mural bursting in shades of blue, purple, and red. Nearly two dozen doves, one for every year that Kevin Johnson lived, soar toward freedom. Below them, there's a portrait of Kevin from before the shooting, dapper in a tuxedo and bow tie, and in the foreground, there's an empty wheelchair. Like those birds, Kevin is shown free from this world and that chair. Janice, his dutiful mother until the end, is featured, too. Her head is lowered, and her eyes are filled with the kind of sorrow only a mother knows.

As distinctly as we live and die, there's a shared way in which we've ritualized our grief and mourning. There's this way that Black folks come together in death, with a dignity that often defies the level of disrespect their loved ones faced in dying. Mourning is perhaps the purest, rawest form of human bonding. And African Americans have had plenty of such ritual, holding tight to some of the bereavement traditions that date back centuries, from before the first of our Black bodies were sown in American dirt. But we've also developed new rituals in response to the changing manner and frequency of Black death.

We pour libations for our ancestors, the long gone and just gone. We sing over caskets—songs that have carried us through time and dimensions, like "I'll Fly Away," whose lyrics reach back to the days that Black folk toiled in cotton fields and on chain gangs, and sang to carry them to another place.

> *When I die, Hallelujah, by and by,*
> *I'll fly away.*
> *Just a few more weary days and then,*
> *I'll fly away.*
> *To a land where joy shall never end,*
> *I'll fly away.*

There's a myth carried over from the slavery times, spun into folklore, that some enslaved Africans had the power to fly and that some of them flew back home to Africa, far away from their tortured fate in the Americas. In death, so many of our people got their wings.

We dance out of funerals to the beat of brass bands to wash

the weeping away. We fill our bellies with food and our faces with laughter, at repasts on burial day. And the young ones, they put names, dates, and portraits on T-shirts like wings on the backs of their angels. None of these mourning rituals erases the pain of death, but they remind us of why death hurts in the first place. That for a blink in time, we shared life and love together, and then it was gone.

Being Black and American means to be in a perpetual state of limbo, holding in one hand the joys of life steeped in the beauty of the cultures and traditions we've carved out of our peculiar Americanness, drenched in the residue of our lingering Africanness. And in the other hand, our perpetual closeness to death and dying, which often comes way too early. In our death rituals, those hands come together.

You see it in how we've buried our dead; in some regions, mounds are covered in conch shells. And in the music we play at funerals, a blend of centuries-old gospel, rhythm and blues, and jazz. You see it in how we save and archive funeral programs as if they're historical documents, because they are. And you hear it in the language that we use to describe the afterlife. We call funeral services *homegoings*, because it's believed that life here is just a pit stop, that there's something greater later, beyond this earthly realm.

Death and mourning are not always private, closed matters for Black families. They often don't have that privilege. Death for us, at least the violent kind, has long been a public spectacle. The way the world watched those officers in Minneapolis press the life out of George Floyd, minute by minute, through the lens of a cell phone camera on a public street in front of a busy convenience store, and then replayed on a television news loop for months on end, is little different from the old black-and-white snapshots of Black men lynched in public squares, surrounded by smiling white men, women, and children, then circulated across the country. The latter would often be sold as postcards. The former drew millions of eyes to cable news screens, where higher ratings mean higher ad revenue. The collective mourning, in agony, grief, and rage, was also done publicly.

As we've relied on our broader communities during times of tragedy, we've also faced the challenge of grieving in the public eye while searching for meaning in our mourning.

Mamie Till-Mobley, mother of Emmett Till, a boy whose murder at the hands of white supremacists after allegedly catcalling at a white woman in Money, Mississippi, helped spark the modern civil rights movement, chose to memorialize her son with an open casket. That open casket offered a window into the gruesome handiwork of American hate. The boy's face, swollen and badly mutilated by fists and a bullet, revealed the undeniable violence deployed to keep Black bodies within bounds. Mamie Till decided to force America to mourn with her family and see what those white men had done to her boy. The image of Till in that casket, the long procession of mourners streaming past it, and Mamie weary under the weight of it all would be seared into the consciousness of a whole generation of Americans, Black and white alike. Uncensored photos of the young Till's mutilated face and his funeral were published in the Black press, spreading to homes across the country. His was a cautionary tale, a reminder, an illustration, an unveiling.

Tell Me What You See

One of the first questions Black folks will ask after someone passes is: "Who's doing the body?" This is as much a factual inquisition as a value judgment. A good mortician works a quiet kind of magic, restoring dignity to the departed, sending them into eternity with grace.

The Black funeral home is a sanctuary, a place where grief and reverence and tenderness sit in the same pew. But often, in violent deaths, they become a place of physical reconstruction, where Black morticians have become masters of the so-called restoration arts. So often Black bodies are disfigured by the violence that snatched them from life. Morticians stitch, paint, and rebuild. Their makeup brushes and glue guns do the work of surgeons and sculptors. These artists patch gaping wounds in faces and restore structure to shattered or missing limbs. They work wonders with balms and wigs. One funeral home director described himself to me as "basically a plastic surgeon, but one who works with dead flesh."

That mortician's name is Ronald Jones, and years ago, I spent a couple of days with him at his funeral home in North St. Louis, one of the most violent neighborhoods in one of America's most violent cities. Jones has been in the funeral business for decades. He's one of the go-to funeral homes for many of the Black churches in North St. Louis. Jones said about one in five of his funerals are tied to gun violence. He was preparing for three or four funerals that week, nearly all of them for young people.

From the corner of one of the parlors in Jones's place, I watched as a little boy sheepishly edged nervously toward a casket placed in the center of the room, a few feet away from rows of collapsible chairs. The boy wasn't tall enough to look inside of it, so his mother grabbed him by the waist and hoisted him high enough to peer inside. His eyes grew wide at the sight of the man, his daddy, lying in the smoke-gray casket. The boy squeezed his eyes tightly and buried his face into his mother's neck as a flock of his aunties drew to the boy like moths to bright light.

Lenny Hogan, the young man tucked inside of the fancy box, nestled atop a cloud of ivory bunting, was shot and killed just about a week earlier. He was just one victim in a string of homicides of twentysomething-year-old Black men in a particularly bloody stretch. His Burberry print shirt was carefully buttoned up to the top, its brown-beige hues matching the warmth of his cafe-con-leche skin.

A little while after Lenny's family left the parlor to prepare for the service, Jones pulled me close to the young man's casket.

"Tell me what you see," Jones asked me, his hands gliding across the casket's edge. I leaned in. Lenny looked immaculate, "casket clean," as the old folks say when someone's so well put together, it's as if they're ready to meet the Lord in their Sunday best. "Look closely. What do you see? You don't see nothing, do you? He was shot here, here, and there. All in his face. But you don't see a scratch on him."

Jones lifted the lid of another casket, revealing another young Black man who looked just a few years younger than Lenny. Another gunshot victim. Another face pocked with bullet holes now undetectable beneath Jones's work.

He took me downstairs, through a wood-paneled parlor where families hold repasts—the traditional post-funeral meal—through an office strewn with files and paperwork and receipts, to a set of heavy doors. Behind them, all along the walls, were bodies lying on metal shelves in various stages of readiness, their heads propped up on blocks. People like Jones work in the tedious, matter-of-fact realm of violence. Jones is a barber and a cosmetologist, with 1,500 different types of makeup, because "no two human beings have the same hue or color." And if a skull is shattered, Jones says you have to work it back together like a puzzle.

It's a challenging job," Jones said. "The only reward that I get is the fact of being able to meet the challenge of giving that person an opportunity to bring closure because, you know, a closed casket brings a lot of doubt. We're able to eliminate closed caskets about seventy-five to eighty-five percent of the time."

An open casket is part of the African American funeral tradition, a tradition challenged by the destructive nature of gun deaths. Closure is part of what families come to Jones for—an unspoken contract to see their loved ones rest in dignity, no matter how violently they were taken.

The harsh truth of being young and Black in cities like St. Louis means growing up close to death, so close that many young mourners will attend a funeral at Jones's and window-shop for a coffin of their own. They'll walk into the casket display room and say, "'This is the casket that I want.' And it only tells me that they have nothing in life to look forward to but a grave," Jones says. "And that's the sad part about it because rather than saying, 'I wanna be a football player, a doctor, or a lawyer,' he's saying that 'I'm looking forward to a grave,' you know."

Regardless of how they die, there's something about the funeral of someone not old enough to vote that is incredibly unsettling. Their still, youthful faces contorted in death. All of the could've beens and should've beens buried with them, lost in forever's silence. The wailing of mothers and fathers forced to undertake the unfathomable duty of burying their babies, be those babies fifteen months or fifteen years, is wrenching.

Yet amid that coarseness of pain, there's a specific choreography to an African American funeral. Black women, long the backbone of the Black church, not only fill the pews but also the usher boards that operate as a kind of service corps for the congregation. They're often the first people to greet you at the doors of a funeral, handing out programs and guiding mourners to their seats. Most ushers are dressed in uniform, something like a traditional white nurse's outfit with crisp white gloves. They provide tissues or water or hand-waved fans as needed and ensure the orderly flow of attendees, assist with family processions, and help maintain the dignity of the service. They are the church's matriarchs, frontline ambassadors, and its sentinels.

Then there's the music. Not the staid stuff of white Catholic hymnals. A gospel choir is the beating heart of a Black funeral service. In the Christian tradition, these choirs sing songs to remind mourners that the dead have left the worldly realm to be in a better place. These songs wash through the sanctuary like a balm, soothing but unflinching, recalling the faith that has led Black people through the darkest times. My favorite of these funeral songs is one I first heard at my wife's grandmother's funeral in Baton Rouge, Louisiana. It's called "New Life" and speaks of transcendence, a powerful journey into what's next. It's a slow-building celebration of leaving behind an old life for a new one, that by the end erupts in joy.

> *I moved from my old way of strife . . . can't you see I'm a new man*
> *Don't you know I got a new name, and one day I'll live in that new land*

At the front of the church, the casket rests on its bier, as loved ones deliver words of remembrance. Of better days, of childhood memories, of lessons learned. Sometimes those words are funny or profane. Too many of us have cringed at that one uncle who just can't help but offend someone, including the dead. But other times there's wisdom passed from the pulpit to the people. Decades ago, at my stepbrother's funeral, the preacher warned us to take heed. His violent death was a ringing alarm, the preacher said over his body. "How many times are y'all going to keep hitting the snooze button?"

After the pastor delivers his eulogy, and with the family sitting in the front row, mourners form a procession past the open coffin to lay final eyes on the dead. Some Black families will have a crowning ceremony, where a crown is placed on the deceased's head, in a final act of grace. When the service comes to its close, the pallbearers, usually male family and friends of the deceased, step forward, solemn and steady. The casket is lifted and wheeled down the aisle, the congregation rising as one in silent respect. Outside, a hearse waits to lead mourners to the cemetery where loved ones will say their final goodbyes, punctuated with flowers laid upon the coffin as it's lowered into the ground.

In many poor Black communities, funerals have become weekly or monthly times of ritualistic mourning, fellowship in grief where the teenagers and twentysomethings arrive with freshly inked tattoos with sunrise and sunset dates. They shun formal dress for jeans and T-shirts, often adorned with the airbrushed faces of their fallen friends. In the 1970s and 1980s, young people started memorializing their lost friends on T-shirts, jackets, and jeans. Local shops sprang up dedicated almost entirely to the RIP business. At the same time, young artists started painting huge murals of lost youth on public-facing walls in their neighborhoods. The iconography of mourning young, violent death was evolving, becoming brighter, bolder, belying the solemn finality of death. In this way, the fallen might live publicly forever, or at least until the paint fades or the T-shirts shrink. These have become markers of a generation's togetherness, a reminder that we are not alone, that we have a history and community. But I can't help but also believe the ubiquity of not just the deaths themselves but the glorification of those who were killed has helped normalize what should never be normal.

4

(G)un-Civil Rights

Perhaps the most underappreciated and overlooked response to the *Brown v. Board of Education* decision of 1954 and the signing of the Civil and Voting Rights Acts of 1964 and 1965 is the rise of the modern American gun rights movement. When the Supreme Court ruled that systemic legal segregation in schools was unconstitutional, the court mandated that states end school segregation with "all deliberate speed," a vague and deliberately unquantifiable time frame that allowed any hope of true integration of America's classrooms to wither on the vine. A decade after *Brown*, it would take the assassination of President John F. Kennedy in Dallas in November 1963 to put the passage of the Civil Rights Act of 1964 within reach. President Lyndon B. Johnson used his deft political acumen, familiarity and comfort with racist Southern sensibilities, and the collective grief of Americans following Kennedy's murder to push its passage. It was a watershed moment, outlawing discrimination based on race, color, religion, sex, or national origin in employment, voting, and public accommodations. The push for desegregation provoked a reactionary response from white politicians and voters, particularly those in the South, who perceived racial progress as a radical encroachment by the federal government and the Supreme Court.

This backlash evolved into a reshaping of the Second Amendment. Conservative lawyers began framing the right to bear arms as a source of individual "counter rights" that could be a wedge against progressive groups on issues such as racial segregation. The appeal was pitched not only to white men but also white women; promises to safeguard the traditional family from perceived threats of feminism attracted white women to the cause.

In June of 1968, *Time* magazine ran a cover story under the headline "The Gun Under Fire." It had been just weeks since the assassination of Robert F. Kennedy and months since Dr. Martin Luther King Jr. met the same tragic fate. Forget for a moment, the piece suggested, America's steady democratic process, our judicial system, and our vast wealth. "Remember, instead, the Gun," it said. "That is how much of the world beyond its borders feels about the U.S. today. All too widely, the country is regarded as a blood-drenched, continent-wide shooting range where toddlers blast off with real rifles, housewives pack pearl-handled revolvers, and political assassins stalk their victims at will."

The social tumult of the 1960s—the fight for civil rights and racial justice, the Vietnam War—had bubbled to a bloody crescendo with increasingly public violence. Racial tension was exploding across America. A series of political assassinations, all by bullets, began with President John F. Kennedy in 1963, Malcolm X in 1965, and then the president's brother, Robert Kennedy, and Dr. King in 1968.

This climate set the stage for the passing of the Gun Control Act of 1968. While the primary aim of the bill was to cinch and regulate interstate and mail-order gun sales, it was also a largely symbolic bipartisan effort to show the American people that Congress was willing to act in the face of great national tragedy.

By then, America had not just fallen in love with its guns, it had deified them along with the white men who handled them. History is full of the antisocial misfit heroes who used lawlessness to bring revenge and dark honor—à la Jesse James and Billy the Kid. Or the noble cowboys and lawmen whose six-shooters tamed the West and the "savage" red and brown people who filled it. The myths that grew from the frontier spread from the dusty towns to the big city, migrating with the population, from John Dillinger to dime novels to the romanticized gangsters of TV and film. White, mainstream pop culture collided head-on with the real-life racial politics of the '60s.

Up until 1968, there had only ever been two pieces of federal gun legislation in American history. The first was the National Firearms Act of 1934—in response to the bloody "tommy gun" era of Al Capone and Bonnie and Clyde—which levied a $200 tax on the manufacture and sale of machine guns and required all sales to be documented in a national registry. And four years later, the Federal Firearms Act of 1938, which required interstate gun dealers to be licensed and to record their sales. It also prohibited gun sales to people under indictment or convicted of violent crimes.

Three decades later, with the killings of the two Kennedys and King, President Johnson managed to secure passage of the Omnibus Crime Control and Safe Streets Act of 1968 and the Gun Control Act of 1968. The Gun Control Act put further prohibitions on who could and could not purchase firearms, including convicted felons, drug users, and the mentally ill. It also boosted the age requirement to buy a handgun from a federally licensed dealer to twenty-one and expanded licensing requirements.

Johnson called the legislation "the most comprehensive gun control law ever signed in this nation's history" and pointed a finger at America's growing mountain of firearms: "160 million guns in this country—more firearms than families."

"Some of you may be interested in knowing really what this

bill does:—It stops murder by mail order. It bars the interstate sale of all guns and the bullets that load them. It stops the sale of lethal weapons to those too young to bear their terrible responsibility," Johnson said in his White House speech. "It puts up a big 'off-limits' sign, to stop gun runners from dumping cheap foreign '$10 specials' on the shores of our country."

But Johnson knew even then that the bill fell short. He'd asked for a national registration on all guns and licensing for those who carry them.

"If guns are to be kept out of the hands of the criminal, out of the hands of the insane, and out of the hands of the irresponsible, then we just must have licensing. If the criminal with a gun is to be tracked down quickly, then we must have registration in this country. The voices that blocked these safeguards were not the voices of an aroused nation. They were the voices of a powerful lobby, a gun lobby, that has prevailed for the moment in an election year," Johnson said.

As the civil rights and burgeoning gun-control movements were churning out their respective social and legislative victories, the National Rifle Association shifted its focus from hunting and sport shooting to promoting the view that the Second Amendment protects an individual's right to own firearms for self-defense. This message resonated with many white Americans who feared the loss of their white privilege and white power as Black Americans gained access to a fuller kind of American citizenship. Meanwhile, in the urban North, on the heels of a decades-long influx of Black Southerners and declining investment, the social and economic conditions of redlined slums were growing increasingly volatile. Into the 1970s, poverty, crime, and deteriorating infrastructure were hallmarks of many of the communities where large poor Black populations lived. They faced various forms of discrimination and limited opportunities for social and economic mobility. Housing was often overcrowded and substandard, with inadequate access to basic services such as clean water and sanitation. Unemployment rates were high, and those who did have jobs often worked in low-paying, unstable positions without benefits. Crime rates were also high, with drug use and gang violence increasingly more prevalent. The lack of investment in these communities by the local, state, and federal governments fueled a cycle of poverty and marginalization that persisted throughout the decade. To make matters even more volatile, widespread police abuses and the assassination of Dr. Martin Luther King Jr. sparked fiery riots and rebellions that would tear through some of America's largest cities, east to west. Detroit, Los Angeles, Newark, and New Orleans would all glow in the embers of America's seething war with itself and the never-ending so-called Negro Problem.

After the 1967 riots in Detroit, gun sales skyrocketed. The city issued four times as many handgun permits in 1968 as it did in 1965. The city's white suburbs issued five times as many permits. White paramilitary neighborhood protective associations began to spring up along with more explicitly white supremacist militia groups. They began stockpiling weapons. In the first half of the twentieth century, an average of about ten million firearms were manufactured for the civilian market in each decade. But between 1958 and 1968, the height of the civil rights movement, nearly thirty million guns were added to the civilian stockpile. In 1969, a congressional commission on gun violence found that the steepest increase in privately owned guns took place between 1963 and 1968, "a period of urban riots and sharply rising crime rates," in which annual rifle and shotguns sales doubled and handgun sales quadrupled. The commission's conclusion was that fear of violence was pushing people to buy more guns. What they didn't say was who were the feared and who were the fearful.

Many of the economically isolated northern urban communities, home to much of America's Black population, settled into a kind of plantation-style policing system, where mostly white officers living outside of these communities, along with their Black counterparts, served as the armed overseers and proxy for the white power structure. Others, like those white civic and neighborhood associations and militias, were deputized to keep Blacks in their place, through blockbusting, racial housing covenants that kept white people from selling houses to non-whites, and sometimes physically pushing Black people out. The strictures of this system were always reinforced with state-sanctioned, vigilante, and mob violence.

Few places in the US have been more misshapen by structural racism, segregation, and violence than Chicago. On August 5, 1966, when the Reverend Martin Luther King Jr., dressed in his customary dark suit and polished shoes, arrived in the city as part of a campaign to fight against poverty and de facto segregation in the North, he certainly expected some degree of white rage. King was becoming one of the most reviled men in America. In his final year, he faced overwhelming public disapproval ratings. One early poll from 1968 showed that 75 percent of Americans viewed him unfavorably. It wasn't just the deep resentment that many whites had built up for King's shaking of the country's racial order. It was his fierce criticism of the Vietnam War and his call for cross-racial economic justice through his Poor People's Campaign. What made King so dangerous, so hated, wasn't that he shifted his principles. It was that he expanded them.

But what King found that day was shocking even for him.

He was met with a line of police and an angry mob of white people snarling in rage. As he walked toward a group of his supporters, someone threw a rock, hitting King in the head, knocking him down to his knees. As they marched, his aides did their best to shield him from the barrage of bricks and bottles launched at him by the furious crowd. Racial violence was nothing new to King, but to experience it here, in Chicago, was jarring. The open violence of the white crowd that day was with the tacit approval of some of the city's most influential citizens and institutions.

Chicago was a prime end point of the Great Migration, one of this country's great Black meccas, where Southern transplants would reshape themselves and, in doing so, reshape America. They'd create new music, new politics, and birth a new generation of thinkers and doers, some who would leave Chicago for other cities, taking with them their brand of Black tenacity. It's hard to overstate the importance of Chicago in creating and elevating a specific kind of Blackness in America.

But Chicago would also offer unique new ways for Black freedom, citizenship, and humanity to be challenged. This city, more than most, went through tortuous lengths to shrink Black possibility. Residential segregation was mastered in Chicago, a kind of Jim Crow reimagined with even more venom. Racist white citizens formed block associations and other organizations purely to prevent Black people from encroaching on white neighborhoods. All while the government played a complicit role in keeping Black residents cloistered.

"I have never seen, even in Mississippi and Alabama, mobs as hateful as I've seen here in Chicago," King told reporters the day he was attacked. "Yes, it's definitely a closed society. We're going to make it an open society."

Chicago Black

Time and again, I've been drawn back to Chicago. The first time I went, more than a decade ago, it was to report on gun violence as a generational curse. I wanted to show how gun violence spread from family to family, neighbor to neighbor. I'd come across some research that likened gun death to a communicable disease. The closer you are to a gun violence victim, the more likely you were to become a victim yourself. Despite the troubling frequency of shootings in Chicago in particular, the violence was largely concentrated in a handful of blocks in just a couple of neighborhoods. Black folks had migrated here a century ago, and red lines and covenants were designed to keep them there.

For years, I'd be in and out of the city, spending much of my time on the city's historically Black South Side and to a lesser degree the equally Black West Side. Here I'd meet a wide cast of people from different walks of life, on both sides of the law, who carried their own stories of how gun violence had touched them and their families: The young brother paralyzed by a party-crashing gang member. The young sister left handicapped in an attempted hit on her boyfriend. The mother who'd lost one son to gun violence and another son to prison for a separate shooting, her mind racked by the emotional chaos of it all. The wheelchair-bound former drug dealer who turned his life around, but not before his own son was shot and left paralyzed. The mother whose daughter was shot and killed in a robbery, whose grief settled so deeply inside of her that to this day she carries the girl's ashes around in a gold urn. The white police sergeant who was so blinded by his blue loyalty that he struggled to separate Black perpetrators from Black victims and Black innocents. The mother who watched a stray bullet crash into the windshield of her parked car and strike her ten-year-old daughter in the head, killing her instantly. The pediatric emergency room chief who's had to stitch the little limbs of preschoolers back together after they'd been torn to pieces by bullets. The teachers who've resigned themselves to the fact that any number of classroom seats will be vacant come the school year because surviving summer is a privilege that too many Black boys and girls in the city aren't afforded.

But threaded between all the heartbreaking stories of life, death, and survival in Chicago are many stories of surprising resilience even by Black American standards of indomitable survival. Here are people who find the will to keep on keeping on in the face of extraordinary hurt.

It's a beautiful city, rich in history and culture and a kind of Blackness that feels essential to understanding a broader sense of American Blackness. The migrants who poured into the city from the South during the migration brought with them many of their cultural and political sensibilities, which were eventually shaped and molded to their new realities up North.

The Chicago Defender, at the time one of America's preeminent Black newspapers, aggressively urged Black people to flee the South. The paper launched an all-out campaign, championing migration as essential for Black people to gain true agency as American citizens. *The Defender* was widely circulated throughout the South, and it strummed folks' hopes and stoked their fears. In any given issue, sensational headlines screamed above dramatic stories of lynching and other brutality at the hands of whites. The paper published testimonials from African Americans who'd successfully made the journey. There were job opportunities, social listings, and even northbound train schedules. Regular columnists included Langston Hughes and Ida B. Wells-Barnett.

The Defender called the migration "the Flight Out of Egypt" and during its height ran photos of train stations packed with folks waiting to board toward "freedom." At the same time, many Southern newspapers were angered by the loss of cheap or free Black labor. An editorial in *The Telegraph* of Macon, Georgia, warned that big-city labor agents in the North were "stealing" Blacks from the South. It even went so far as to say that Southern Blacks would freeze to death in the North's cold winters. *The Defender* would later write of the warnings: "To die from the bite of frost is far more glorious than at the hands of a mob."

Chicago became one of the most important end points of the Great Migration. The African American population grew from 2 to nearly 35 percent of the city. The migration slowed a bit during the Great Depression, as jobs dried up and competition for those that remained grew stiff. Still, by 1930, Chicago was home to almost 200,000 Southern-born Blacks, about 73 percent of the city's Black population. Chicago would continue to be a top destination for Black families migrating northward. World War II would usher in a labor boom, accelerating the draw of migrants to Chicago's industrial hub. In just one decade between 1940 and 1950, the city's Black population grew by 77 percent, to 492,000. It grew by another 65 percent in the following decade, and by 1970, there were 1.1 million Black Chicagoans, almost entirely due to the Great Migration.

By 1970, there were more people from Mississippi living in Illinois than in all other Southern states, according to James N. Gregory at the University of Washington. A host of social, economic, and geographic phenomena ripened the vine between Mississippi and Chicago. Because the migrants followed the existing train, bus, and highway routes, Black Chicago was populated from the states along Highway 51 and the Illinois

Central railroad tracks—Arkansas, Louisiana, and, most important, Mississippi. In the '50s alone, Mississippi lost more than a quarter of its Black population, much of it to Chicago. It's no wonder that the Delta blues became the Chicago blues in the late '40s and early '50s. Black people today still sometimes call the South Side of Chicago "North Mississippi."

As these new arrivals flooded into the city, a new culture, a new Black culture, was taking shape. If blues music wept in the Mississippi Delta, it got over its lament and puffed out its chest in Chicago. The music became more raucous, reflecting the frenetic pace of city life. The Chicago style of blues music is characterized by its electrified sound, with amplified guitars and bass guitars. This style emerged in the late 1940s and early 1950s when Southern musicians had trouble throwing their sound above noisy club crowds, turning to electric guitars and amps to blast above the din. The city became a major center for jazz and blues, with venues that attracted some of the greatest performers of the era. Chicago was also home to the Chess Records label, which captured the sounds of legends like blues artists Muddy Waters, Howlin' Wolf, and Willie Dixon. From this musical ecosystem, other genres would emerge and evolve, including rock and roll, soul, and, much later, house and hip-hop.

Served alongside these developing musical traditions were plentiful platefuls of soul food. Black migrants brought with them a rich culinary heritage that included staples like fried chicken, collard greens, and sweet potato pie. Soul food joints like Gladys Luncheonette and Army & Lou's were important gathering places for the Black community in Chicago.

Around these tables, a new generation of Black politicians would find their voices and their power. In the 1930s and 1940s, Chicago's Black community began to organize politically.

The first African American politician elected to Congress in the post-Reconstruction era was a Chicagoan named Oscar Stanton De Priest, who took office in 1929 and represented Illinois's first congressional district. Around the same time, after years of struggle and organizing, the city's majority-Black plant workers formed the interracial United Packinghouse Workers of America, one of the first and most powerful unions of its kind, representing a rare cross-racial power play. The organization worked to address issues such as discrimination in housing and employment and helped to lay the groundwork for the civil rights movement of the 1950s and 1960s. In the late 1960s and early 1970s, Chicago was home to a vibrant Black Power movement, with organizations such as the Black Panther Party led by charismatic leaders like the late Fred Hampton and others. The Black Panthers advocated self-defense against a white political and police system that they saw as an enemy of Black people. When Hampton was assassinated in his sleep during a predawn ambush by police in December 1969, his death cleared the way for a different kind of Black organizing on the street level.

As Chicago—like other major American cities—was being remade by deindustrialization, homegrown gangs were growing in size, influence, and power. The systematic marginalization of the city's Black population, pressed into increasingly poorer and increasingly overcrowded neighborhoods on the city's South and West sides, created an ecosystem of deprivation and disinvestment that—coupled with the white power structure's sheer brutality—made poor Black communities ripe soil for street gangs to thrive. No longer would the racist Chicago police regime be the sole enemy of a particular class of Black youth. Black gangs would emerge as a source of belonging and protection, but also of bloodshed and destruction. Disillusioned Black youth, disenchanted with a society that had time and again cast them aside, found solace within the ranks of these highly organized neighborhood gang networks. With their allure of power, protection, and economic opportunity, gangs became a rallying point for a whole generation of young people scraping to survive.

As the gangs grew in strength and influence through the '70s, '80s, and '90s, their presence cast an ever-darkening shadow over Chicago's proud but marginalized communities. Largely disconnected from the city's political and economic engines, these disillusioned youth became trapped in a cycle of violence that haunts the city to this day.

Gang-related violence engenders a cycle of retribution. The trigger becomes an arbiter of power, leaving both gang members and innocent bystanders caught in its crosshairs. This chilling reality is worsened by the ease of access to firearms, nudging personal disputes into fatal encounters.

As the blood was spilling, the gun industry grew more lucrative and influential. The industry's gatekeepers were politically savvy and unrelenting. In 1972, the Republican platform supported gun control measures that aimed to limit the availability of "cheap handguns." But it wasn't the first time the GOP supported gun control measures. In 1967, then–California governor Ronald Reagan signed the Mulford Act, which banned people from carrying loaded firearms in public without a permit. The act was signed in an effort to disarm the Black Panther Party. That same year, dozens of Black Panthers took to the steps of the California statehouse to protest, armed with pistols and shotguns in hand. "The time has come for Black people to arm themselves," they said.

However, just three years later, in 1975, Reagan, who was preparing to challenge Gerald R. Ford for the Republican nomination, wrote in *Guns & Ammo* magazine that the Second

Amendment was clear and left little room for gun control advocates. By 1980, the GOP platform stated that the right of citizens to own guns must be protected, and federal registration of firearms should be opposed. As a result, the NRA endorsed Reagan for president in 1980, marking the first time it had ever endorsed a presidential candidate.

Over the coming decades, record numbers of firearms poured into America's streets, a seemingly endless supply of which would be siphoned from the pipeline between gun factories and gun shops all across the US and into the hands of illegal gunrunners and shooters.

Murder Math

The generations-long struggle of Black folks to secure peace and safety in Chicago, one of America's most historic and important cities, has become a cliché. The city has become a poster child, a (Black) whipping boy in the seething national politics around gun rights and gun control. In many ways, the media and academics supply the kindling with our murder math.

We do a great job of counting the dead. After long, bloody weekends, the media tallies up the carnage and prints it in headlines and streams it across the nightly news. The police fill out paperwork, and criminologists turn statistics into trends. We note the age and manner of death. It's gunfire, mostly. Sometimes a stabbing or a beating. But almost always gunfire. We mark the location of the dead using color-coded maps. We keep a tally of the murdered and maimed like a box score in the most inhumane spectator sport. We note the time of year. The shootings spike in summer or when it's unseasonably warm. Winter's chill sometimes cools the violence. And the later the hour, the more violent, though many have died before noon. And if no race for a victim or victims is given, it's assumed. In recent years, as many as 78 percent of the city's shooting victims have been Black. The gunfire is typical in a handful of poor, neglected neighborhoods. We call them "bad neighborhoods." *Bad* is a wrought shorthand for Black. The yearly tabulation from Chicago and cities like it across the country is sifted through like a ritual to anoint America's murder kings. There's a brief collective gasp at the bloody math. Some hand-wringing. Then the counting continues. The formula is then politicized, weaponized, and sermonized.

End of the Line

Modern Chicago has become the poster child for gun violence in this country, a straw man for the anti–gun control set, who point to its über-restrictive gun laws yet maddeningly high number of shootings. But the dire state of gun violence in Chicago isn't simply a result of good guys hamstrung by local gun laws while the so-called bad guys have free rein and an endless supply of weapons (which they do). The fact is that the Swiss-cheese nature of gun laws in this country, with their wide, gaping holes that vary from state to state—county to county, even—have created an iron pipeline that stretches from nearby and far-off states with lax gun laws, leaving Chicago and other midwestern cities in particular awash in illegal weapons.

The long history of police violence aimed at Black Chicagoans, the lack of justice-oriented, restorative policing in hard-hit communities, along with the economic deprivation of those same Black neighborhoods on the city's South and West Sides specifically, has made the city a powder keg that hasn't stopped exploding. As the author Jill Leovy writes in her searing examination of murder in Los Angeles, *Ghettoside*, "Where the criminal justice system fails to respond vigorously to violent injury and death, homicide becomes endemic." It's not just that an ill-equipped justice system has failed to deliver justice to Black crime victims; Chicago's (in)justice system has been structured to abuse its citizens, particularly the city's Black poor. These colliding forces, along with the lingering social and economic wreckage from the crack epidemic of the late '80s and early '90s, were magnified by reckless and sensational media coverage that had gone crack-crazy, helping to weaponize police in a so-called war on drugs, leaving Chicago to wither beneath the weight of it all.

Chatham

Over the years, Chicago has become a kind of North Star for me, a guiding light that has allowed me to shine attention down into some of the darkest places. In hundreds of hours of reporting, I managed to stitch together a portrait of America that most at best willfully refuse to acknowledge, or at worst exploit to disparage Black people. Certainly, much of my work reveals the kind of Black pain all too common inside the community. But I also want to believe that these stories speak to the humanity of Black folks and the inhumanity of the system.

But there's one story I have never been able to get my arms around—perhaps the most important story I have never told. This particular story, of one Chicago family, takes place in one of the city's most important, traditionally well-heeled Black communities, from which generations of leaders, politicians, and business elite have emerged. But it's also a story so thick with pain and emotion that I've had to piece it together without the participation of those closest to it. It's a story that sadly illustrates the brief yet violent timeline of a single gun in America.

Tommy

A writer once called Chatham, a historically Black middle-class enclave in Chicago, "Mayberry of the South Side." It was the kind of place that Black families flocked to in droves post–World War II. They filled sturdy, well-kept houses on tree-lined streets, joined social clubs and neighborhood organizations. And built community on a foundation of upward mobility, Black pride, and socioeconomic stability. Chatham was the opposite of the Chicago slums that many other Black Chicagoans were pushed into.

In a prior lifetime, the neighborhood was a suburb of mostly ethnic white immigrants—Protestants and Catholics from Hungary and Ireland and Jews from Eastern Europe and Germany. But as Black migrants began streaming north to Chicago, communities like Chatham began to transition. Between 1950 and 1960, Chatham's Black population went from 1 percent to nearly 64 percent. These new Chatham residents were a blend of professionals and working- and middle-class folks, who'd work in union-protected industries, government jobs, and small businesses they built from scratch. Their efforts would bear fruit. There was the Johnson Products Company (of Ultra Sheen fame), and financial institutions like Independence Bank and Seaway National Bank, which, at their respective peaks, were the largest Black-owned banks in the country. Churches, schools, and social organizations nurtured generations of residents proud to call Chatham home—among them, luminaries like the writer Gwendolyn Brooks, baseball great Ernie Banks, and gospel singer Mahalia Jackson. Chatham's prominence, its brick bungalows, and strong economic footing made it an island of the Black middle class in a sea of stubborn economic strife and violence. As Chicago's industrial luster dulled, huge swaths of the city started to decline. Already poor and underserved Black neighborhoods fell further into crime and dilapidation. By the end of the 1990s, Chatham started to feel its once-sturdy foundation trembling as its population grew older and fewer, falling from a high of 47,287 in 1970 to 37,275 in 2000. Just as Chatham's protective buffer against the world beyond began to erode, it was hit with one of its greatest challenges—the Great Recession of the early aughts. The recession of 2007–2009, ignited by a housing market collapse fueled by reckless and predatory banking practices, ravaged the global economy, wiping out $2 trillion in retirement savings, leading to millions of home foreclosures, and plunging the US into its deepest economic crisis since the Great Depression. The economic collapse eroded jobs, wealth, and a huge chunk of the middle class. The Great Recession hit Black Americans especially hard, widening the racial wealth gap. Black families lost 53 percent of their net worth, destroying decades of progress. By the end of the recession, nearly 35 percent of Black families had either zero or negative net worth.

The recession plunged Chatham into a free fall from which it has struggled to recover. The recession didn't just strip away jobs. It tore at the fabric of Chatham's identity. Foreclosures swept through the area, and vacant homes became the silent markers of a neighborhood in decline. During the recession, Chatham's foreclosure rate was fourteenth highest out of eighty Chicago neighborhoods. Local businesses that had thrived for decades were struggling, and some longtime residents, facing unemployment and shrinking retirement funds, were forced to leave. The sense of safety and pride in homeownership that had defined Chatham waned, replaced by a creeping sense of loss. In the shadow of these economic woes came violence.

On a drive through Chatham some years back, I couldn't help but take stock of a neighborhood fighting to hold on to its bygone days of prominence. Many of the old, tidy brick homes and well-manicured lawns remain, while unkempt yards and broken-down homes on nearby blocks showed the deep wear of time and loss. The old commercial strips are now dotted with big national brands like Target, Nike, and local Chicago favorite Garrett Popcorn. There was Mather's More Than a Café restaurant, which closed since I last visited, with its modern décor and brightly colored orange and yellow walls, buzzing with the chatter. In a small conference room with big recliner chairs at the back of the shop, a book club was meeting, and the elderly female members of the club came dressed to the nines in full faces of makeup and pearls. "It's not like it was before," customer Lonnie Smith said while eating BBQ ribs. "They have guns, but seniors, we don't have guns, so we can't fight back. Things change, and we just have to accept it."

While trying to wrap my mind around the connection between violent crime and the economic woes of post-recession Chatham, I stumbled across a name in the *Chicago Tribune*—Thomas Wortham IV. I remember thinking that his name had a ring to it. Wortham. It reminds me of my own people's noble-sounding surname, Worthington. Tommy, as family and friends called him, was a son of Chatham, featured in an article about violence closing in on the neighborhood. Much of it was happening around a popular public park, Cole Park. Tommy was the president of the Cole Park Advisory Council. The shootings and fights at the park disrupted those nostalgic memories of the place that Chatham families like the Worthams had known. Older residents lamented what they saw as a cultural shift, a sort of social and economic erosion that drew a wide chasm between generations. That divide was animated by the demolition of the notorious Robert Taylor Homes, a vast and dangerous public housing complex, in the mid-2000s. The former residents of the Taylor homes were flung throughout the South Side, many to Chatham. Worlee Glover, who ran the *Concerned Citizens of Chatham* blog, noted with disdain the markers of this new, degraded public life: "Loitering out on 79th. Walking up and down the street, eating out of a bag. Eating out on the porch." Another resident wrote that this "once proud community is allowing our own children to bring us to our knees." A spate of shootings around the park had sent fear coursing through the neighborhood. Old folks who'd been around long enough to know couldn't fathom the kind of violence that neighboring communities on the South Side had long endured. The bloodshed of that spring chipped away at that steady sense of sanctity.

Tommy had gone off to war in Iraq, only to return home to find Chatham under siege. But he was determined to do something about it. I couldn't help but linger on his words. "It's starting to feel like it's expected in this community. When people think of the South Side of Chicago, they think violence," said Tommy, then thirty. "In Chatham, that's not what we see. We're going to fix it, so it doesn't happen again."

Wortham's family is one of those longtime anchor families in the community. His grandfather built the family's home right across the street from the park a half century ago, brick by brick, with his own hands. Over the generations the basketball courts at Cole Park had drawn local standouts as well as a number of future college and NBA stars. Thomas was no basketball star, but he grew up running up and down those same courts and chasing his sister through the neatly kept grass that kissed the blacktop on either side. On any given night, when the weather is right, the place comes alive with neighborhood residents, lining the courts to watch the ballers ball. Relatives gather for reunions and barbecues there. Families pool beneath the summer sun, and young lovers, hand in hand, steal not-so-private moments in the park of whose namesake, the singer and Chicago native Nat King Cole, would be proud.

For most of Wortham's life, he had a front-row seat to that theater. After he graduated from Brother Rice High School in 1998, he enrolled at the University of Wisconsin at Whitewater. A year later, he enlisted in the Wisconsin National Guard. After his first tour ended in 2007 or so, he went back home and joined the Chicago Police Department. He was then called back into duty in early 2009 to serve a second tour in Iraq with Troop A of the 105th Cavalry. He joined 3,200 other guard troops in the Wisconsin National Guard's largest deployment to a combat zone since World War II. In a gallery of photos from his time in Iraq, posted to his Facebook page, Wortham is strapping and serious, almost always with dark shades over his eyes and a gun in his hands. Every few photos or so, Wortham's bright smile seems to leap from the page, illuminating the pixels like bright embers in the sky. In one, he's shown running in a black T-shirt, drenched in sweat under a #210 bib above a caption reading, "The Army 10-miler in Bucca, Iraq."

After his final ten-month deployment, Tommy was back home in Chicago, picking up where he left off. He rejoined the Chicago PD, following in the footsteps of his father and other relatives who worked as officers or on the civilian side of the department. His father, Thomas Wortham III, by then retired, had the distinction of serving in the security detail of the legendary Harold Washington, the city's first Black mayor.

Tommy returned to a community grappling with new levels of violence. On most evenings those days, the old family vibe at the park was replaced by something more raucous. Rivals gathered where relatives once held reunions. Young lovers too often replaced by young gunners. The old folks stayed away. The children were kept inside. In the weeks prior, there'd been two shootings at the park and a number of others that rang out not too far from it. In one incident, a nineteen-year-old ball player was shot on the basketball court after trying to break up a fight. He was one of fifteen people shot across the city in a six-hour period. On another evening not long after, a gunman opened fire on a crowd of teens hooping on the same court. One of the teens was shot in the neck, another in the hip and calf. The night of the second shooting, Freddrenna Lyle, then an alderman for the Sixth Ward and now a state appellate court judge, had the basketball rims removed from the courts. She said that it was unfair for the taxpayers and to the "good kids," but "I had to do it because we can't afford to have another child shot."

If the neighborhood was flinching from the uncharacteristic bloodshed, panic hit a crescendo weeks later when a twenty-month-old girl was shot and killed less than a mile from the park. Little Cynia Cole was in her father's car when a bullet crashed into the back seat where she was sitting with her siblings. The shooter was aiming for her dad, an alleged rival gang member, but instead struck the baby in the back of her head. The girl's father was unhurt, but the shot that took his baby signaled something of a mortal wound to the psyche and soul of the community. By the time of her killing on April 21, 2010, homicides in Chatham had doubled from the same time the year before, from eight to sixteen. A third of those homicides were believed to be gang related. In the days and weeks following, community groups, activists, politicians, and police would all offer a similar hue and cry. The Reverend Jesse Jackson urged local political officials to declare "a state of emergency in Chicago."

"It is time for a massive petition drive. Now is the time for mass action, mass litigation, mass legislation, and mass demonstration," Jackson told a crowd during a press conference in Cole Park that May, where he assembled a group of local ministers and church folks to call on leaders and residents to step up to do more in the face of growing violence. Among those in the crowd that day was Thomas Wortham III, who served as vice president of the Cole Park Advisory Council with his namesake son as president. "The main thing is we need security and more supervision," the elder Wortham told a reporter that day. "The Park District hasn't recognized that there has been an influx of people visiting this park. On any given night, you might have one hundred people in the park watching basketball. This is the only neutral park between Seventy-First and Ninety-Fifth Street."

"All we want to do is to preserve the quality of life that we had as children," Carolyn Wortham, Tommy's mother, added.

Few longtimers in the neighborhood could recall the last time there'd been a shooting in the park. But in a matter of weeks, there'd been two, including one in which someone fired into a crowd with dozens of onlookers. Just a week after Tommy Wortham and other members of the Cole Park Advisory Council met in the park, gunfire would again ring out. This time, closer to home than the Worthams could've ever imagined.

In a social media post from May 12, 2010, Wortham

announced a trip to DC and New York for a pair of police memorial events dedicated to officers killed in the line of duty. The trip was an opportunity to pay respect to those police who paid the ultimate price, and a time to bond with those still serving across the country. Wortham soaked in every moment. During a candlelight vigil, the twenty-second annual in honor of each year's fallen officers, then–attorney general Eric Holder addressed the thousands gathered, honoring the 325 men and women who'd been added to the national law enforcement memorial, 116 of whom represented cops killed just the year before. "Unspeakable tragedy may be what brings us here," Holder said. "But our unending appreciation—for the unsung work of law enforcement—is what binds us, and binds all Americans, together. So, while we may grieve, we must not despair."

Holder referenced the killing of four police officers from the Lakewood, Washington, police department, a few days after Christmas in 2009. The officers were ambushed at a coffee shop by a felon armed with a pair of guns, who'd been released from the county jail just days before the shooting. Their killer, Maurice Clemmons, had days earlier cut a GPS tracking bracelet off his ankle in hopes of triggering a response from police. He told a friend, "When they come to this door, I got something for 'em," according to police accounts. When that failed, he took "something" to them. He walked into Forza Coffee Company in Parkland, Washington, and opened fire on the officers as they sat together filling out paperwork. Two were hit in the head. A third was shot in the neck as he stood to confront Clemmons. The fourth officer managed to shoot Clemmons in the gut before Clemmons shot him in the head.

The handguns Clemmons used in the shootings, a 9 mm Glock 17 and a Smith & Wesson .45-caliber revolver, had both traveled long, dark paths to the shop that day. A federal trace of the weapons revealed they'd gone dark, or disappeared into the underground market, several years earlier. The Glock was purchased from a Seattle-area pawnshop in the summer of 2005. The man reported the gun stolen the following year, saying it was taken when his car was broken into at a parking garage. It resurfaced more than three and a half years later during the coffee shop shooting. The Smith & Wesson had gone dark in 1981. That year, it was shipped to a now-closed gun shop, but federal authorities were unable to turn up any records for the gun. So, they had no idea when it was sold, to whom, or to how many owners it was passed.

Two days later, during an event that Saturday, Wortham joined thousands of other officers and their families in front of the Capitol. Among them were members of the Chicago Police Department. They posed for photos and consoled the loved ones of their fallen brothers and sisters. Wortham handed the mother of fallen Chicago police officer Alejandro "Alex" Valadez a patch he carried overseas in remembrance of him. Valadez was a fellow graduate of Brother Rice High School who was shot and killed on duty the previous summer. Valadez was twenty-seven, and an expectant father who transferred to the troubled Englewood District hoping to make a difference. He was killed just after midnight while responding to a call of shots fired. Dressed in plain clothes that night, he was questioning a man when three reputed members of the Gangster Disciples drove up and opened fire. The trio were arrested, convicted, and ultimately sentenced to a collective 350 years in prison. One was on probation for armed robbery at the time of the murder. Valadez had grown up in the heart of a gang-infested Chicago neighborhood and was touched by gun violence long before he was killed. He was just three years old when a gang leader out for revenge murdered one of his older brothers.

Valadez was one of 116 police officers who were killed in the line of duty in 2009, 49 of whom were shot dead.

The next day, Wortham and a group of other Chicago police officers made their way to New York for the NYPD's annual memorial run, a 5K that cuts through lower Manhattan in honor of the more than 860 and counting New York City police officers who have been killed in the line of duty. Days after the race, Wortham was back home in Chicago and eager to tell his parents all about his trip. He spent much of the evening going through his photos, as well as showing off his new motorcycle, a 2005 Yamaha R1.

Just before 11:30 p.m., Wortham said his goodbyes. It was a clear and cool night. A streetlight shone down from its perch above, pushing away the darkness on that stretch of the block. Wortham strode down the steps and toward his motorcycle.

At the same time, an older-model red Pontiac Grand Prix crept slowly down the street, stopping not far from the Wortham house. Four men sat inside—cousins Marcus and Brian Floyd, along with Paris McGee and Toyious Taylor. They'd spent much of the evening driving around Chatham looking for someone to rob. They found him in front of that tidy, low-slung home on the corner, across from the park.

The Floyd boys got out of the car, lurking as the Pontiac's creeping slowed to a crawl. From his porch, the elder Wortham watched as the Floyds approached Tommy. Beneath the cascade of light, he could see a flash of metal. It was a gun. This was a stickup. They wanted the motorcycle.

Wortham's father yelled out, demanding they leave his son alone. Then he disappeared back into his house. Clad in her robe, Wortham's mother, Carolyn, watched from the front door. Just then, Tommy yelled out, "Chicago Police!" and pulled his gun, a 9 mm Glock. The next few moments whipped like a whir in time. A burst of muzzle flashes lit up the night, crackling the Chatham calm. Brian Floyd shot Tommy Wortham over and over. As he returned fire, his father burst into the gunfight from his front door, firing back at his son's attackers. As the Worthams and the Floyds exchanged gunfire, Taylor spun the Pontiac's wheels, he and McGee yelling for the Floyds to get in. The elder Wortham crouched behind a car, firing his gun in one hand and his son's, which had fallen to the ground, in the other.

"They're shooting at him!" Wortham's mother said in a frantic call to 911. "My husband's out there, too. Oh my God!"

The Pontiac finally screeched away, running over a fallen Tommy Wortham, dragging him down the street before he was finally knocked from the car.

"I shot with both hands," his father would say later. When the shooting was over, three men lay bleeding. Brian Floyd, twenty, was dead. Marcus Floyd, nineteen, was critically wounded and clinging to life. Tommy Wortham was fading several yards down the block.

A neighbor rushed out into the street, where he found father standing over son.

"It's going to be all right," the father said. Sadly, he was wrong.

About a half hour later, just after midnight, Tommy Wortham was pronounced dead at Advocate Christ Medical Center. He survived two tours in the Middle East only to be killed in his hometown of Chicago, which by then had been derisively nicknamed Chi-Raq.

Within twenty-four hours, police had accounted for all four suspects in Wortham's murder. Brian Floyd was dead with at least ten bullet wounds. Marcus Floyd was clinging to life with at least five of his own. Paris "Payroll" McGee, twenty, turned himself in to police. Toyious Taylor, twenty-nine, was arrested during a traffic stop.

Police say the Floyds and Taylor were affiliated with the Gangster Disciples. McGee was a Cicero Insane Vice Lord. McGee, who boasted on his Facebook page that "I hav no promlem wit pullin da trigger!!!!" and listed his interests as basketball, dice and "robbin," had been out on probation on a previous gun charge when Wortham was killed.

Years after the shooting, on December 15, 2015, Marcus Floyd was condemned to life in prison, the same sentence doled out to Taylor and McGee months earlier. At his sentencing, Marcus Floyd insisted that he wasn't the one who pulled the trigger that night. Rather than apologizing, he asked Wortham's father why he shot an innocent man. Floyd claims that because of his extensive injuries, he suffered from amnesia and couldn't remember the shooting.

What the shooters took that terrible night may never be made whole. They ended the story of a young man who the judge in Floyd's sentencing called—along with his father—"brave and selfless." In his victim's impact statement, Thomas Wortham III spoke of his joy at watching his boy grow into a man.

"As a father, I could not have been prouder of the man he turned out to be."

Wortham's mother lamented that her son "does not get a second chance to do anything—build his career, have children, make a difference in his community, or just enjoy the life he had worked so hard to create. And I will always miss that."

His shooters took so much. A son. A brother. A committed young police officer from a city in desperate need of men and women just like him.

Months later, then–attorney general Eric Holder invoked Wortham's name the way he had the others during Police Week in DC. Speaking at the International Association of Chiefs of Police annual conference in Orlando, Florida, Holder said that in the year since the last conference, 163 officers had been killed, with more than a third by gunfire.

"These losses—of mothers and fathers, spouses and siblings, children and colleagues—represent an alarming increase in police officer fatalities. After reaching a fifty-year low in 2009, the number of US law enforcement officers killed in the line of duty has surged," he said. Wortham was one of five Chicago police officers killed in 2010; three were killed during robberies.

In the coming years, the family would indeed set out on a mission, tough work they hoped would prevent killings like the one that took Tommy.

But the killers also left something behind. Its own dark path would track back more than a thousand miles, and with each of those miles, it would take on a bit more of its own sinister, violent life. That gun, a matte-silver .45-caliber Smith & Wesson 457s, serial number VJH755, was born out of forged steel in Massachusetts, crossed to the dark side in Mississippi, and fulfilled its fate on the streets of Chicago, taking the life of Officer Thomas Wortham, badge #6181.

5

Trouble Man

I held the gun in my hand and hoped more than anything that I wouldn't have to use it. But at that moment, the decision was already made. I'd empty the magazine if I had to. I looked over at my older brother, Oliver, who was behind the wheel, for some sort of guidance or assurance. But his eyes were fixed in the distance as we zipped through the city streets. It was the first time I'd ever held a gun; it was much heavier than I'd imagined.

Memories of my grandfather's murder had been etched into my family's collective consciousness, a cautionary tale about the wickedness of guns. Yet there we were, the grandsons of a murder victim speeding toward what I was sure was going to be another homicide.

The Philadelphia cityscape melted into a blur of adrenaline and streetlights and concrete. My brother, who I have always called by his childhood family nickname, Lil Man, or by the one he picked up in the streets, O, was about twenty-seven, which would have made me twenty-two. The last thing either of us needed was trouble of any kind, but especially gun trouble.

After years of bootstrapping through my college career, from a fumbled Division II football scholarship at Shippensburg University to Camden County College and by then at Rowan University, that illustrious bachelor's degree finally seemed within reach. I worked hard in school and was a strong student journalist, all while holding down various odd jobs—call center guy, bouncy house operator, seasonal postal mail sorter, temp office worker, occasional weed seller. I kept my nose clean for the most part and managed to avoid the kinds of legal pitfalls that tripped up so many of the guys I grew up. O had jumped off the porch and into the streets early. As a teenager, he declared he'd make his own money and not ask our mother for a single penny. For the coming decades, he'd do just that with entrepreneurial zeal. Yet he'd never been jammed up with the police. But that night, trouble rushed past my open window in a whir of whistling wind. I just wanted to make it back alive and without killing anyone.

All the drama had started a few minutes earlier. We'd just left Palmer's, a four-story behemoth of a nightclub in downtown Philly. Each floor of the place played a different kind of music—hip-hop, reggae, house music, and R&B. It was the first club I'd ever been to with coed bathrooms. There were suede couches and an unspoken policy that encouraged flirting between the sinks and the stalls. But the best part was the let-out, when the lights were flipped on, doors swung open, and hundreds of partygoers poured onto the street outside. The sidewalk became the after-party, providing your last chance to talk to the young ladies you'd just spent the last couple of hours dancing or trying to dance with. The sky would be lit up with stars almost as bright as the ones glistening from all the bumping and grinding back down on earth. Blunts were lit while liquor bottles were pulled from trunk car bars.

It was about 2:30 in the morning, always a beautiful but dangerous time. From my brother's car parked across the street from the club, we watched as Palmer's emptied onto the sidewalk and into an adjacent parking lot. The sounds of bass-heavy hip-hop spilled from the cars that lined the block. We laughed and cracked jokes and ran through the play-by-play of the night—who danced with us, who gave us their number, who dissed us, who we planned on calling on the way home. It was one of the first times that I can remember feeling less like a baby brother and more like one of the fellas. I was warm off the liquor and the brotherly love. Just then, over my brother's shoulder about thirty feet away, I saw some dude arguing with two young women.

"I said no!" one of the young women barked.

"Chill, shorty, I'm just trying to holler at you for a second. Chill," the man responded, unfazed by the ferocity of the woman's reproach.

"Damn, just leave us alone!" the second woman yelled back.

That's when James (which is not his real name), one of my brother's boys, part-time drug dealer, part-time pimp, full-time hustler, walked over with a big smile on his face and his arms open wide.

"C'mon, man. It's all good, playboy. You heard what they said. Just step," James said to the man.

"This ain't none of your business," the young man snarled back.

James's smile faded to a crooked smirk as he shook his head incredulously. Staring deep into the stranger's eyes, James grabbed a fistful of his own T-shirt and lifted it to reveal a handgun tucked in the front of his waistband. "I said step," he said, drawing out each letter.

"Aight, aight, aight, man. All good," the man said, throwing his hands up while slowly backing toward the curb. In what seemed like slow motion, the man swiveled around to a black SUV parked right there on the corner, popped the trunk, and pulled out the biggest gun I'd ever seen. It was black with a pistol grip and took two hands to hold.

"Now what, nigga?!" the man yelled at James.

James yanked his gun from his jeans and aimed it at the man as he dashed around the back of my brother's car to the passenger-side window, where I sat slack-jawed. James tossed the gun through the window, and it landed in my lap. In no more than three hops, he'd bounded onto the back of his motorcycle parked a few feet away and peeled off. Seconds later, the black SUV was screeching down the street behind him.

Without a word, my brother jammed his foot on the gas, and we were speeding behind them. I never asked my brother if he was armed that night. But it didn't matter. I guess I was.

James was weaving in and out of traffic, trying to dodge the big black truck. When he bobbed, the truck bobbed with him. When he weaved, same thing. It was like they were engaged in some angry pas de deux, one that I was certain would end up with someone dead.

I had no business with that gun in my hand, from Lord knows where. But I knew that if that guy started shooting at James, I was going to have to fire back. In just a matter of seconds, life could've changed for all of us. Just like that. Fortunately, that's not what happened. James faded into the night. His pursuer gave up and dipped out of sight. And my brother and I crossed the Ben Franklin Bridge and cruised back into New Jersey unscathed.

My brother and I never talked much about that night or what he ended up doing with that gun. I often think about how things could've turned out very differently. But I also wonder what kind of violence that gun saw before or after that night. So many others just like it have passed through the hands of young Black men just like us. These guns, which so often take life, also have lives of their own. From hand to hand they travel, collecting the energy of each palm from which they're passed, and delivering their own kind of kinetic resonance.

Many years after that night, I'd stumble upon a story that would have me bound and obsessed. It's the story of a well-traveled gun that would upend a web of Black lives it came in contact with, the gun that was used to shoot Tommy Wortham.

Bleeding the Blues

It wasn't yet noon and already it was scorching hot outside of the federal courthouse in Greenville, Mississippi, a Delta city known as much for its moody blues music as it is for tough justice. Inside, Judge W. Allen Pepper Jr. was about to sentence twenty-seven-year-old Quawi Gates on a host of gun-trafficking convictions that threatened to put him behind bars for many years.

A Chicago native, Gates wound up in that neck of the Delta several years earlier by way of Rust College, a historically Black college in Holly Springs, Mississippi, about three hours northeast of the courthouse. In a moment that could've been scripted in a television crime drama, Pepper lifted a hand, holding a photo high enough for everyone in his courtroom to see. A boyishly handsome young Black man, not too much older than Gates, gazed out into the gallery. "Have you ever seen this picture?" Judge Pepper asked.

"Today, sir," Gates responded.

"Today is the first time?"

"Yes, sir."

"You want to look at it again?"

Seemingly agitated, still holding the photo, Judge Pepper got right to it.

"There is a very strong possibility that but for your actions—you didn't pull the trigger, you just got the gun to somebody that did—this man might be alive today."

Though they'd grown up just a few miles from each other back in Chicago, the two young men, the one in that photo and the one being blistered by the judge, had never met. The only thing the two shared was a single gun, their fates sealed in a burst of gunfire.

Gates was facing up to ten years in prison. Not for murder but for his role in a ring that funneled firearms from gun shops and gun shows in Mississippi to gang members in Chicago. Gates's guns, at least the eight that prosecutors were able to trace back, had passed through a number of hands before being picked up at crime scenes all across the South Side of Chicago.

Months before that day in the courtroom, Gates had pleaded guilty to two of ten federal counts, including multiple counts of aiding and abetting another to cause a federal firearms dealer to keep false records. That's longhand for his involvement in a classic straw purchase, which is when someone buys a gun for someone else and lies about who it's for on the legal forms required for the sale. Straw purchases move legal guns into the shadows of the underground gun market, where many end up in the hands of criminals. This was the foundation of the prosecutors' sprawling case against Gates, who they said was the mastermind behind an interstate gunrunning operation that stretched from Holly Springs to the ganglands of Chicago.

Gates enlisted a network of friends and fellow college students to buy guns to supply his growing operation, which delivered an untold number of guns from Mississippi. But despite prosecutors laying out chapter and verse on how Gates was the brains behind an interstate trafficking ring, the only chargeable offenses they were able to pin to him were having people lie to gun shops to facilitate the purchase of five of those guns. Of the five, one was used in the killing of the young man in Judge Pepper's photo—Tommy Wortham IV.

The Connection

Gates's journey from Chicago's Englewood neighborhood down to Mississippi, and eventually to the courtroom, took as many twists and turns as the weapons he'd eventually smuggle back up north. By all accounts, Gates had been a smart young man, but one filled with as many problems as promise. As a child, he and his two younger brothers were taken from their drug-addicted mother and placed in Illinois's notorious foster care system. The trio would eventually be adopted in the early 1990s by an emergency room technician. She did what she could to mend the many broken pieces of their lives, but even with all his potential and all the hopes she had for him, Gates, who along the way picked up the nickname "Red," always seemed drawn to trouble. Englewood, like so many other neighborhoods in Chicago and in hardscrabble cities across the country, is filled with trapdoors, especially for young Black men. Between the often abusive, sometimes corrupt police and the gangs and perpetual violence, those trapdoors are rigged to snatch the young straight from city blocks to cell blocks or graves.

Gates was ripe for the snatching. The instability of his youth fed a resentment that grew into anger in his teen years. Still, he was a father figure for his younger brothers, always prodding them to do the right things even when he seemed incapable of doing so himself. By 2000, his sophomore year at Bogan High School, he started getting in serious trouble. He was charged with burglary, pleaded guilty, and was sentenced to community service. As a stipulation to his guilty plea, he was also referred to a social service agency that worked with troubled youth and families. At that point, things started to look up. He graduated from high school, and on a college tour sponsored by the agency, he found himself on the campus of Rust College in Holly Springs. He fell in love with the school. And his adopted mother loved the idea of getting him as far away from Chicago as possible. He enrolled at Rust in 2002. Gates's journey south symbolized a kind of rebirth. His arrival on Rust's campus that fall marked the end of one chapter and the beginning of another. At least, it could have.

Unlike the forever-in-flux Chicago, Holly Springs is a place of staid consistency, of relics, tangible remnants of times long past, with its antebellum buildings and folksy town square where locals gather to mark celebrations and enjoy parades. On steamy summer nights, when the stubborn sun begins to fade, blues bands set up in the square. This is where the blues were born, stitched together by lifetimes of lament and regret from hard-living, hard-surviving Black men and women. Those old blues songs reflect life in our most hobbled stretches, from the bowels of the Mississippi River up through America's guts, rhythms that ride all the waves of pain, violence, racism, and sorrow that Black folks have experienced since we were dragged across these Southern shores.

Of all the hallowed ground and history in the Delta, Holly Springs holds a particularly special place. It's the birthplace of Ida B. Wells, the African American journalist and anti-lynching crusader. Wells attended Rust College, which at the time was called Shaw University, founded during Reconstruction as a school for newly emancipated African Americans. Wells, like so many thousands of Black people before her, headed north to Chicago after blowback from her searing exposé of Southern lynching forced her out of the South. It would take a hundred years for Black folks to begin a reversal. In recent years, more and more Northern-born Black people, whose families had joined the Great Migration generations ago, began returning to the South. They were seeking greater opportunities and safety from growing police violence in many northern cities.

Those old, sturdy ties to that Southern soil may have been weathered over the decades, but they never truly withered away. They were kept strong with stories of ancestors, their travels and travails. In that oral tradition, connections to the South were not just passed in the stories themselves but in the tongues telling those stories. It doesn't take long to hear the Mississippi stuck to the Black Chicago accent like red dirt on Delta work boots.

But those deep and binding connections, which allowed the free exchange of culture, food, and music, also bound Chicago to something else: the South's vast supply of guns. The pipeline follows the Interstate 55 corridor and its tributary highways, which bend and twist along the Mississippi River for most of the 964 miles from where it begins at the laces of Louisiana's boot, snaking up through five states before emptying into Chicago. It's the favored route for gun traffickers moving hardware from the Magnolia State to Chi-town. The pipeline, laid over generations, is a prime source of firepower for Chicago's gangs; Mississippi provides an almost unlimited supply of weapons to people who wouldn't be able to get them any other way. While in recent years investigators say the source for the state's illegal guns has shifted a bit from Mississippi to nearby Indiana, hundreds of guns used in crimes each year still can be traced back down the I-55 corridor.

A Homecoming, a Plan

The chaos of Chicago proved too hard to shake for Quawi Gates. On trips back home, he picked up where he'd left off. In 2006, Chicago police caught him with an assault rifle outside of an apartment building in his old neighborhood. Investigators found another gun, a Glock handgun, at Gates's residence. Two years later, he beat the charges. Back in Mississippi and back on his hustle, he started to put together a moneymaking scheme to capitalize on a simple equation: the wide availability of guns in Mississippi and the unquenchable thirst for firepower back home in Chicago. He had connections back home and slowly built a small network of locals to help him acquire the weapons he wanted.

Mississippi, like all its Southern neighbors, has incredibly lax gun laws. To buy a gun in Mississippi, you don't need a permit, registration, or a license. For private sales, there's no background check required. At gun shops, you simply need a state ID and to be able to pass a background check to confirm you don't have a felony. More so, state law dictates that no county or municipality can institute ordinances that in any way restrict the sale, transportation, or ownership of firearms. As a result, the state has long been a hub for gunrunners.

Gates had a criminal record, so he couldn't legally buy a gun in Mississippi. Instead, he recruited accomplices with clean records, offering them between fifty and one hundred dollars to purchase guns on his behalf. The buyers were then instructed to report the guns as stolen and were assured that their hands would be clean once the guns were taken up north and their serial numbers were obliterated. At the same time, a war was brewing between various gang factions back home in Chicago. Gates allegedly had deep ties to gang members in his

Englewood neighborhood, specifically, the Gangster Disciples, known as the GDs. Federal investigators say Gates used those ties to fuel his budding enterprise as a gunrunner.

Have Guns, Will Travel

Quawi Gates's ring is just one of a countless number of gun-trafficking operations that use the vast supply of guns in the South—and well beyond it, for that matter—to feed demand in other parts of the country with more restrictive gun laws. The guns come from throughout the region, including Alabama, the Carolinas, Mississippi, Georgia, and Virginia, and end up in northern states like Illinois, New Jersey, New York, and Pennsylvania as well as the District of Columbia. Other routes flow up west, while other networks ping-pong between states in upper New England down to Boston and into New York.

The trafficking routes have been called the "Iron Pipeline" or "firearm freeways." The guns are purchased relatively inexpensively and often sold for a steep profit. The Bureau of Alcohol, Tobacco, Firearms, and Explosives (more commonly, ATF) describes this relationship as "market" and "source." The economics are simple: a low-quality handgun that sells for a few hundred dollars in the retail market can be sold for three or four times that on the black market. But a proliferation of later-model, moderately priced, high-quality guns push the dark profit margins even higher. Among the most famous of the gun pipelines is the one that follows I-95 from Florida into the mid-Atlantic, New York, and then New England. In recent years, new corridors have opened, including the I-75 pipeline that's used to pump guns from Kentucky, Ohio, and Tennessee into Detroit. Another circuit of highways in the Southwest and West feed California. From Las Vegas, it's I-15. Phoenix, I-10. From the Northwest, it's down along I-5 from Washington and Oregon.

But of all those routes, Mississippi to Chicago has been one of the most entrenched. Mississippi is among a group of just ten states that in recent years have supplied nearly half of the country's guns that've been trafficked across state lines, were used in crimes, and later recovered by police. In recent years, 60 percent of the guns recovered in crimes in the city and traced by the ATF were originally sold in other states.

Collision

Beyond the layers of inequitable tragedy, Gates's sentencing provided a close look into the infrastructure of gun violence and the overlapping worlds of police officers and ATF agents, the catch-as-catch-can work of chasing down gunrunners and trying to cinch the pipeline between Chicago, with its überstrict gun laws, and loose supply states like Mississippi.

"Chicago has no gun shops. For somebody to run guns up and down the highway, it's despicable," said then–Chicago police commander Keith Calloway, who drove seven hundred miles to the courthouse in Greenville to testify. During the sentencing, assistant US attorney Susan Bradley questioned ATF agent Russell Johnson on the dynamics that keep Chicago's underworld armed with Southern firepower.

Bradley asked Agent Johnson if he frequently encountered cases where guns were trafficked from Mississippi to Chicago.

"Yes, ma'am," Johnson said. "Very often."

"During the course of your employment with ATF, have

you learned about factors that result in trafficking, reasons why that may be true that guns move between Mississippi and Chicago?" Bradley asked.

"Yes, ma'am, there are several reasons why Mississippi and Chicago—there is a lot of firearms back and forth. First is familial ties. Lot of individuals throughout time have moved to Chicago for work. Began several decades ago when they went up to Chicago for work, they left behind family in Mississippi. They come back for holidays or special events."

Judge Peppers chimed in: "You said there is not a gun dealer in Chicago?"

"There is not a federal firearm licensee in the City of Chicago. The firearms laws are strict in Chicago and Illinois as a whole," Johnson said. "Just to possess, you have to have a firearms owner identification card. Therefore, every gun that is legally possessed in Chicago is supposed to be registered. In Mississippi, everybody has firearms. You can have them in your car. There is no registration."

The Hustle

Gates got the gun used in Wortham's killing back in May 2007, after he talked to a guy named Michael Elliott, who he knew from around the Rust College basketball courts, into buying it for him. It wasn't a hard sell. Elliott was struggling to find a way out of a dire financial situation. The twenty-five-year-old worked as a forklift operator in Holly Springs, making $7.50 an hour, not nearly enough to take care of his gravely ill eighteen-month-old daughter. The little girl was born with a brain tumor and was back in the hospital. For months, the young father shuttled back and forth between Mississippi and Memphis, Tennessee, where the girl was being treated. The stress was beginning to take a toll, emotionally and financially. Afraid of losing his job, Elliott was desperately trying to hold it all together.

In this moment of vulnerability and desperation, Elliott ran into Gates at a local gas station. "Want to make a hundred bucks?" asked Gates. Elliott had never been in trouble with the law, but cash was cash. The plan Gates laid out seemed simple enough. Elliott was the perfect straw buyer. He had a clean record and a state driver's license, all he needed to legally purchase a gun in the state of Mississippi. He'd be given a list of guns to buy and a wad of cash. After he made the buy, he'd hand them off to Gates, who'd be waiting nearby. Gates promised that the guns wouldn't be traced back to him and instructed him to report the guns stolen in the coming weeks to cover his trail and to separate him from the weapons.

On May 25, 2007, the two drove about twenty miles west of Holly Springs to the town of Byhalia, Mississippi, a rural, blip of a town best known for being where the writer William Faulkner died in 1962. They were headed to Ed's Pawn Shop, which traded in the kinds of goods that desperate people pawn off to make frayed ends meet. Located on a busy corner, Ed's typically saw a rotating cast of regulars. Elliott was a stranger, but a stranger who cut a clean figure when he strode into the place that spring day. He was polite and good-looking, workers at Ed's recalled years later. Nothing about his manner sent up any immediate red flags. Though, perhaps, they weren't looking closely enough. Elliott was anxious, his mind racing between the plan and his baby girl dying in that hospital bed just forty-five minutes away in Memphis.

Elliott found a small menagerie of pistols—some new, some old—lined up in a glass display case. He did a quick mental inventory, running through the guns on Gates's list. He asked about three of the newest guns in the case—a Glock .45-caliber, a KelTec .40-caliber, and a Smith & Wesson .45-caliber, all semiautomatics. A worker dug down behind the counter and came up with a paper document, ATF Form 4473. Anyone buying a gun from a federally licensed gun seller has to fill out the form. Elliott handed over his driver's license, and the worker called state authorities so they could conduct a criminal background check through the National Instant Criminal Background Check System (NICS), another federal requirement when making a purchase from a federal firearms licensee.

Name. Address. Date of Birth.

Then Elliott came to Box 11a, which asked if he was the "actual" buyer of the guns. He marked that he was. His background check came back clean. He handed over $1,500 in cash and walked out with the three guns—the .40-caliber and the two .45-calibers. Gates got his guns. Elliott got his $100.

Elliott was just one of several locals recruited by Gates, whose roster also included Garrion Liggins, as well as McKenzie Young and Jacquisha Denise Sims.

On the same day in 2007, Young bought a pair of 9 mm Jimenez Arms pistols from Ed's. She told investigators that Gates had approached her on at least four or five separate occasions about buying guns for him. She was only nineteen at the time and too young to legally purchase one in the state. The legal age is twenty-one. But she said he continued to press her. Young eventually acquiesced, and Gates told her to come up with someone else's ID, someone old enough to buy a gun. She eventually found an ID left by a friend in a basket at the college library. She had a handwritten list of which guns to purchase, as well as instructions on where in Ed's she'd find them.

Months later, Liggins, who was a member of the Mississippi National Guard, bought a Jimenez Arms 9 mm pistol. A few weeks later, he bought a Smith & Wesson .40-caliber. On two days the following month, Liggins purchased a .45-caliber Glock 36 and an Intratec AB-10 9 mm from Ed's.

House of Cards

Gates used Sims to purchase four guns—three at a gun show in Tupelo, which were private sales where no background checks or paperwork were required—and one from a licensed dealer, complete with all necessary documentation, including ATF Form 4473.

It was the purchase from the licensed dealer that brought Gates's house of cards crashing down. That gun, a Taurus International .45-caliber pistol, serial number NAW53584, resurfaced in Chicago just months after Sims purchased it, by a resident doing yard work. The police and ATF traced the gun back to Mississippi and Sims. That short time between its purchase and recovery piqued investigators' interest and was the first clue that the gun may have been trafficked. When agents got to Sims, she lied and said the gun had been stolen, before admitting that she'd bought that gun and others for Gates. When pressed by investigators, Sims detailed step-by-step how she became involved in the ring. She was the first to identify Gates, but eventually, each of the others would implicate him as well.

Sims told police that the day she bought the Taurus, Gates asked her to stash a duffel bag of guns in her dorm room. She said Gates often moved guns between dorms to evade routine school searches. But that day, her roommate became concerned. Fearing a mass shooting, Sims's roommate called campus police. Sims ended up getting kicked out of school. Not long after talking with Sims, investigators headed back to Gates's Chicago neighborhood, where they cultivated an informant. The informant picked Gates out of a lineup and identified him as Red, a gun supplier to Gangster Disciples. Investigators began making the rounds in Mississippi and to Gates's associates.

The Takedown

Six months after investigators first spoke with her, Sims agreed to help them nab Gates. In the months since she'd been expelled from school, she moved out of town and was desperate to wriggle out of the jam she'd found herself in. First order of business, Sims had to set up a meeting with Gates to talk about guns and how he was moving them. On November 7, 2008, Sims met with ATF agents and members of a special task force not too far from campus. They snaked a wire up her shirt and through her bra, equipped with an audio recorder and a small camera built into a button on her shirt. After being hooked up, she headed to campus to try to find Gates. The officers were holed up in surveillance units just off campus, far enough away to be inconspicuous but close enough to pick up her signal from their devices. Sims was supposed to tell Gates that the police had come to talk to her several times and to ask him for guidance on what she should tell them.

Nothing went according to plan.

Sims tracked down Gates at his dorm, but as soon as she opened her mouth to talk, he told her to shut up. All the agents could hear was the click-clack of her shoes tapping the ground as the pair quickstepped across campus. Several minutes passed. The agents had absolutely no idea where the two were going and completely lost contact with them once they made it to the middle of campus. They were headed to the campus library. It was a Friday night, and the yard was humming with activity. But the library was virtually empty; a lone student was leaving as they walked in. The library is a cavernous old building with thick walls and expansive corridors. The deeper the pair went into the place, the weaker the signal became. For about fifteen minutes, the line was silent but for the intermittent screech of popping static. Then the transmitter went completely silent. The agents scrambled to get close enough to catch Sims's signal or a glimpse of her.

Meanwhile, Gates had grabbed Sims by the arm, dragging her down into a basement bathroom. He pressed her against one of the bathroom stalls, tore open her shirt, and found her wire. Sims would later tell the agents that Gates emptied her pockets and her purse and threw her cell phone into the toilet. He took the audio/video recorder attached to the wire and shoved it into his pocket before storming out of the library. Minutes later, Sims stumbled out into the early evening. She was distraught and crying, clutching at her torn white shirt.

When she got to the front of the campus, the agents were waiting for her, parked near the dean's office. They whisked her off to the Marshall County Sheriff's Office. The entire plan had crumbled. Now, they had to move fast. Three agents and the chief of the Rust College police ran back to the dorms, where they found Gates in a small room just off the foyer of his building. During a pat down, the officers found their recorder in his front pocket. Because he admitted that he was high on weed, Gates was taken directly to the sheriff's office. Once there, the agents told him that they wanted to talk with him about firearms trafficking—specifically in guns moving from Mississippi to Chicago.

"I ain't into that anymore," Gates said that night. "I just sell weed."

The officers were well aware of Gates's run-ins with police. The previous spring, on May 31, 2007, he had been pulled over and then arrested by state police in Illinois after the officers discovered $16,000 and two guns in his car. Gates said that he'd gotten them back in Holly Springs. In another incident not long after, police in Chicago were responding to a shots-fired call. They found Gates in the front yard with an assault-style rifle and gave chase. They seized the rifle, and during a later search, they found a .40-caliber Glock handgun they were able to trace back to Mississippi. According to investigators, Gates admitted that he frequented gun shows in Tupelo and Ripley, Mississippi. Police traced the .40-caliber Glock back to a Mississippi man named Cameron Bateman, who purchased the gun two years before it was recovered during the car stop in Chicago. Bateman didn't have the gun long. He sold it to a friend named Pat Cooper, who would buy and sell guns at flea markets and gun shows. When investigators tracked him down, he wasn't completely cooperative, though he did recall selling the Glock. When shown a photo lineup, which included Gates, Cooper said he thought he might've done business with him. When agents pressed Gates to name who he'd sold guns to in Chicago, Gates asked how cooperating was going to help him and on at least two separate occasions said he needed immunity to sing.

In July 2009, Gates, Sims, Liggons, Young, and Elliott were all indicted on various charges related to the straw-purchased weapons. In January 2010, Gates would plead guilty to two counts. In court the day of Gates's sentencing, prosecutors projected a large map of Chicago onto a blackboard. The map, Government's Exhibit #4, detailed where guns connected to

Gates were recovered as well as where he'd had run-ins with police. The city was outlined in red, and the city's twenty-five police districts were outlined in blue. Agent James Ferguson with the Chicago ATF pointed to Gates's Chicago home address. Sprinkled all around it were triangles, squares, and circles noting where the guns were picked up.

- 7342 South Merrill Avenue—A homeowner doing yard work found what he believed to be a toy gun in his backyard. It was the Taurus .45 originally purchased by Jacquisha Sims. It was this gun that brought investigators to Mississippi.
- 7038 South Sangamon Avenue—Responding to a fight on a porch at this address, police encountered a man who said he had a gun, before the man ran off and into a nearby residence, where police found the gun in a bathroom. That gun was originally bought by McKenzie Young.
- 3515 South Cottage Grove Avenue—Police executing a search warrant at what they described as the home of a Gangster Disciple. They arrested a man in possession of a gun.
- 6919 South Racine Avenue—Gates was caught with the SKS assault-style rifle.
- 2115 West Seventy-First Street—Gates's home address, where police found the Glock that went from Cameron Bateman's hands in Mississippi to Pat Cooper, who sold it to Gates at a gun show in Ripley. Gates later admitted that the Glock was his.
- 1230 North Larrabee Street—Police responding to a shots-fired call and another viewing the location on a pole-mounted camera station there watched a group of

people toss guns into the trunk of a car. When police searched the vehicle, they found four guns, one of which was purchased by Liggons.

The Gang Ties That Bind

All but the gun turned in by the homeowner, the one initially purchased by Sims, were somehow connected to the Gangster Disciples street gang. The label "gang member" can be a dubious one. Out of ignorance, racism, or indifference, authorities have used gang affiliation as a tool to target specific demographic groups—namely, young Black and Hispanic men. Often, that affiliation, like the label itself, isn't by choice. In many of the most disadvantaged neighborhoods in America, there's literally no one to protect you, certainly not the law. The people with the most clout, and the willingness to fight for you, to feed you, to respect you are those closest to you. Sometimes those people are in a gang.

There's no doubt just how much cultural and criminal power gangs have in Chicago. When police rounded up the people caught with Gates's guns, they used their arrest records, in which many of them admitted their gang affiliation, to connect the dots. In court testimony and interviews with law enforcement, Gates denied any connection to the gangs of his city, including the Gangster Disciples:

> "It's your testimony here today that you don't even know any Gangster Disciple members?" asked Assistant US Attorney Bradley.
>
> "Yes, ma'am. If I do, I'm unaware they were in a gang," Gates said.

"So we don't have any explanation as to how all these guns that people say they purchased for you ended up in Chicago in the hands of Gangster Disciple members?" she pressed.

"No, ma'am, I don't have any involvement with any gangs, ma'am."

"You said a minute ago . . . that you took some guns to Chicago?"

"Yes, ma'am."

"Can you give this court an estimate of how many guns you might have taken to Chicago?"

"At the most, 6. When I read my report, it said 20 something guns. I've never . . ."

Bradley cut Gates off.

"That's all I have for Mr. Gates, Your Honor. One more thing I didn't ask you. Of those guns that you took to Chicago, what did you do with those guns?"

"Two of them, they were—I was on the way to Chicago, I was stopped by state troopers, as I said earlier. They was taken from me by the state troopers," Gates said. "One of them was recovered from my house. Two of them—no—yes, two of them, I sold to an old man I knew."

One Gun Left

Of the cache of guns that federal agents were able to track back to Gates and his Mississippi connections, just one remained unaccounted for.

The .45-caliber Smith & Wesson purchased by Michael Elliott in 2007 bounced from state to state and hand to hand. Its journey finally ended on a quiet street on a well-kept block in

Chicago almost three years to the day that it was purchased. This is the gun that was used to kill Tommy Wortham. It was the final starred piece of evidence on the government's map.

That gun, serial number VJH7557, was shipped from the Smith & Wesson factory in Springfield, Massachusetts, in November 2002. Number VJH7557 would be shipped to a store in Shreveport, Louisiana, and end up in Mississippi through the hands of a regular customer who sold it to Ed's Pawn Shop. It would take a few years after that, passing from Elliott to Gates, then between unknown hands, for its journey to finally end.

At the time of Wortham's killing with the Smith & Wesson, Gates had already been locked up for several months on the other gun charges. Of the two counts Gates eventually pleaded guilty to, one was for the straw purchase of the gun used in the Wortham case.

"Is there anything you wish to state before sentencing occurs?" Judge Pepper asked Gates.

"Yes, sir."

"All right," Pepper nodded.

"I would like to say I apologize for decisions I made. I know they were stupid. I should have thought wiser, wisely, and I should have made better decisions," Gates said. "I ask the Court, look at the fact that I had a somewhat rough upbringing and that I'm not a criminal. I'm not a violent person at all. I'm not a gang member, leader or any of that, and I would ask the Court to have mercy on me, sir."

Bradley, the US attorney, asked Pepper to give Gates the maximum sentence allowed, sixty months, or five years for each of the two counts Gates pleaded guilty to:

"I was struck by the statement that the Defendant made that he is not a violent person. He may not be a violent person. But by his actions, he has enabled others to be violent. In fact, I think the testimony and the evidence has shown that he has put guns in the hands of people who intend to be violent and intend to do bad acts," Bradley said. "Oftentimes, we have very sympathetic straw purchasers involved. But we always worry that—and we always prosecute people because, we say, regardless of how sympathetic they may be, the crux of the matter is that a gun that is purchased here and trafficked to Chicago or elsewhere in the worst-case scenario could be used to kill somebody or do harm. . . ."

On that August day in 2010, Quawi Gates was sentenced to the maximum he could receive—ten years in prison. In some ways, that's something like justice, but there's little that could ever be done to mend the wounds that Gates helped deliver to Wortham's loved ones. Though I tried time and again to get that part of the story from Wortham's still-grieving family, they wouldn't or couldn't bring themselves to share it with me. For years, I wrestled with the decision to tell this story without their blessing. I didn't want to cause any more pain than they have already experienced. But as more and more families just like theirs were dealt senseless death by guns just like the one that took Tommy, I felt even more compelled to shine a light not just on his story but the story of the gun itself. These two stories are inextricable. It's impossible to tell one without the other.

6

The Way of the Gun

On a windless summer day some years ago, I sat with a woman named Reba Askew, on the front porch of her bullet-scarred house in the West Pullman neighborhood on the far South Side of Chicago. One of her grandchildren, a shirtless boy still in diapers, stood watch from a second-floor window. The one-year anniversary of her oldest son's murder was just days away. Dovone was shot down just blocks from where we sat. The pain of her loss cut as deep on day 360-something as day 1.

"I'm not taking it very well at all," Reba told me, her eyes locked on some distant point somewhere below her feet. "Like I tell everybody, they see me, but I ain't really here." She lost more than forty pounds, and her eyes would flood at the mere thought of her son, who was all of twenty-three years old when an argument with his daughter's mother's new boyfriend turned from words to fists to gunshots in short order.

A therapist I'd gotten to know in the city, Nosheen Hydari, once told me that of all the Chicago families she's sat with over the years, an unexaggerated 100 percent of them have been affected by gun violence. "There's a sense of normalcy around these experiences of life for these communities," she said. "I think we are just now starting to talk about what could help."

Experts say that witnesses, victims, and their loved ones all need mental health attention. They need their voices and experiences validated. They need someone who can identify the symptoms of post-traumatic stress disorder, anxiety, and depression. This help is often in short supply in communities that don't have adequate health infrastructure, let alone easily accessible mental health care. "If your brain is constantly under some sort of threat, be it emotional or physical, and you're in a constant state of awareness, you're just kind of waiting for something to happen," Hydari said. "It could be the slightest thing, and people can become incredibly emotionally reactive." Chicago offers some services for young people and families affected by gun violence, but few people in neighborhoods like Reba's say they've been touched by the city's outreach efforts. "That's all people do is talk to me. Only keep talking. I'm trying to steady make it, and it's really tearing me apart," she said, pushing through tears. "I don't think they understand until they lose one they self."

Of all the devastation that gun violence has heaped on people in Chicago's most vulnerable neighborhoods, it's likely the psychological scars, the trauma of war-level exposure to violence, that cast the longest shadow. In recent years, there's been a growing catalog of research around soldiers returning from war with post-traumatic stress disorder. Federal funding has been set aside, and programs have been launched to treat them. But what happens when the war is at home and the wounded are civilians and the trenches are city blocks, playgrounds, and even front porches?

A study by Chicago's John H. Stroger Jr. Hospital of Cook County (formerly Cook County Hospital), a Level I trauma center that treats many of the city's badly injured residents, found that 40 percent of patients showed symptoms of the disorder. Those wounded by gunfire were about thirteen times more likely to suffer symptoms of PTSD, which includes anxiety, isolation, anger, and sleeplessness. Experts say you don't have to be the one injured—or even a witness—to suffer from PTSD. People indirectly exposed to violence can experience debilitating social and cognitive injury. Repeated exposure to violence can rewire a person's brain. People in neighborhoods like Reba's often remain in a perpetual state of fight or flight, with the sections of the brain that control the release of stress hormones locked in overdrive. A study by a pair of Yale sociologists suggests that just being friends with someone who has been the victim of gun violence increases the likelihood that you'll also become a victim. In poor Black neighborhoods on Chicago's South and West Sides, it's harder to find someone who hasn't been impacted by gun violence than someone who has. In 2012, a year before Reba's son was killed, Chicago led the entire country in murders with 506. That same year, former mayor Rahm Emanuel closed half of the city's twelve mental health clinics. Those clinics were among the scant resources available to people in neighborhoods under the deepest clouds of trauma.

Reba said there was nothing she could do to slow the spiral that her life has taken since her son was killed. "I'm not even coping," she said. "Sometimes I can eat, but I have to force myself. The depression pills, they work sometimes and sometimes I get tired of taking them." She couldn't find work. She could barely keep her mind straight, let alone remain positive. To make matters worse, her surviving son, who was twenty-three at the time, the same age his older brother was when he was killed, was locked in a violent beef with nearby rivals. "My son, he wants to give up on everything, too. He just don't care about nothing. He don't even care about life, I don't believe," she said. "I worry about him a lot." Fresh from a stint in prison, her younger boy was shot while walking with his girlfriend just up the block from the family's house. He survived. His girlfriend did not. The young woman died two days before Christmas from a bullet to the head, bleeding in a patch of grass not far from her own home. For months, the girl's mother would go down to that patch where her daughter died and she'd lie there, dying all over again, offering her life for her baby girl's. "One night, she spent the night out there," Reba said. "Like I told her, it's not going to bring Natasha back, but I can't tell her much, because I'm walking in her shoes, so I know how she feels. And when others come up like, 'Get up. Get up. Get up,' y'all can't tell her that. Y'all are not walking in her shoes."

    I felt guilty, as I often do, about dragging the worst experiences of a person's life out of them. I do it to understand and with the hope that others will, too. But there's guilt nonetheless. All I could offer was a meal, and silence or more words, whatever she'd prefer. We decided to exhale over lunch at a nearby Chili's restaurant with the mutual friend who'd introduced us. As we pulled away in my car, she pointed into an alley. It was her younger son. He was walking through the alley, headed to the next block over. A few minutes later, her phone rang. It was a neighbor with frightening news. A group of young men ran over to her house after we left and began shooting. In the five minutes we'd been away, her son had gone to the next street over, homebase of a rival crew. They chased him back through the alley. Had we not left when we did, our names might've been added to the endlessly long list of gun victims on the South Side of Chicago.

Trainspotting

There's an urban legend that I've heard time and again from Black people in cities all across the country, but especially in

Chicago. And it's not just from the mouths of your average conspiracy-minded barbershop denizens but from rational folks in their right minds. The legend goes that there are powers whose desire to see the Black community destroyed is so great that they'll allow guns to fall off the back of trucks and trains to get them into the hood.

The legend goes hand in hand with another popular Black adage: "Ain't no gun factories in the hood, so who's bringing them in?" Or another version that rings just as true: "How many Black-owned gun factories are there? None. So where are they coming from?"

In my travels, I've heard from people who say they've either witnessed or know people who have seen people finding bags of guns in Black neighborhoods. Somewhere amid the rumors, myths, and legends about how so many illegal guns end up in Black neighborhoods—like those speckled across Chicago—is a measure of truth.

Many of America's major firearms manufacturers use trains to move guns city to city. In Chicago, some of these train depots have stops in some of the neighborhoods where illegal gun activity and violence is heaviest. In recent years, there have been a slew of train car robberies, where thieves have made off with hundreds of deadly weapons, many of which eventually ended up being used in violent crimes.

You would imagine that the pure economic value of firearms as products would require no small number of guards, security dogs, or at the very least very high fencing topped with razor wire. But at the Norfolk Southern railroad located on the South Side of Chicago, thieves have cut locks, ripped off chains, and practically walked into what one reporter called "a gangster's jackpot: box after box of brand-new guns."

In one heist in 2015, thieves boosted 111 .45-caliber Ruger revolvers that had been en route to Spokane, Washington, from Sturm, Ruger & Co.'s New Hampshire plant. Thieves made off with dozens more weapons in two other unrelated hits at the city's Sixty-Third Street rail yard. Police said those three robberies alone sparked a massive wave of gun violence. In 2014, in another train break-in, thieves made off with thirteen guns, and before that, in 2009, with 319 guns in a train car robbery. In 2021, gang members in Los Angeles broke into train cars passing through East LA and stole eighty-two guns, including thirty-six handguns and forty-six shotguns, raising security concerns about transporting commercial firearms. An LAPD captain who oversaw the LA rail yard area told a newspaper that with his twenty-four years on the force, his military experience, and his secret clearances, he has to wait ten days to get a new firearm, "and these guys are going into these containers with no locks and getting guns . . . These guns were unguarded, unprotected . . . God knows how many guns have been stolen that way." Few of the stolen guns have been recovered.

The guns that end up at crime scenes in urban America are truly manufactured worlds away.

The gun that took officer Tommy Wortham's life in Chicago was produced on an assembly line at Smith & Wesson's once colossal gun factory on Roosevelt Avenue in Springfield, Massachusetts. Here men like Joe Lewis have carved out a living building guns that are sometimes used to kill.

One Sunday night several years back, Lewis shook himself from sleep. He looked over at the alarm clock, bleary-eyed. It was already 9:00 p.m. He'd managed to hush his mind long enough to eke out a few hours of sleep. Now, it was time to hustle. He slipped on his clothes: work boots, sweatpants, an old T-shirt. He packed a lunch: a piece of chicken and some vegetables. Outside, he hunched against a biting chill, climbing into his two-door Honda for the ride to work. He had his routine down to the minute. From his home in Chicopee to Springfield in sixteen to seventeen minutes. For all but a fleeting window in late June and early July, when there might still be a whisper of blue twilight on the horizon, it's a ride in darkness. Cross the city limits, over Interstate 291 and then the railroad tracks that flank the highway, past a squat, art deco security building off Roosevelt Avenue that served as a checkpoint to vendors and visitors pulling up to Smith & Wesson, one of the world's largest and most iconic gunmakers.

This was years before Smith & Wesson uprooted for Tennessee in 2023. Back then, Lewis was one of about 1,500 employees at the company's old fifty-acre plant in Springfield. Through the checkpoint, he'd drive another 650 feet to the beginning of an obstacle course of gates, checkpoints, and scanning stations, where he'd wave his badge umpteen times throughout the night: to lift a gate, open a door, or trigger a mechanized turnstile to get in and around the building. He'd march through a metal detector and send his bag, with his chicken-and-vegetable dinner tucked inside, through an x-ray machine.

From there, he'd walk down a tunnel and up into a second building, where he worked in the polishing department for the company's revolver line. Then, a deep breath and a pep talk with himself: "All right, you gotta stay up. I know you don't really want to work, but you know, you got bills to pay. You got a good job. So just go ahead and knock it out."

It was 9:40 p.m. And it was the same routine each night, Sunday through Thursday. The drive in darkness. The labyrinth. Positive self-affirmation.

"And then when I get there—boom," he said. "Get my job done."

Back then, Lewis was a member of one of the factory's six-person polishing teams. They worked with the revolver frames, using belts to smooth out the trigger guards, and polishing jacks—fitted with rag wheels that had been twice bathed in glue and coated in emery—to dig out the milling marks and grooves left by earlier steps in the machining process. A prep guy handled forty-two boxes per shift, twelve revolver frames to a box. He was responsible for smoothing the trigger guards. When he was finished, he sent twenty-one boxes each to two side roll workers. They were on the rag wheels. The roll workers then passed the frames to three plate guys who got fourteen boxes each, who passed the frames to the final assembly line, where they'd get triggers and hammers and everything else that makes a gun a gun.

A paper schedule kept Lewis and his coworkers on track. On a good night, it was mostly aluminum frames, and the polishing wheels wouldn't wear down as often and he wouldn't lose time gluing up the wheels and applying emery and waiting for it all to dry and then doing it all again. If they got hit with a lot of steel frames—especially X-Frames, used for the company's largest revolvers—the work slowed down, and they might not make their numbers.

At 5:30 a.m., Lewis was sweeping up pieces of dried glue and getting ready for the ride home. By the end of his shift, he'd polished 252 revolver frames—252 of the 1,260 he'll do in a week, and of the 65,520 he'd do in a year if he never took a day off.

The sheer volume of soon-to-be guns that went through his hands begged the question with which he and some of his coworkers wrestled: "Who's buying all these guns?"

Big Guns, Big Business

In 2021, the gun and ammunition industry generated approximately $18.4 billion in revenue, with about $9 billion in profit. The industry has also been a boon for the government, generating an estimated $7.4 billion in state and federal taxes. The National Shooting Sports Foundation, the firearms industry's trade association, estimates that the firearm industry added $80.3 billion to the economy in 2022. Over the last decade, the industry has seen tremendous growth, up from $31.8 billion in 2012, an increase of over 152 percent. The industry employs 390,000 workers who manufacture, distribute, and sell firearms, including various suppliers and those who work in ancillary businesses. These jobs pay an average of $65,000 in wages and benefits.

In many cases, gunmakers are the backbones of local and regional economies; they serve as good neighbors, contribute philanthropically, and provide smooth pathways into the middle class without requiring a college degree. These jobs are spread across industry towns throughout the South and all the way up through New England, where gun manufacturers have carved out wide economic and civic lanes for themselves, providing much-needed jobs. Much like college or prison towns, these gun towns lean heavily on the industry for the steady jobs and incomes, benefits strong enough to cut through even the toughest political beliefs. Massachusetts is among the most consistently liberal states with some of the toughest gun laws. But like a number of its neighbors, the state benefits greatly from a healthy gun-manufacturing industry.

"We're a liberal state delighted to supply conservative states with all the guns they want," writes John Hahesy, a former reporter–turned–political strategist. "We who live under the

Route 128 bubble too often forget that the making and the marketing of deadly weapons is a big, booming business in the Bay State."

The economy of western Massachusetts has been steeped in the production of firearms since 1777, when George Washington selected Springfield as home to the nation's first arsenal. Into the twentieth century, a long list of gunmakers, including Colt, Marlin, Mossberg, Ruger, Savage Arms, Smith & Wesson, and a slew of peripheral and associated businesses have woven themselves into the fabric of the region's social, cultural, and economic life.

Smith & Wesson, recently renamed American Outdoor Brands, is among the largest gun manufacturers in the world and considered one of the "big three" US gunmakers—including Sturm, Ruger & Co. and Remington Outdoor Company—which in total, between 1986 and 2010, produced about forty million firearms. These three companies have accounted for about 40 percent of the guns produced in America each year. Smith & Wesson has a long list of police and military contracts, around the country and around the world, to say nothing of its legions of private buyers. Known for its pricey but high-quality guns, Smith & Wesson has long been held in high regard among American gun owners.

From the Revolutionary War until it shut down in 1968, the national armory operated on a hill in the heart of the city, churning out muskets and rifles for the nation's military. Gunmakers at the Springfield Armory would gain world renown as innovators in firearms technology, in developing assembly line mass production and interchangeable gun parts. Springfield offered a prime location for the distribution of weapons, as it sat at the intersection of three rivers and a number of major routes to New York City,

Boston, and Montreal to the north. While Springfield, the third-largest city in Massachusetts, bills itself as a "City of Firsts"—claiming pioneer status from gas-powered cars to frozen foods—it is perhaps best known for two extremely popular exports: basketball and guns.

Smith & Wesson's reputation for well-made guns goes far beyond the world of legal gun owners. It has also gained a following among America's criminals. A massive study, conducted by Everytown for Gun Safety, and including 171,501 recovered guns, found that between 2017 and 2021, four manufacturers—Glock, Smith & Wesson, Taurus, and Ruger—accounted for more than half of the crime guns recovered in thirty-one major American cities. In all, Smith & Wesson came second in the sheer volume of recovered crime guns only to Glock. Smith & Wesson later told the House Committee on Oversight and Reform that it doesn't "monitor or track" what crimes their products are used to commit once they get into consumers' hands. In 2018, shareholders of Smith & Wesson and Ruger, which are both publicly traded companies, voted on proposals that would require the gunmakers to track and disclose information related to how their guns are used in crimes. But Smith & Wesson rebuffed the notion, saying that most of the public and the company's business partners "understand that the manufacturer of a firearm is not responsible in any way for its illegal misuse."

We Need Guns

East Springfield, home to the former Smith & Wesson factory, remains one of the few city neighborhoods still steeped in manufacturing. The economy of the place has yet to give in to the new major fields of employment, such as health care and finance, or to the poverty that has crept over huge swaths of the city, block after block of multifamily homes, apartment buildings, vacant foreclosures, and burned-out Victorians.

Escape the gated acres of the once-sprawling gun factory and take a left, like Joe Lewis did as he headed home before the sun rose most mornings, you'd soon hit a set of lights next to the tangled steel and wires of an electrical substation. Another left and you'll run into Page Boulevard, East Springfield's main drag. There's a machine shop across from a sign shop, a paint shop and an American Legion post, an auto parts shop and union halls for electrical and sheet metal workers. A weekday morning finds workers for the city's water commission holding court at a Dunkin' next door to a company that makes ice. Workers file in for coffee and head back to work at a $95 million Chinese-owned factory with contracts to make subway cars. The gray factory, with a single row of windows running just below its roofline, covers a little under five acres off Page Boulevard—about one-tenth of the site once occupied by Westinghouse Electric, where thousands of workers found jobs during the heart of the twentieth century's boom years. Past the railcar plant, toward a city neighborhood known as Hungry Hill, Page Boulevard swings left and comes full circle: back near the highway, in an industrial area where Rolls-Royce and the Indian Motorcycle company once operated plants. For decades there, Smith & Wesson ran Smith & Wesson Academy, a firing range for company employees and law enforcement officers and members of the military. Before shutting down when the company moved to Tennessee, the company had closed off public access to the range—where, previously, anyone could rent a gun for an afternoon of target practice—after a federal investigation in 2012 found a handful of convicted felons among the shooters there.

The side streets off Page Boulevard remain lined with modest, single-family homes with neat yards. On an unseasonably warm Sunday one early January day, men on ladders were taking down Christmas lights and Christmas wreaths. And on Fresno Street, a guy in a paint-spattered sweatshirt leaned into the passenger window of an SUV emblazoned with a paint company's logo, talking to the driver. There was a tan toy poodle at his feet.

"It's a sweet neighborhood," he told me, adding that despite the proximity to Smith & Wesson and the many company workers who live here, nobody owns guns. As if running through a mental Rolodex of neighbors, he points at the houses, one by one: "This person, this person, this person—all no," he said of their status as gun owners, before continuing to work his way down the street. From the driver's seat, his friend chimed in: "Nobody here owns guns. We don't need them."

"We're hoping it stays the same with these guys coming in," the man in the sweatshirt said, nodding toward the railcar factory still rising two blocks away. The driver added, "Let's hope they hire people from the neighborhood." The manufacturing corridor of Page Boulevard has long been the neighborhood's lifeblood. "That's where these families all came from."

The colossal building that once housed Smith & Wesson still looms large over the area, visible from the other side of the neighborhood. Way across the railcar company land, a tan smokestack at the gun plant rises above the trees and billboards that line the highway. But like an old ghost, the factory building disappears as you walk another block to Edendale Street, out of sight behind one of the last traces of the Westinghouse company: a long, two-and-a-half-story brick building where the words WESTINGHOUSE ELECTRIC appear in a slab of marble above a metal door. The old company office building faces off against a one-story strip across the street where there's a local office for a state representative, a Jamaican restaurant, a tattoo-and-piercing shop, and, at the corner of Edendale, Vito's Barber Shop. The shop's namesake, Vito Ricciardi, came to America to cut hair. But on the way toward opening the business that his sons operate today, he made guns.

Born in Striano, Italy, Vito followed his wife, Concetta Robustelli, to Springfield after she took a job at a relative's shop in the city's Six Corners neighborhood. The gun factory was hiring machinists. It was work, and Vito needed to hustle up some money, fast. He had four kids to feed.

Vito and Concetta bought a two-family house in the city's South End—a traditionally Italian enclave where you can still find men playing bocce on the roof of a neighborhood market. For three years, he made guns at night and cut hair during the day, until he finally had enough money saved up to open the barbershop in 1974. Vito Ricciardi died in 2012. His son Ciro now runs the shop with his brother. Inside, a couple of barber chairs are separated by one for kids, shaped like a fire truck; it sits high enough off the ground so that a barber won't have to break his back bending over to cut a kid's hair. Old, white, white-haired men still come in for haircuts and to banter in Italian. A Norman Rockwell painting of a barbershop scene hangs on the wall next to photographs of soccer teams. Vito played until he was nearly sixty.

"A lot of the immigrants from Italy ended up going to work in factories, and they didn't even speak the language," Ciro said. And that included his uncle, who worked at Smith & Wesson for twenty-eight years—"without learning a lick of English."

The barbershop's proximity to the former Smith & Wesson plant—as well as Vito's brief tenure there—meant that the gun factory still plays a role in the brothers' business. Some customers have been regulars since Vito worked at the plant, over forty years ago. The way Ciro saw it, Smith & Wesson was a business with little downside.

"I don't think we have an issue. I think it's good. It's good work; we need guns for protection for all of us. American citizens should have guns, I think. I'm for guns, not against, and I think Smith & Wesson's doing a great job." When his father needed work, Smith & Wesson was there.

"We need manufacturing," Ciro said. "Any manufacturing in this area is excellent for our community." Not far from where Ciro clipped at the head of one of the Italian white-hairs, sitting on the counter, next to a cash register and business cards and lollipops, the lead headline on the day's newspaper carried news out of Miami: 8 SHOT AT MLK PARADE.

A Good Job at the Gun Plant

Joe Lewis took the long, scenic route through various part-time, temporary, and low-wage jobs on his way to landing at Smith & Wesson. During high school, his mother moved to North Carolina, and he lived outside of Charlotte for several years. Bouncing between the South and Massachusetts, he held tight a dream of someday making a career out of music (his mother is a singer, his father, a bass player). He completed a yearlong recording arts program at Full Sail University in Winter Park, Florida. As he bounced between regions, he worked as a cashier at a Food Lion grocery store, at a Subway franchise, at a photo-processing company, at a Family Dollar warehouse, and, briefly, as a firefighter.

He landed his first temporary job at Smith & Wesson in 2010, banging small metal plates carrying the company logo into revolver frames, three hundred per shift. At $10 an hour, he said he was grinding it out, working all the overtime he could get. His supervisors cut his overtime back after a stretch when he put in over eighty hours several weeks in a row and found himself exhausted. When he moved back down South again, working as a night manager at a CVS—a job he hated—he kept an eye out for openings back home at Smith & Wesson. He ended up landing a third-shift assembly job at a defibrillator company in Chicopee. Then one day, a coworker mentioned that she'd applied to Smith & Wesson, so he gave it another try—finally landing a permanent, full-time job in the revolver frame division. He started out in loading, working with the machines that cut the frames, for $15 an hour. In the polishing department, $30 an hour worked out to over $60,000 a year, in a city where the median annual income back then was $34,728 and the per capita income was $18,553. In Upper Hill, the neighborhood where he grew up in a house on Norfolk Street, the poverty rate is 35 percent; in other parts of the city, it soars above 60 percent.

Upper Hill has also seen its share of gun violence. In one of the most notorious cases, a fourteen-year-old girl was killed in 2007 in a drive-by shooting as she sat on a porch on Wilbraham Road, a block from Norfolk Street. Lewis was raised here in Springfield and said three people he grew up with were shot and killed. Two were stepbrothers—one slain in Springfield, and one killed in Charlotte. A female classmate was fatally shot by an ex-boyfriend who then took his own life after breaking into her home on Wellington Street, four streets away from Norfolk. The shooting paralyzed the woman's boyfriend at the time, who'd been a standout athlete at the city's High School of Commerce. Lewis knew other kids who had guns back then, and he still doesn't know where they got them. In thinking about weapons that leave the factory where he works, only to turn up after someone's been shot, he wonders: "So how did a fourteen-year-old get a gun in Chicago, or whatever city they're in? Well, there had to be a bad apple somewhere who scratched off a serial number, who could get a gun. And then say, shit, I could make double the money selling it on the street." He believes there will always be bad apples, so it's important to examine what he calls the "deeper issues" driving people to shoot. As he sees it, society sets many inner-city kids, Black kids, up to fail. Poor schools. No jobs. Racism. Bad parenting. Questionable decision-making. All reasons why a kid might feel the need to carry a gun in the first place.

Though he wrestles with competing notions of the role that guns play in society, he said, "I'd rather be able to have that choice to be able to purchase a firearm as opposed to not having a choice. And even though those firearms may end up in the wrong hands—that's pretty much—that's life," he said. "Anything, with anything that we do, anything could end up in the wrong hands."

Where Do the Weapons Go?

DeShaun L. Woods grew up in Springfield, and his mother worked at Smith & Wesson when he was a kid. She still worked there as a machinist. When he applied to the company through a temp agency in 2010, he didn't tell her.

"Before I knew it, we was walking by each other in the hallway," the Marine Corps veteran said. He had long thought of the gunmaker as one of what he calls the "big three" in the Pioneer Valley: Baystate Health, MassMutual, and Smith & Wesson. Places where, if you were lucky enough to land a job, you'd have a good life. He was in his mid-thirties and hoped to parlay the gun manufacturing gig into something bigger, a stock portfolio or a way to help jump-start his way into real estate. "You want to have that nest egg and build on it rather than break it and cook it," he said. "It was a job where I was gonna go there and make it shine. I was gonna make it work." His first position at Smith & Wesson was in assembly; he moved on to loading, then to a position as a CNC machine operator. But unlike a lot of the older guys, he had little interest in the buddy-buddy "picnic" approach where guys hang out and make friends. "It was a no-brainer to get your butt out of bed and go to work, and when you're done, go home," he said.

Working the CNC machine, Woods had little connection to the finished product. He cut tools that were used in other machines to make slides and barrels. At first, he didn't spend a lot of time wondering about where the guns went when they left the factory. But then came the Elliot Perez incident. On November 8, 2012, Perez, a truck driver for Stratford, Connecticut–based Pace Motor Lines, was dispatched to pick up five unmarked cases of semiautomatic handguns and revolvers at Smith & Wesson. He'd been on the job for just over a month and had collected packages from the gunmaker before. This time, though, he loaded three extra cases onto his truck. The cases contained 111 guns.

From Springfield, Perez drove to his home in Bridgeport, Connecticut, stopped for thirty-five minutes, then drove to Pace headquarters to drop off the five expected cases and ended his shift. On November 20, after Smith & Wesson notified Pace of the suspected theft, the company's owner confronted Perez, who said he didn't know anything about the guns. A special agent for the Bureau of Alcohol, Tobacco, Firearms, and Explosives interviewed Perez later that day, and eventually, the investigators caught a break: a man arrested in Bridgeport was carrying a Smith & Wesson gun with a serial number matching one of the weapons reported stolen. The suspect offered information that led the investigation back to Perez and an accomplice. Perez ultimately pleaded guilty and was given over seventeen years in federal prison—but when he was sentenced nearly two years after the theft, only forty-six of the guns had been recovered. Many turned up in Stratford, West Haven, New Haven, and Hartford—in neighborhoods "plagued by gun violence," a sentencing memo notes. Other guns were recovered in North Carolina and the Bronx. The sentencing memo ticks off the circumstances under which the stolen guns were found: a man arrested firing shots outside a Hartford nightclub; in the home of the alleged leader of a Connecticut drug ring; another was found stashed at a convicted felon's aunt's house.

"Perez has poisoned these communities and deserves to be severely punished for doing so," the document reads. "With over sixty-five stolen guns unaccounted for, Perez's crime will continue to impact negatively Connecticut's larger towns and cities for a long time."

For Woods, the case was like an alarm. He began to question where the guns went—beyond the military and police contracts, beyond the soldiers and cops and hunters and imperiled homeowners featured in television ads. He began to notice when Smith & Wesson guns crept into news stories about violent crime, thinking, *How many more do we need?* He noticed the kids in his neighborhood who, after learning where he worked, would ask him about specific models like the Governor—a revolver that fires shotgun shells—and half-joke, "Yo, you gotta get me one of them." As a hip-hop fan, he noticed how many times his company's name slipped into song lyrics, and he wondered: What kind of marketing role does that play, creating demand among all those people the company doesn't consider its customers? "A business is a business, and it has to run. I don't blame them," he said. "But a business has to have a good amount of people who buy and another good amount of people who *want*."

For all the commercials Woods saw on hunting and outdoors TV shows, he thought, *What I don't ever hear them talking about is the most common thing I hear their name on*—namely, songs that glorified gun violence. He was also curious about what his coworkers thought: "I need to know if I'm working with a bunch of knuckle-dragging Neanderthals who don't care where the weapon goes." And, of the company: Were its sights set so narrowly on military and police contracts that there was no concern about gun violence? The questions weighed on him and finally, about five years into his employment, at a meeting held in the company cafeteria—one of the company's periodic gatherings with workers to discuss its financial position—Woods broached the subject. Company executives Woods describes as "basically anyone who could sign my paycheck" were taking employee questions. Woods stood up. He talked about the popularity of hip-hop culture in the neighborhoods where he grew up, about the frequency with which he heard the company's name appear in verses or songs about gun violence. He talked about the toll of guns on the streets of Springfield; he'd recently seen a close friend lose a godson to a bullet. He asked, "What is your feeling about having your name dropped in so many songs, and your influence on the gun culture in inner-city neighborhoods? Is it something you feel like you can stop? Do you want that association?"

The meeting's leaders said it was something to look into and quickly steered the discussion back to quarterly earnings. "That told me there's a level of expendability that comes with this place," Woods said. Three months later, supervisors started picking apart his performance. There were trips to HR, visits to the employee assistance program. Eventually, the company let him go.

"Maybe I caught everybody off guard, I guess, because I asked a question that had nothing to do with money," he said, reflecting on the meeting. "It was like, I'm asking a question that has to do with my neighborhood. I'm asking a question that has to do with kids. I'm asking a question that tickles your moral fabric."

Woods said he didn't begrudge anyone who chose the work as a way to make a living. His mother, a gun owner herself, was still employed there. "It's one of those jobs where you can work at and make that money and forget about everything else," he said. "I wouldn't knock anyone for that." And he didn't dispute the good Smith & Wesson has done in terms of providing economic security, contributions to local charities, and sponsoring some of the basketball tournaments he played in growing up.

That good, though, can easily be overshadowed by the next headline, he said. And for Woods, the prevailing philosophy—that the explanation for a life lost on the streets can only be traced as far back as the shooter—didn't align with what he hoped for in his colleagues. "It makes it hard for me to work with you if that headline comes up and your reaction is, 'Well, he shouldn't have had the gun in his hand,'" he said.

On his way to his new job, at a factory in Chicopee, headed in for a twelve-hour, 7:00 p.m.–7:00 a.m. shift, Woods drove through a steely winter rain that punished his windshield. Though he's moved on to a new job, many of his questions remain. He still lives in Springfield, still hears about people getting shot, still sees the company's name pop up in the music he hears every day. "Sooner or later, it's like—you're not going to say anything about this? Nobody has anything to say? Nobody said anything remotely close to, 'Let's not have rappers say our name.'" He goes on, "Y'all have stood up there as Republicans, who push the NRA and all that—and yet you all turn your nose up at inner-city violence and say that's a Black problem. But you don't care about the free advertising. You don't care about the name you put in people's heads."

It's the silence that bothers him, that makes him wonder whether to interpret it as tacit approval—approval of the brand's high status on the streets, approval of the idea that some level of gun violence is acceptable as a cost of doing business, especially when it comes to Black people killing or wounding other Black people. When he heard about the shooting that killed his friend's godson: "First thing I'm wondering is, is it one of ours? Second, how did it get there? Third, what does the job have to say about it? What does Smith & Wesson have to say about it when someone gets shot in Springfield?"

Politics, Payback, and Punishment

A gunmaker's brand is a fragile thing, and acknowledging a role, any role in the problem or even the solutions to gun violence, can put a company in the crosshairs of the gun lobby and its own customers. Smith & Wesson found out as much in 2000, when the company agreed to a settlement with the federal government in order to be released as a defendant from a number of lawsuits. The agreement, announced by President Bill Clinton on March 17, 2000, came after a decade that saw a proliferation of gun violence. Beginning in 1998, thirty-two cities and counties filed lawsuits against the gun industry, most of which claimed negligence on the part of gun manufacturers. New Orleans was the first to file suit. Then Chicago and a flood of other cities. The City of Boston was among the plaintiffs, alleging that Smith & Wesson and other gunmakers were negligent in their distribution and marketing strategies, and that the company and its peers had been unjustly enriched by the use of guns by juveniles and criminals. A suit from the City of Atlanta claimed the defendants' guns were "unreasonably dangerous" because they could be fired by unauthorized users. When Chicago mayor Richard M. Daley joined the lawsuits, he said, "You can't expect the status quo on businesses which make money and then have no responsibility to us as citizens." The city of Bridgeport, Connecticut, sued twelve American gun manufacturers (including Smith & Wesson), three handgun trade associations, and a dozen gun dealers in the state, seeking damages in excess of $100 million, arguing that gun shops were an essential part of the "stream of commerce" in the gun industry and that the trade groups promoted the false idea that personal gun ownership makes gun owners safer.

"We had a level of frustration that we couldn't build political momentum for any type of gun safety legislation," said Marc Morial, president of the National Urban League, who back then was the mayor of New Orleans. "But look, these were the days when we had just passed the Brady Bill, and when the assault weapons ban was in place, we decided that we needed to look at different options." The '90s, he said, were full of "gutsy people who were not afraid to be aggressive." Working with teams of lawyers, the group decided that they could challenge the gun industry in court on some issues related to the design of guns and how they were manufactured and marketed. The blueprint had been taken from lawsuits on the state level against the tobacco industry, which successfully argued that cigarette makers marketed a product that they knew caused disease, disease that cost the states billions of dollars in increased Medicaid costs.

The state lawsuits against tobacco companies resulted in a $206 billion settlement. Rather than claim negligence on the part of manufacturers, the Chicago and New York lawsuits claimed the gun companies oversupplied the market in states with lax gun laws. The inevitable surplus of weapons ended up in the hands of young people and criminals in cities with more stringent gun laws. Morial said the cities were trying to coordinate a simultaneous filing, but he eventually decided to break rank and file his first after it had "become clear that you had a handful of people that thought they could negotiate with the gun industry."

In the end, the lawsuits failed. "We were up against a highly organized, well-financed opposition, and the opposition was really the gun manufacturers and the people that made money making and selling guns and munitions—that's the real interest group here," said Morial. The National Rifle Association would hardly exist but for sponsorship dollars coming from the industry. The second component are the retailers, everything from small gun stores to the big retailers and sporting goods stores that sell guns and have cultivated close relationships with hunters and sport shooters. Morial and others say the gun lobby and industry leaders have conflated interests and causes to fortify their political wall against any gun control efforts. Under the fiction that gun control disarms hunters and sportsmen, the NRA has thwarted legislation that might slow the flow of weapons from the factory to the illicit market.

"I got more hate mail as a result of the gun lawsuit than anything else I did in my career," said Morial. He read off the typical responses:

> *You're trying to confiscate my guns and impose socialism.*
> *I'll never visit your city again. We'll boycott New Orleans forever. We'll wreak economic havoc.*

Sentiments like that typically came with a healthy sprinkling of racial slurs and insults, Morial recalled. At the time of the Clinton / Smith & Wesson deal, the gun company was owned by a British engineering company, Tomkins PLC, and the accord saw company executives agreeing to a number of concessions. Some were explicit safety measures, such as external and internal locking devices, and the development of "smart gun" technology that would limit a gun's use to its authorized owner—the latter innovation to be funded by the company earmarking 2 percent of its annual revenue toward development. Other measures were specifically aimed at helping to trace guns, such as imprinting each gun with a second, hidden serial number that couldn't be removed.

The agreement also required the company to "make every effort to eliminate sales of firearms that might lead to illegal firearm possession and/or misuse by criminals, unauthorized juveniles, and other prohibited persons" by cracking down on straw purchases, sales of multiple weapons, and sales without background checks.

The backlash was swift. Three days after Clinton's announcement, the NRA released a statement calling out Smith & Wesson's British ownership, saying the company had become "the first to run up the white flag of surrender and run behind the Clinton-Gore lines, leaving its competitors in the U.S. firearms industry to carry on the fight for the Second Amendment." The statement was careful to note: "Of course, there is no Second Amendment in Britain, where subjects are barred from owning handguns and many long guns." Rather than combating the criminal use of firearms, the NRA said, "The price of S & W's maneuver falls primarily on others—lawful firearm dealers, distributors, other manufacturers and law-abiding American citizens." James Jay Baker, the NRA's chief lobbyist, claimed Tomkins had engaged in "a futile act of craven self-interest," seeking to get out from under lawsuits as they prepared to sell off Smith & Wesson as an "inconvenient asset."

A boycott followed, and sales of Smith & Wesson guns plummeted. The company's workforce had already dwindled to just over 700, and in July 2000, the factory on Roosevelt Avenue shut down for four weeks—a month without pay for the workers. Later that year, the company laid off 125 employees, including many who'd worked there for the better part of their adult lives. Just over a year after the agreement was announced, Saf-T-Hammer Corporation, an Arizona-based manufacturer of gun locks, bought Smith & Wesson for $15 million—a fraction of the $112 million Tomkins paid in 1987. When the George W. Bush administration assumed office in 2001, it deemed the Clinton / Smith & Wesson agreement nonbinding. Free from stringent regulations, Smith & Wesson worked to reestablish itself as an industry leader, introducing a slew of new products. Those new offerings included its first-ever assault-style rifle and the Model 500, a .50-caliber revolver that at the time was "the most powerful handgun in the world." A headline in the *Los Angeles Times* in November 2003 read: NEW REVOLVER TOO BIG FOR "DIRTY HARRY." The company said it hoped the new gun would help it win back market share.

Pride and Problems

The tenuous nature of the company's place in the market still weighs on the minds of people like Jim Welch, a former state senator whose district was home to Smith & Wesson and a number of the company's employees. In 2014, Welch was one of thirty-seven state senators voting in favor of an update to the state's gun laws that legislators hoped would make Massachusetts safer. The gun bill, signed into law by former governor Deval L. Patrick, sought to standardize local practices for issuing firearms identification cards. It required gun dealers to run criminal background checks on new hires and set fines for failing to report lost or stolen guns.

On a Friday morning a while back, in his old office on Hampden Street in downtown Springfield, Welch recalled growing up in neighboring West Springfield, where he first learned Smith & Wesson's name, ubiquitous around town, before learning what it made. "I just remember one of my hockey coaches as a kid worked at Smith and Wesson, and he always had this Smith and Wesson jacket," he said. "And there seemed to be a pride to working at Smith and Wesson."

A day earlier, Springfield's police department had issued a press release about a Smith & Wesson .38 Special seized during the arrest of a twenty-seven-year-old man after a car and foot chase. It was one of more than twenty times over a period of about three years that the department's crime blotter updates specifically mentioned the recovery of a Smith & Wesson gun.

"It's something that I think about a lot," Welch said, reflecting on the bloody by-product of the gun industry. He brings up the 2014 gun bill and the knee-jerk response to it. "What's the social impact of what we're doing, and then, oops—wait a minute, what's the impact on one of our largest employers?" But there are other questions, too. What role does Smith & Wesson have in keeping tabs on the guns once they leave the facilities?

But trying to engage gun manufacturers in a discussion of those questions seems challenging at best. The companies operate in a highly regulated industry where scrutiny and missteps can bring a firm to the brink of bankruptcy. Putting himself in the shoes of a Smith & Wesson executive, Welch muses,

"'Maybe we're just better off not getting involved in that kind of debate.'"

It's Personal

Working at Smith & Wesson made Joe Lewis feel like he was part of a bigger mission. Something that mattered, as the recruitment spot advertised. "It's cool that I'm a part of something that makes people feel safe," he said. "That can have them go to sleep at night."

But Lewis isn't a gun guy—never has been: "To be honest with you, I'm not even into guns." He passed a test for a permit to carry a handgun, but he never went downtown to the police station to follow through—and despite having a hand in the creation of tens of thousands of guns, he's never bought one.

When he sleeps, he keeps a knife under his bed.

7
Gigglebox

Every now and then, a fragment from my early days as a police reporter in New Orleans drifts back to me. It's not just that it's one of the sadder stories I've ever covered. Or that when I covered it, back in my formative cub reporter days, the work was a never-ending scramble of crime scenes and deadlines, steep learning curves and after-hours sourcing, tequila and casual friends on a loop. It's because it's something of a Janus for me. Janus, the Roman god of gates and doors, held the key to what was and what was to come. It's the what's-to-come part that plunges me back into this story time and again.

In 2005, on a sweltering mid-August day in New Orleans's Hollygrove neighborhood, a man with a gun pushed his way into a house where a young woman named Tefany Dickerson lived with her seven-year-old daughter, Ta'Lasia. He then shot them both in the face. Ta'Lasia died at the scene. Her mother died at the hospital about four hours later. A police source told me the little girl must've been looking up at her killer when he shot her because of the damage that was done, a treacherous act even by New Orleans's treacherous standards of violence.

Murder is common in New Orleans. But this felt like something different. The murders shook the neighbors as folks tried to make sense of the senseless. The Dickersons' killer walked in and out of their traditional shotgun-style home like a shadow, leaving little evidence and not much of a trail for police to follow. What he did leave behind would be a seeding of even more terrible things to come.

Ta'Lasia had been a standout student at nearby Lafayette School. She was the kind of child who teachers pour their whole hearts and hopes into. They know just how tough the road ahead will be even for the best and brightest Black children. The day after the shooting, I headed over to Ta'Lasia's school and found India McDougle, one of the girl's summer program teachers, shuffling through a handful of photos. They were of the silly second-grade variety. Little brown faces, some with gap-toothed smiles from where their baby teeth had recently fallen out. The smiles were goofy and happy and hopeful. Many of the photos were marked with gold, silver, red, or green stars. Some were already tattered at the corners where tape or pushpins had kept them in place on corkboard, or in holiday collages that stretched from one season into the next.

"I used to call her Gigglebox," McDougle told me that day, just a week before the start of the new school year. "Gigglebox, that's just how she was. Always smiling and always, no matter what, giggling."

Gigglebox. I said it in my head a dozen times before I left her classroom. Gigglebox.

"We have no idea what we've lost in that little girl," Rosalyn Kelly, another of the second grader's teachers, said. "I just keep thinking that whoever killed her had to put that gun to her smiling face before he did it."

I went from class to class, strumming up memories of the giggly girl gone for no good reason. Ta'Lasia's teachers wiped away tears as they tidied up their classes for another crop of Black babies with rocky roads ahead of them. Back in the neighborhood, I stood across from 3120 Leonidas Street. A memorial of stuffed animals had climbed up the steps and onto the rickety weatherboards of the Dickersons' shotgun-style house. Narrow-framed, open-floor style, found mostly in New Orleans, they are called *shotguns* because you could fire a load of buckshot through the front door and out the back door without hitting a single wall. But the blasts that day, the ones that took momma and daughter, tore through those walls, leaving their typically busy street silenced but for the sound of the men cutting grass in nearby lots and clearing debris along Leonidas.

Up and down the block and around the corner, at mailboxes and driveways, from lawn chairs and other weather-whipped front porches, I began picking up bits and pieces of the lives lost that day. Neighbors recalled seeing little Ta'Lasia riding her bike on the block, her mother sitting on the front porch, dutifully watching. Nothing stood out as odd or off about the family.

"You just keep thinking, what if that would've been my child?" one neighbor remarked. "Just a baby," said another.

In so many ways, the talking and door knocking were in vain. Everybody knew there was no keeping check on the wanton gun violence in New Orleans. No questions could be posed succinctly enough to elicit an answer that could make sense of this kind of murder. The ground here is hallowed by a history of bloodshed that dates back centuries, a polar and parallel track to that of the true warmth and zest for life that also embodies the city's culture. Deep poverty, easy access to guns, revenge culture, a perpetually broken education system, hard-drawn racial and class lines, and a criminal class as brazen and ruthless as they come.

The dark shadow over this city, broken only by its indomitable spirit of resilience and resurrection, dates back to the 'eighteenth and nineteenth centuries, when enslaved Africans were subjected to brutal forced labor, spawning a culture of oppression and violence that continues to linger. The French. The Spanish. The Americans. All added their twist in systematizing racialized violence in the city. Later, Jim Crow calcified that system by legally institutionalizing racial segregation and creating deep communal rifts. Gun violence, police corruption, and brutality, and failures in education, health care, and justice, are all direct descendants of these sweeping historical injustices. It's a wild recipe that continues to throw New Orleans in the mix of most dangerous, most gun-deadly cities in America.

The year before Ta'Lasia was killed, New Orleans had the nation's highest murder rate with 57 murders per 100,000 residents. It also had the highest gun death rate among women and children. In 2022, almost two decades later, New Orleans still had the highest murder rate, with nearly 72 deaths per 100,000.

That afternoon back in Ta'Lasia's neighborhood, a young guy named Jason Brooks stood on a front porch around the corner from the scene and assured me that the slaying, even of a child, "ain't nothing new."

"They don't care if you're seven or not, especially if that seven-year-old is a witness," he said. Brooks lifted his white, ribbed undershirt, displaying a scar left by an AK-47's bullet that shredded his gut on an August day just like this one two years earlier. It was a drive-by shooting. "I mean, I feel bad about a kid getting shot, but it's going to keep happening," he said. "Know why? Because they want a nigga to get a job, but ain't no jobs for a nigga. So everybody hustling, and some fall off. They see the next man making his money, and they get jealous. And they'll kill him, his kin, whoever. It's like tradition, and ain't no such thing as stopping."

Ain't no such thing as stopping. I couldn't find the lie. It wouldn't stop with the killing of Ta'Lasia. There were too many guns, too much bad blood between neighbors, too much hunger and economic isolation.

I'd only been in the city a few months. I left my job as a police reporter at *The Trentonian* newspaper in Trenton, New Jersey, for the police beat at *The Times-Picayune* in New Orleans. I was growing accustomed to heinous acts of gun violence here. Accustomed, but not comfortable. From the city's hardest wards and most unforgiving streets, I met some of the most honest and open people I'd ever come across as a reporter.

People can be understandably skeptical of media, especially big-city media staffed with few people who look like people in the communities they cover. Local newsrooms all across the country remain overwhelmingly white. And many of those operations cover politics, crime, and violence in Black communities patronizingly and paternalistically. So even though I was Black like the people I most often covered, I had to work to disprove some of the preconceived notions folks had of reporters. Historically, mainstream media has perpetuated negative stereotypes and biased narratives that misrepresent these communities, and worked to alienate the people who live in them. Every time a news reporter described something terrible happening in a so-called bad neighborhood, the message conveyed was clear: that bad things happen to "bad people" in "bad places." So these things should be expected. Coverage is regularly skewed toward sensationalism rather than addressing systemic issues like racism, economic inequality, police brutality, and inadequate access to quality education and health care. This lack of fair and comprehensive reporting fuels mistrust, as these communities see the media as another entity that fails to advocate for their interests or convey their stories accurately. I consciously worked to counter all of that.

It wasn't always easy. The newsroom gatekeepers, like the majority of newsroom staff and leaders, were white. Many were professional, a lot of them really good at their jobs with a keen sense of the news and storytelling. Still, there were often social, cultural, and political blind spots their professionalism could never overcome. One of my white colleagues, a veteran city hall reporter, once told me that New Orleans, with all its "Black crime," had a way of making good white people turn to racists. People with ideas like these had the power to green-light or kill stories or certain kinds of coverage. A newspaper's values are reflected in what they cover and how they cover it, but also what they don't cover at all.

In many ways, it has always felt like we were operating within a plantation system. The newsroom was like the Big House where white folks served as overseers. And every day, as a Black journalist covering issues concerning those who live and work in the fields, I'd have to go in the house and ask for permission to tell those stories. But the white bosses lived so far away from the field, were so comfortable within the Big House and how it served them, that they often met the truth of Black life *out there* with skepticism. And on the other end, even though my people came from the field, too, some Black folks out there were equally as skeptical. With all that time I was spending with the white folks in the house, was I really one of them? I found myself doing the same thing. In those early days, I wore my working-class roots like a badge and had my own misgivings about the middle- and upper-middle-class Black people that occupied the newsroom. I sometimes antagonized those I felt were too comfortable with the plantation system of the newsroom. I recognize now that this was my own insecurity moving through an alien, white professional world. As confident as I was as a reporter, writer, and thinker, there was always tension. I'd come from a completely different rung on the social ladder from the vast majority of people I worked with, both white and Black. And while I had full command of the English language, I sometimes stammered while speaking in groups, self-conscious of the way I pronounced things or conjugated verbs or used hundred-dollar words I'd never actually used in conversation. I never let it get me down. And fortunately, I found support from a diverse spectrum of folks who believed in journalism or believed in me. In fact, I'm not even sure any of them ever sensed what I was wrestling with.

I masked it all with the work. I was on a mission. I'd dive deep into neighborhoods and the ground-level institutions that buoy them. I went to all the churches, all the meetings, I drank at hole-in-the-wall bars and ate at the greasy-spoon joints. I was doing hyperlocal reporting before hyperlocal was a thing.

The hardcore realities of how people in these communities experience violent crime and the injustice that so often follows were mind-blowing. Beyond so-called no-snitch culture where cooperating with police is frowned upon, it can be dangerous. In fact, the number one reason murders in New Orleans go unprosecuted is because witnesses are reluctant to talk, let alone testify. People don't often want to talk to police or even reporters about what they've seen or heard because sometimes witnesses to killings end up dead themselves. It's happened enough to send a chill across communities that most deserve justice and accountability. Fear of retribution is real. So people have grown accustomed to keeping tight-lipped. Silence is a survival mechanism. From my first days on the police beat, I heard the tales: witnesses killed days before they're set to testify; the message-sending murders of relatives of witnesses; the folks dragged into housing project courtyards and offed execution-style; the hired killers whose sole job is cleaning up the mess made by people who saw too much.

But violence against witnesses hasn't only been the domain of drug dealers and killers. A particularly shocking case of police violence from 1994 rocked the city and exposed the dark depths of police corruption in New Orleans. NOPD officer Len Davis hired a hit man to kill a woman named Kim Groves, a thirty-two-year-old single mother of three who witnessed Davis beating up a teenager in her Lower Ninth Ward neighborhood and filed a complaint against him. Fearing that Groves's testimony would expose his criminal ties, Davis orchestrated her murder. Federal agents who were already investigating Davis's role in an alleged drug ring inadvertently recorded him ordering the hit. Before they could intervene, Groves was shot in the head while she waited at a bus stop.

But in New Orleans, I also found an openness and honesty in folks that was as endearing as it was jarring. I found wisdom in the weariest corners of the city, even in the most unexpected voices.

Once, after a shooting at a block party that wounded a bunch of bystanders, including a sixty-one-year-old grandmother shot in the leg, I met a wheelchair-bound man named Robert Wilson. Wilson had been paralyzed from the waist down after a rival's bullet bit into his back three decades earlier. He told me that, in his day, he and his partners would often resort to violence against foes, but there was a code, he said. No women. No children. No innocents. There were rules of engagement then that made sure the right men bled. The bullets were not sprayed aimlessly into crowds or at family functions.

Fast-forward to the early aughts, and the rules of engagement had been torn up and tossed to the wind. Wilson, a convicted felon who served twenty years in prison for a crime he declined to disclose, said an unspoken code of honor among thugs has disintegrated. "They ain't no men," Wilson told me, shifting in his wheelchair. "They ain't no real men." While he was locked up, younger relatives passed along stories of how the streets were changing. In each letter or phone call, they told tales of frequent and bloody shootings, of crack cocaine and high-caliber firearms landing in the hands of younger and younger hustlers. Wilson got out back in '97 and was blown away by what he saw. "When I left, it wasn't like this, like Vietnam," he said. "Now we're in a war nobody's safe from." With everything he'd been through, he said the mass shooting that happened the night before, the one that drew me out to his Central City neighborhood, was far more callous than the ambush that left him paralyzed and an innocent woman dead in 1974. "And I can sit here and tell you about that because I lived it once," Wilson said, his hardened life illustrated across his upper body in faded blue-green prison tattoos. "And I'm in this chair because of that foolishness."

The Red Pill

"I always felt like that case changed you," Deborah Cotton, an old friend from my pre-Katrina days in New Orleans, told me a while back.

The story she was talking about was the killing of little Ta'Lasia and her mother. I hadn't talked to Deborah in more than a decade, but it felt like a lifetime. In some ways, it'd been a couple of lifetimes since our days in the city together.

We met over shots of Patrón in the spring going into summer of 2005, at a dive bar called Club Decatur in New Orleans's French Quarter. She was vivacious with an easy laugh, bound only by the whims of her free spirit. She had just moved from California and had applied to a cooking school in New Orleans. She was short and thick bottomed with a head full of curly brown hair. Her café-au-lait face didn't hide one bit of her Black and Jewish ancestry. I was maybe five seats down the bar from her, but I could feel her presence just radiating. It sounds like a cliché or granola or gemstones and horoscopes, but I felt her deeply and in the most ethereal way. We became fast friends over too many drinks to count and the occasional home-cooked meal. Deb grew up in Texas. She was funny and vibrant and sassy in the most endearing way. She loved music, art, and cooking. She's the first person I'd ever known who had her own stone mortar and pestle. I'm not sure I'd ever actually seen either in real life before she busted hers out of a bag she lugged into my kitchen one night to cook up something special for me. If anyone would've sensed a change in me, it was Deborah.

It wasn't just the little girl's death that altered something inside of me. I'd seen so many young stars crash to earth that it began to feel as if the sky, my world, was growing darker. There was just so much killing in those early days. Had to be some kind of early-onset PTSD. It felt as though I'd slipped into the Matrix: "You take the blue pill, the story ends. You wake up in your bed and believe whatever you want to believe. You take the red pill, you stay in Wonderland, and I show you how deep the rabbit hole goes."

I'd taken the red pill. Day in and day out, it was more of the same. Less than two years into my career and I'd already covered dozens and dozens of killings. I'd collected stories of the murdered like colorful strips of construction paper for a grim kaleidoscope that contorted American life and death. And I remember all the hues, vividly.

The teenager, an urban equestrian enthusiast, who was killed alongside her mother and her mother's boyfriend, rolled in carpet and left in the basement as their killer ordered pizza and watched *Monday Night Football*.

The three-year-old girl who caught a stray bullet to the chest as a moving gun battle tore through the streets, also wounding her five-year-old brother.

The boy who blew a hole in his head while showing his friends a gun he'd found tucked between the cushions on his living room couch.

The young military veteran turned do-gooder-gang-member gunned down after trying to get a drug dealer to stop dealing crack to his aunt.

I'd gone from Philadelphia to Trenton to New Orleans and had witnessed much of the same in every city. But there was something a bit different about gun violence in New Orleans. There was brazenness about it. The unabashed violence was not only aided by some of the unique cultural and historical factors but also by stubborn corruption at nearly every stop between law enforcement and the local criminal justice system.

On that August day when I was out canvassing the neighborhood in Ta'Lasia's name, I'd only been in New Orleans about four months. And I was just beginning to understand all the nuances of gun violence in the city, a counterbalance to Bourbon Street and its pomp and revelry. My skin was feeling thinner by the day then, and I could taste the resin of each death.

A Great Flood

Down the street from the Dickerson crime scene, Willie Collins, a forty-six-year-old machine operator, lorded over his front yard like a Black sentinel, peering from behind the wrought iron railing that guarded his stoop.

"The Bible says these are the last days," he warned me. "The great flood is here for the Black community. We have the murder of that seven-year-old to tell the story."

I could never have predicted just how prophetic his words were. A little more than two weeks later, a great flood would indeed drown the city, killing off pieces of Black New Orleans that would never be resurrected.

When Hurricane Katrina struck on August 29, 2005, just weeks after that little girl and her mother were killed in Hollygrove, the storm did, for a time, cleanse New Orleans of the great wrath of bloodshed. What had been as much a daily part of life in the city as beignets and rice and red beans was now a haunting memory of the past. More than three thousand people would die during Hurricane Katrina. Some drowned in attics or in the streets while trying to escape the torrent from broken levees. Hundreds of thousands of others would be figuratively washed away, some to far-off alien cities. Many would never return.

The night before the storm smacked down in New Orleans, I took refuge in the newsroom of *The Times-Picayune* with dozens of my colleagues. The *TP* building on Howard Avenue became a sort of shelter of last resort for staff. I remember pacing back and forth; outside, the winds started to whip as night faded into the early morning. Then there was the sound of shattering glass. A century-old tree anchored outside came crashing into a large window at the front of the building. It was the first sign of violence. But it wouldn't be the last. Soon, the levees around the city would break, and the city, like a soup bowl, would fill with floodwater. Later the next day, I was dispatched to city hall to keep track of the city's disaster efforts. I grabbed a pen and notepad, and one of my editors handed me a ham sandwich and another gave me marching orders. "We'll come get you tomorrow," he said. "Just report what you see and hear."

I climbed into one of our newspaper delivery trucks, the kind with the oversize wheels, and we headed through feet of floodwater until we were downtown on Poydras Street. Some 80 percent of the city was underwater by then. There were reports of many dead and many others trapped on rooftops and in attics. It didn't take long before I saw my first body bobbing along the flooded streets. I talked to one after another of the flood victims who'd fled their homes and neighborhoods for what they were told were safe spaces and shelters downtown, including the Superdome and the Ernest N. Morial Convention Center. They were a wet and beleaguered mass. Some had waded through miles of deep floodwaters with small children in tow on makeshift rafts or in plastic tubs. Others had made harrowing escapes from rooftops or from trapped vehicles. I spent that first night in a random office at city hall, on a green military cot with no blanket. Every hour or so, officials would gather in another office nearby to give updates on what was going on and where. The city's infrastructure had crumbled. Communication lines were virtually nonexistent. Countless people were still trapped in their flooded neighborhoods, including the mostly Black Lower Ninth Ward, which suffered more than most. There were also early reports of widespread looting, including by the police.

By the next morning, as I waited for a call from the newsroom about getting picked up, cell service stopped working. But text messaging was going through, though spotty. I got a text from a friend back in New Jersey asking if I'd evacuated *The Times-Picayune* with the rest of the staff. She heard on CNN that the basement of the newspaper building was taking water. And at the same time, city officials had evacuated the flooded jail nearby, moving the prisoners to a stretch of highway uncomfortably close to the paper. Apparently, while I was at city hall, *The Picayune* relocated to Baton Rouge, some forty-five miles north of New Orleans. I was stuck in the flooded city.

Later the next day, city hall began to flood. We were told to make our way over to the Hyatt hotel across the street. Many of its windows had been blown out by the hurricane, and knee-high floodwater was barely being kept at bay by rows of fraying sandbags. Inside the hotel's darkened, musty lobby, the flicker of orange backup lighting bounced off the walls, casting odd shadows like something out of one of Plato's caves. It was hard to imagine that any of this was real. A few steps in, I saw a slender Black woman with her arms wrapped around a brawny white emergency worker; a handful of his sweaty blue T-shirt rippling from each of her fists.

"Thank you, thank you, thank you!" she cried out, her face pressed against his chest. She had barely gotten out a fifth thank-you when the emergency worker whispered into her ear that "it was going to be okay" and that "it was our job to save lives."

Her name was Lucrece Phillips, and when the worker left her standing there, I went and put an arm around her and asked her how she was doing. My simple question opened up another kind of floodgate. Tears poured from her bloodshot eyes as she shared a story of death and survival. She was haunted by what she had seen in the flooded Lower Ninth Ward. Every waking hour was filled with the images of dead babies and women, and young and old men, all of whom had been floating along the streets of her neighborhood. She had relatives in town for a family reunion, and she and her daughter, her niece, and her uncle and his wife and their tiny two-year-old daughter, along with a friend, took refuge in her attic as the water knocked the front door off its hinges and swiftly swallowed much of her home. She said she could hear her downstairs neighbor and the woman's five-year-old son banging for help as the water crept higher. Then the banging stopped. She and her group were in the attic for hours, and they grew more and more frantic. The water kept rising. They saw it inching up. Lucrece told me she didn't want to die like the little boy or his mother or the others who couldn't or wouldn't leave the neighborhood in the face of Katrina. So the group pounded, kicked, and pulled at the wooden boards in the roof. At last, the boards around a vent near a trestle broke open. When they heard the din of boat propellers in the distance, they screamed and waved shirts from the roof. Finally, they could see men in a boat drawing near, until it was close enough to climb aboard. A few of them got in, and then another boat arrived and picked up the others.

"The rescuers in the boats that picked us up had to push the bodies back with sticks," Lucrece said, sobbing. "And there was this little baby. She looked so perfect and so beautiful. I just wanted to scoop her up and breathe life back into her little lungs. She wasn't bloated or anything, just perfect." I stood there, hands shaking, as I scribbled her words in my notepad. I began to cry with her, the ink on my notepad smearing with each fallen teardrop.

"I know this storm killed so many people," she said. "There is no Ninth Ward no more. No Eighth or Seventh Ward or east New Orleans. All those people, all them Black people, drowned."

It took a long time to get the image of that perfect little baby out of my head. To this day, when I tell this story, every emotion I saw in Lucrece's eyes wells up in my own.

After camping out that night at the blown-out Hyatt, I ran into a colleague who said that not everyone from the paper had fled to Baton Rouge. A handful of reporters stayed in the city to keep reporting. The next day, we met up, and for a second, I exhaled. It was as if the floor of the entire city had crumbled. But the reporting gave me something stable to hold on to. I was glad to be reunited with my people.

We spent the next couple of days at the home of one of our photographers' parents. It hadn't flooded. And a neighbor had a generator. It's there I typed up the story about Lucrece Phillips and that perfect little baby caught in the flood. It was also where I had my first shower and change of clothes since I'd left *The Times-Picayune* for city hall days earlier. After a few days sleeping on the floor of the *Houma Courier*, a *New York Times*–owned newspaper about forty minutes out of New Orleans into the marshland, we relocated to another colleague's house back in New Orleans. Her uptown neighborhood was dry and largely emptied of neighbors. The city had worked for weeks to get everyone who remained in the city out. There was an eerie calm there, especially at night, with little to no electrical power or lights.

One day, we heard a loud banging at the door. We opened to find one of our photographers, along with a police officer standing on the front steps.

"Are you guys armed?" the cop asked.

The four or so of us crowded around the door all gave some version of *no*.

"Well, you should be," he said, handing us a revolver and a shotgun.

It was one of those moments in post-Katrina New Orleans that blurred the lines between ethical and unethical, criminal and survival.

Day and night, we'd climb into a car to move around the naked city. National Guardsmen were deployed to enforce the city's evacuation orders. Armed with assault rifles, they had the power to detain anyone who wasn't supposed to be in the streets. On one of these nights, I was squished in the back seat, the windows wound down and some rock song I'd never heard blaring from the radio. It was so jarring for me, the only Black person in the car, speeding through the streets with armed military men given the green light to eliminate any perceived threat. I tried to imagine how this scenario might play out if five Black men were zipping through the streets of post-Katrina New Orleans blasting hip-hop. We drove over to the West Bank, where a number of stores and restaurants were still open. I can't recall if it was a Fridays or a Chili's or Applebee's, but it was one of those chain restaurants. We met some guys there, sat at a table, and my colleague passed one some money, and he handed something back under the table. After dinner, we went back to our place uptown, which became our post-storm headquarters. Someone lit a joint, and we passed it around. Then someone asked if I wanted a line. *A line?* Before I could comprehend exactly what he was asking, I saw the others sitting at a table sniffing lines of cocaine. It was as if I were in the Twilight Zone. Where I'm from, you're either a hustler or a junkie, with not too much in between. But these professional, respected white boys were getting zooted. The world was flipped upside down.

In the days, weeks, and months ahead, there'd be more bizarre tales. But mostly, these were tales of terror. Some were born from the hurricane and flood itself. But others were born from something less natural but just as destructive.

In the early days after Hurricane Katrina left much of New Orleans in ruins, the city was awash in tales of violence and bloodshed. The narrative of those early, chaotic days—built largely on rumors and half-baked anecdotes—quickly hardened into a kind of ugly consensus: poor Black people and looters were murdering innocents and terrorizing whoever crossed their path in the dark, unprotected city. But what I heard from people in the streets and what was much later confirmed drew a clearer, just-as-ugly picture, of white vigilante violence, police killings, official cover-ups, and a Black population far more brutalized than many were willing to believe. Several police officers and white civilians were later indicted, and the Justice Department launched a sweeping investigation into civil rights violations after the storm.

In Algiers Point, an unflooded, predominantly white enclave on the city's West Bank, armed white militias patrolled the streets and posted signs warning, "We shoot looters." Gunfire there was frequent. One Black resident told me that as he and his girlfriend were walking through the West Bank trying to get to a rescue point, they were confronted by a group of white men who told him, "We don't want your kind around here," before shoving guns in their faces. Although the West Bank escaped the flooding, hurricane winds had toppled trees, and something or someone else had toppled several Black bodies. Passersby discovered the remains of several Black men whose deaths could not be attributed to drowning. One high-profile case involved a man named Roland J. Bourgeois Jr., a former Algiers Point resident, who was convicted on federal hate crimes charges for shooting and wounding three Black men who were attempting to leave the city. Bourgeois had warned a neighbor that any person "darker than a brown paper bag" would be shot. And that's exactly what happened as men like Bourgeois set up checkpoints and barricades along the streets of Algiers Point.

Just a few days after the storm, I was walking along the Interstate 10 overpass, where people had gathered for safety and to pick up dropped-off provisions and water, when a man ran up to me and told me the police were shooting people and pushing their bodies in the river. At the time, there was no way to verify rumors like that. But we'd learn later that there were a number of incidents where the police did indeed shoot and kill people and tried to cover up those shootings. In one especially disturbing incident just six days after Katrina struck, I was down in front of the Harrah's casino, which had been shuttered by the storm and turned into a New Orleans Police Department makeshift headquarters. Each morning, the NOPD would dispatch rescue boats and search teams and deployments from that location. I'd make daily rounds down there to report on the latest.

That day, I heard a crackle over the police radio: "We got five of theirs, none of ours hurt!" And a few dozen cops let out a cacophony of cheers and hoorahs. Earlier, there were reports of a group of armed Black people shooting at rescue workers on the Danziger Bridge over in New Orleans East. Not long after, the same photographer who'd accompanied the police officer who brought that revolver and shotgun to us, arrived at Harrah's with the crew of cops who'd just left the bridge incident. It was well known that he was best friends with several NOPD officers, including some of its leaders. When I asked him about what happened on the bridge, he snapped on me, saying the officers did what they had to do to protect themselves.

I found his response unnerving. First, I felt like punching him in his mouth for his tone. But secondly, we're journalists; we're supposed to be aligned with the people and the truth, not the police or any other arm of the government. He clearly chose the other side, feeding us the unsubstantiated police narrative, the lie, that the cops were in a gun battle and were defending themselves.

The events on that bridge marked one of the darkest chapters in the city's history of police brutality. Officers, crammed in the back of a U-Haul van and wielding assault rifles and automatic weapons, opened fire on a family of four, wounding them and killing two others, including a teenager and a mentally disabled man. Among the victims was Ronald Madison, a forty-year-old man, who was shot in the back with a shotgun while running from the gunfire with his brother. Court documents later revealed the harrowing details of how, as he lay dying, an officer stomped and kicked him. Madison's death stands as a chilling testament to the violence, chaos, and racism that surfaced in post-Katrina New Orleans—a grip and gravity of which have yet to release their hold on the city's soul.

The bridge shootings were not the only examples of police violence my camera-wielding colleague witnessed and kept mum. In the chaotic days after the levees broke, an order began circulating among the city's police force: if they loot, you shoot. The order was given teeth by police leadership. In one instance, Captain James Scott, the former commander of the city's First District, which includes the French Quarter, was captured on video during morning roll call telling a few dozen officers that "we have authority by martial law to shoot looters." Martial law had never been declared in the city. But the rumors spread like wildfire, arming police with the green light to use lethal force on people they thought were stealing in the flooded city. On September 2, 2005, NOPD officer David Warren shot and killed an unarmed Black man named Henry Glover on the city's West Bank. Warren was stationed on a second-floor lookout when he shot Glover in the back. Glover was a floor below and running away. Glover's brother and a friend flagged down a passing motorist, who put the wounded Glover in his car, and sped off looking for help. But help was the last thing the men found when they pulled up to a makeshift police station at a nearby school building. Cops surrounded the men with their guns drawn, handcuffing them as Glover lay dying in the back seat. The officers brutally beat the men before Officer Greg McRae drove off in the Good Samaritan's car with Glover's body still in it. McRae drove to a nearby levee, lit a traffic flare, and used it to set the car on fire, leaving Glover's body to smolder and burn. A federal jury in New Orleans later convicted Officers McRae and Warren and Lieutenant Travis McCabe in connection with Glover's death, the burning of his corpse, obstruction of justice, and the cover-up that followed. "Instead of upholding their oath to protect and serve the people of New Orleans in the days after Hurricane Katrina, these officers violated the law and the public trust," Thomas E. Perez, then the assistant attorney general for the Civil Rights Division, said following the officers' convictions. "And while some officers broke through the thin blue line and told the truth under oath, others were rightly convicted for obstructing justice. Today's verdict brought a measure of justice to the Glover family and to the entire city."

Our photographer was there. During the officers' trial, he testified that he walked into the scene as the officers were questioning the men, that it was "contentious," that Officer McRae told him not to take pictures, and that he obeyed. "It was, for lack of a better term, an order," he said. He testified that he left that part of the compound and never returned to see what happened next. Days later, he said he asked McRae what happened that day. McRae said, "NAT"—NOPD lingo for "necessary action taken"—and swiped his hand across his neck.

The photographer was also on the scene of the police killing of Keenon McCann, another Black and unarmed man. Police shot him as he stood under a highway overpass looking for help. He captured a photo showing Lieutenant Dwayne Scheuermann (also involved in the Glover killing) aiming his gun at McCann.

When I first landed in New Orleans, this same colleague helped show me the ropes. The police scanner over my desk would chirp about the next shooting or fire or mayhem that needed covering, and I'd race to the scene with him, riding shotgun. Every detective and white shirt on the scene knew him well and gave him special access behind the police tape. He introduced me as the new guy, pointed out the workings of the scene, and nudged me to talk to this sergeant or that public information officer. He was a good-natured cowboy, always ready for action. But our buddy-buddy vibe—for me, at least—melted during the heat of Katrina.

Just days after the storm and with thousands of people still trapped in New Orleans without food, water, or shelter, many evacuees tried to escape the city the best they could. One of the few ways out was the Crescent City Connection bridge that joins New Orleans to the city of Gretna on the West Bank. Three days after Katrina, hundreds of mostly Black people amassed on the bridge after being told there were buses on the other side waiting to take evacuees to safety. Gretna was a mixed but mostly white city, traditionally hostile to mostly Black New Orleans. Those gathered that day didn't see salvation on the other side of that bridge. What they saw was a phalanx of white Gretna police blocking the bridge, preventing the primarily Black evacuees from crossing. At one point, Gretna police opened fire, blasting pistols and shotguns just over the heads of the evacuees. The incident amplified an already disturbing chasm of disparity that Black New Orleanians faced in the aftermath of Katrina. Authorities, white civilians, police, all seemed bent on blunting Black survival.

Red Cotton

On an unseasonably chilly afternoon a few days before Christmas 2016, I visited with Deborah for the first time in a decade. I'd only seen her once since Katrina, about a year after. Days before the storm, she left the city for somewhere safer and returned not terribly long after the water receded. All those years had passed, but our bond felt as strong as ever, despite building our lives in different cities. Post-Katrina, Deborah was determined to grow deeper roots in New Orleans. In late 2006, I moved from New Orleans to New York City for a job with *The New York Times*.

We'd emailed each other a few times over the years, and without fail, she'd always ask about the Ta'Lasia Dickerson case. I'd stopped following the ticktock of the investigation years earlier, and the case remained unsolved. It was one of the many that clung to my spirit as the years took me further from New Orleans and the ghosts I left behind. "You were different after that little girl was killed," Deborah said from her couch in New Orleans's Bywater neighborhood, that day in 2016. "I could just feel that something in you had shifted."

By then, I knew she was right. The case had tripped something inside of her, too. She'd bring up the girl's death and the man's prophecy, that her death would usher in a great flood to wash away the city's sins. Or maybe punish it because of them.

In the end, back in May 2008, it was Deborah who had news on the case. Her email subject line was: Gigglebox.

> I hope this finds you well. I was just looking thru some recent TP articles and saw that someone was finally arrested for killing the mother and girl you reported about before the storm.

New Orleans police identified a man named Robert C. Hurst, thirty-four, as the prime suspect in the double murder that claimed Gigglebox and her mom. Hurst, according to police, was shot and killed in an unrelated incident.

"I remembered this case because it was so shocking and horrific—and that her teacher called her 'Gigglebox,'" Deborah wrote. "That name always stuck with me, haunted me. Anyway, it seems like the competency of the police and DA's office is improving—finally. Just thought you might like to know."

Between that last email and our holiday catch-up session many years later, a lot had changed. I'd gone from a four-year stint at *The Times* to *The Huffington Post* and then to MSNBC. I'd cover some of the biggest news stories of a generation, including the killings of Trayvon Martin and Michael Brown Jr. and the rise of the Black Lives Matter movement. I'd gotten married and had my baby girl, Nola, named in homage to the city where her mother and I met.

Deborah had made a number of moves herself; pushing aside dreams of becoming a chef to become a journalist. She wrote under the pseudonym Red Cotton, a combination of her last name and her redbone complexion. Red emerged from the storm as something of a champion for the city's vibrant African

American and Creole cultural scene, especially its social aid and pleasure clubs and the second line parade community, essential aspects of the culture.

The clubs were formed in the late 1800s and early 1900s as a practical response to Jim Crow segregation and systemic racism. When insurance companies refused to insure Black people, the social aid and pleasure clubs would help dues-paying members defray the costs of health care, funeral expenses, and financial hardships. They performed charitable work in the community, hosted social events, and fostered a deep sense of unity among its members and the broader Black community. The second line parades, a vibrant whirl of pomp, strutting, dancing, and imbibing, put all of the above on full display. Clubs would hire brass bands to play at funerals for its members. As the casket was carried from the church to the cemetery, the bands would play somber processional music. But once the dead were lowered into the ground, the music leaving the cemetery would change pace, from somber to joyous. From mourning death to celebrating life. Members of the club made up the main line or first line of the parade. The second line consisted of other mourners turned revelers, high-stepping and dancing through the streets behind the brass band.

The clubs no longer primarily serve as benevolent societies aimed at closing the gap in health care needs, but they remain pillars in the Black community. Before Katrina, various clubs throughout the city held second line parades, sans funerals, almost every Sunday between September and June. These parades would march through each club's respective neighborhood with brass bands in tow, with requisite stops at bars and watering holes along the way. A second line is one of the most beautiful cultural touchstones in America, a living, breathing flourish of

Black life and culture. The clubs rarely publicized or advertised their dates, times, or routes. But those who knew, knew.

Deborah became the go-to source for which clubs were "rolling" when and where. I can't describe how good it felt to see her blossoming from afar. She had this way about her, this glow that was infectious. I read one media report describing her as "a tireless chronicler of the New Orleans brass band and second-line community." She'd tapped into a space that the city's big media just didn't have the credibility to occupy, let alone do justice to. And Deborah did it with a kind of curiosity and seriousness that deserved every bit of ink she got.

In the introduction to her 2007 book, *Notes from New Orleans: Spicy, Colorful Tales of Politics, People, Food, Drink, Men, Music & Life in Post-Breaches New Orleans*, she wrote:

> It is my belief that you don't choose New Orleans—New Orleans chooses you. Those who have fallen for her, live with her, are sprung, lost and turned out in love with her, know exactly what I mean. Ain't no amount of wind, water, gunfire, potholes, "giant" politics or doomsday predictions can pry your death grip from her. Come hell or high water, you stay—or return . . . She makes you high from laughing too much and too long. She breaks your heart till you're crying on the kitchen floor. She haunts you, melts you and is just a damn joy to live in.

Threaded through all of that love and lust for New Orleans was a strong sense of activism and care for the most vulnerable among the city's residents, even the lost and angry who caused so much of its pain. Second line parades have for generations offered a time of unity, goodwill, and celebration. But time and again over the decades, the goodwill and pageantry has given way to bloodshed and violence. With neighborhood residents from all walks of life spilling from their homes into the streets on some of the city's most hardened blocks, they've offered an ideal time for those seeking vengeance. Public, violent, brazen vengeance.

Blood and the Brass Band

On May 12, 2013, two brothers took positions at the intersection of Frenchmen and North Villere Streets, waiting for the Original Big 7 Social Aid & Pleasure Club's annual Mother's Day second line to pass by. They weren't there looking for a good time. Someone had shot another of their brothers two years earlier. Now it was time for payback. As the parade wound its way through the city's Seventh Ward, the To Be Continued Band started to cross the intersection, playing just a few notes, before the brothers opened fire on the crowd. Mayhem followed. Some threw themselves to the ground or dove for cover. Others crumpled in mounds trampled by the scattering mass. Twenty people were shot, in what would be the biggest mass shooting in modern city history.

Deborah Cotton was the most seriously injured of all the victims. A bullet tore into her back, bounced around her abdomen, and ripped through a number of her major organs. She was badly wounded, but she was alive.

The coming years would be long and arduous, steps forward and big steps back. Deborah woke every morning, and the first thing she reached for were the pills for her pain, chased by a ginger ale to calm her constantly queasy stomach. Each day was like this, waking up feeling like a boulder was rolled up a mountain and dropped on top of her. Before eating breakfast, she'd swallow a handful of pain medicine. She had so much internal damage to her gut that when food passed through her digestive system, and knocked against all the scar tissue that had been built up, it sent cramps and pain coursing through her body, like jagged rocks being dragged across her insides. After eating, she had to take the first of umpteen runs to the bathroom.

"That's kinda my life right now," Deborah said.

Deborah had thirty-six surgeries, twelve during her first month in the hospital. She had to have her colon removed and her bowels reconstructed into what surgeons call a J-pouch. Because of the severe damage done to her internal organs, surgeons had to perform what's known as a Whipple procedure. It involves removing large parts of the pancreas and small intestine, parts of the bile duct, gallbladder, and stomach. It's typically reserved for people suffering from stomach or pancreatic cancer.

Her doctors say most people who suffer the kind of internal damage that she did that day don't make it through the night, let alone the week.

"All day long, every day, was just torture," she said of those early days of recovery.

Ultimately, Deborah lost two-thirds of her stomach and was left with an organ the size of a baby's fist. Whatever she ate almost immediately came back up. Every other day or so, surgeons would open her back up to clean out any infection or toxins that might've settled in her gut. Every week, she was dropping five more pounds. When she went into the hospital, she weighed about 183 pounds. But within days, her weight began to drop rapidly. In no time, she was down to a frail 110 pounds. She pleaded with her doctors to place a feeding tube directly inside of her stomach, one that could pump nutrients into her while she slept. It took two months of her pestering before her surgeons agreed to the tube. She would try to eat as much as she could hold down during the day and rely on the help of the tube at night. If she ate too much, she'd throw it all up, losing everything she'd worked to consume all day long. Her weight became an obsession that ran right along with her desire to survive. One doctor had the nerve to suggest that her weight loss was an unintended plus: "You don't know how many of my patients would love to be one hundred and ten pounds," he told her. "You look fine."

It was a smack in the face. She didn't look or feel "fine." She dropped down to a size 0. Each day that she lay in that hospital bed, she withered, her hair was thinning, and her skin was becoming loose and ashen. She didn't eat solid food for more than two months. An IV kept her hydrated, the tube aided in pushing calories into her body. But her stomach needed to be still and under control to allow it to heal. Slowly, she began to pick up a few pounds. By the time she was released from the hospital, she weighed 134 pounds.

Deborah was out of the woods, but every few months, there'd be another setback and an ongoing fight just to stay healthy enough to take care of herself, to run errands, to cook, to live something pretending to be a normal life. She'd go into the hospital for a minor procedure and end up bound there for months. Around New Year's Eve of 2013, she went in to have a small surgery done on her J-pouch, supposedly a four-day stay. But she developed an infection in her stomach, in which the sutures ruptured and fluids leaked through a hole torn into her stomach. What was supposed to be less than a week in the hospital turned into two months knocked off her feet. Doctors couldn't get the infection under control, and it got so bad that they took to hanging gowns, masks, gloves, and booties on her door for anyone who might step foot into her room. She was that susceptible.

Her new fragile physical state took away much of the social verve that made Deb, Deb. She'd not only documented New Orleans famed revelries, she was an avid participant. But now she was enslaved to her feeding machine at home. Every night, she'd have to be home by 9:00 p.m. For twelve hours a night, from 9:00 p.m. to 9:00 a.m., she needed to be hooked up just to maintain her weight.

"It was like I was married to this thing," she said.

Every step in her routine was critical. She had to hit those twelve hours precisely so she could begin her protein shake and peanut butter regimen at 9:00 a.m. sharp. Food became torture.

"It was horrible. I was in a relationship at the time, and we, let me say, we'd been together for like three and a half years. I couldn't be sexual, I was very embarrassed about the way I looked, and he was super supportive and really loving," she told me. "But I couldn't be sexual. I couldn't look in the mirror, I couldn't look at myself in the mirror."

But after a couple of months, she began to pick up weight. As she was getting stronger, her relationship was getting weaker. Around that same time, her boyfriend broke up with her.

"I just said to myself, as hard as I fought to pull myself out of the depths of hell, I am not going to let this relationship, losing this relationship, break me. Like, I spent way too much time being sad, like, fuck that. The night he broke up with me, after we hung up, I sat for like thirty minutes just staring into space like, *I can't believe this just happened.* And then the next morning at ten o'clock, I got on the phone and called Sephora. I booked a makeover for myself, I went to the mall, and I bought all new clothes. I bought this beautiful little leather jacket and some really cute clothes. I bought like four hundred dollars' worth of new makeup. I called it my step-it-up campaign." She had a whole team of girlfriends who'd cochaired her campaign. Along the way, they became more like sisters.

The day after she got shot, about eight of them gathered at one of their homes and divvied up the pieces of Deborah's life. Each would take responsibility for one piece, with the goal of maintaining as much as they could until she was strong enough, physically and mentally, to inherit them back. Linda got power of attorney over her health. Stacy got power of attorney over her money. Meeka organized an online fundraiser with GoFundMe, which raised nearly $40,000. Other friends would come over to clean Deborah's house and keep her fridge stocked with food. Copies of her house keys were made, and everybody had a set. If they hadn't heard from her for twenty-four hours, someone was dispatched to check on her. If one of them called and didn't get an answer, someone would be bounding up her steps in no time. Every now and then, one of her sister-friends would find her balled up on the bathroom floor in a fetal position, retching up her guts.

"That's how I lived for the first year with these eight amazing women," Deborah told me.

A Goodbye, Beneath the Stars

As we talked that day back in 2016, her speech became breathy, her words slowed until she would give me just one or two at a time. She excused herself and disappeared into her kitchen. When she came back, she leaned in the doorway and mustered as much of a smile as she could. She looked as tired as I'd ever seen her. Her eyelids were heavy, but more than anything,

I could see it in the way her cheeks hung down toward her mouth.

"I'm just so tired, baby," she said. "I'm so sorry, I just can't."

I'd only been on her couch for about thirty minutes, not nearly enough time to catch up after so many years, let alone be filled in on the nearly four-year roller coaster she'd been on.

I got back to my Airbnb and the phone rang. It was Deborah. She said she just needed to lie down and catch her second wind. Life, she said, had gotten heavy. Carrying her many burdens—the physical and emotional burdens of her post-shooting life—were never too much to bear, but she wished she could lay them down from time to time.

We spent the next few hours talking and laughing, and at points, I could hear what I could only assume were muffled tears. I'd never imagined her crying. She was filled with far too much sunshine for that.

The next night, her strength had returned sufficiently for me to meet with her and a group of her friends at a place called Café Istanbul to hear another friend of hers sing. We drank and talked and walked down the block, remembering the forever-ago days before Hurricane Katrina. We stumbled upon a brass band playing as it spilled from a barbershop. She quickstepped her way inside and passed a line of patrons, dancing away from a table of red beans and rice, gumbo, chicken wings, and sausage, until she found the owner of the place. I watched from afar as she worked her magic. She was in her element. She was dazzling. She was everything I'd always remembered.

When we left, we hopped inside her Jeep Wrangler, packed from front to back with bags of home-popped popcorn. She shrugged and smiled. Deborah had found yet another hustle, and like everything else she did, she added a bit of her own flavor.

We sat in her Jeep for a long time, just talking about what she hoped to do with the rest of her life. She wanted to give back and to help, to make whole all the tattered pieces in so many people's lives. That included young men like the ones who left her wounded. She wanted to keep her sleeves rolled up and her voice raised on behalf of Black folks in New Orleans, who she said had "the most beautiful spirits in the world." And fight like hell to make sure people in power recognize and respect that spirit and their lives. We dreamed out loud about how one day we'd figure out some way to work together. I told her about a plan I had to create a program to arm young men and women with my weapons of choice—a pen and a pad—to help them take control of their narratives and tell their own stories. We made a deal that we'd hold each other to our grand plans.

Late the next morning, I got a text message from her:

> Good morning. Wanna wish you safe travels and happy holidays for u and the fam. I had such a great time catching up with you last night. I'd forgotten how much we used to get our chat on back in the day and how pumped up we'd get, egging each other on lol. We are good motivators for each other. Let's keep in touch and continue supporting each other's projects. We're both uniquely positioned to make major lasting positive impacts for our community. Take good care friend, see you next year!

When I got back to New York, I couldn't shake the whirlwind of emotions I felt about seeing Deborah. Her spirit was so powerful, yet I could tell it took every last bit of energy she could muster to be there and be present with me.

The hug we shared that night would be our last.

Deborah died on May 2, 2017, at University Medical Center in New Orleans. Her body finally gave in to the injuries she'd suffered four years earlier. When she passed, she wasn't bitter. She wasn't even mad at the young man who'd shot her. But she was angry at a world and a system that made it easy for him to get his hands on that gun and use it so recklessly. She felt compassion for him. He looked just like her nephew, she told me. In a different universe, he could've been her son. But she felt no compassion for a criminal justice system that churns young men like Aiken Scott and his brothers in and out of jails and prisons with little rehabilitation or the possibility of acquiring skills.

"We can no longer take the position, 'Lock them up and throw away the key,'" she said at a local criminal justice forum a couple of months before she died. "We have to ask, 'How can we be our brothers' keepers?'"

"He is redeemable," she said of her eventual killer, having refused to testify at his trial. "We need to find that point of humanity and begin to build there."

In one of her final public acts of defiance, Deborah wrote an op-ed that appeared in *The New York Times* two days after her death.

In it, she decried local prosecutors' efforts to prosecute victims and witnesses who refuse to testify against their attackers, calling tough-on-crime approaches dated and dangerous and for policy that prioritized safety and economic investment in the community:

> When it came to my own cooperation with the prosecutor, I was reluctant. I'd finally clawed myself out of a pit of grief, despair and PTSD and I wanted to live again. Why should I risk my health to testify for the prosecution? In my case, there were more witnesses and victims than

normally would agree to cooperate. The outrage caused by perpetrators opening fire into a crowd of innocent New Orleanians on Mother's Day broke down the community's reluctance. Additionally, our United States attorney, not our local district attorney, prosecuted the case. That made a difference, too.

I also didn't want to be part of the machine that sent men from my tribe to prison. As a Black woman working on criminal justice reform, it breaks my heart to watch scores and scores of Black and brown men in orange jumpsuits going into the tunnel of no return.

We need our prosecutors to be community prosecutors. We need prosecutors who will work with us so that we can build trust. We must believe that our prosecutors see lasting public safety as the end goal, not jail. District attorneys must promise to listen to the needs and desires of crime victims and never ever arrest a survivor who is too scared to testify.

The last time I saw Deborah, we hugged a long hug and I kissed her on the cheek. As I stood on the corner, under the never-ending night sky in New Orleans, I watched her whip her Jeep into the street, her waving hand a glint snapping from the window as if she were trying to swat away the stars.

8

"Let the Water Heal Our People"

This land will keep the score when our memories fade. There will be no forgetting. There will be no confusion, no whataboutisms or bad faith equivocating about what was done here. This is hallowed ground, soaked in Black blood that's been spilled in the name of white supremacy and the violence baked into its maintenance. And try as we might, on bended knees, hands weaved in prayer, our tears haven't washed away our suffering. There is no absolution. Our fingers have been worn raw from tracing over Bible verses like shattered glass for scripture, our hope only cutting deeper into our wounds.

We still bleed. We've clenched our eyes, laid hands upon the afflicted, and spoken our forgiveness in tongues, yet salvation from America's violence has remained out of our grasp, like trying to put shape to the wind.

Body Memory

Beneath the radiant glow of grocery store lighting and the din of squeaking sneakers and shopping cart wheels, I planted my feet and straightened my spine, pulling my notepad from my back pocket. Then I read their names aloud, low enough to become one with the clatter.

Roberta A. Drury was thirty-two and moved to Buffalo a

decade earlier to care for her brother, who was recovering from a bone marrow transplant.

Margus D. Morrison was fifty-two, a father of six and a bus aide for Buffalo Public Schools.

Andre Mackneil was fifty-three and picking up a birthday cake for his young son.

Aaron Salter was fifty-five, a retired Buffalo police officer and security guard who was a bridge between law enforcement and the community.

Geraldine Talley was sixty-two and engaged to be married.

Celestine Chaney was sixty-five and a grandmother of six who had survived breast cancer and a brain aneurysm.

Heyward Patterson was sixty-seven and a deacon at his church; he drove the church van to pick up congregants who didn't have transportation.

Katherine Massey was seventy-two and a longtime civil rights activist who tirelessly advocated for Buffalo's Black community.

Pearl Young was seventy-seven and a dedicated substitute public school teacher.

Ruth Whitfield was the eldest of this group at eighty-six. She was the mother of a former Buffalo fire commissioner; she made daily visits to her husband in his nursing home.

It had been just two months since an eighteen-year-old white supremacist walked into that grocery store, the Tops Friendly Market in East Buffalo, New York, and murdered those folks, each of them Black and killed because of it. Somewhere between the redesigned checkout lines and the gleaming new produce and baked goods sections, I felt their spirits rising where their bodies had wilted under gunfire.

If the corporate owners of Tops hoped that new linoleum

floors, a paint job, and a fancy modern layout might cover up what happened here, they were wrong. A wide-open wound needs more than a Band-Aid. And East Buffalo had been a neighborhood full of hurt that refused to heal long before that white boy came shooting.

For decades, the Jefferson Avenue Tops has been the only full-service supermarket in East Buffalo. The area was a food desert, a community without consistent access to affordable and nutritious food. Tops aside, it's still relatively barren.

Food deserts don't happen by accident. They're created. During the Migration, scores of Black folks settled in Buffalo, and East Buffalo became a mostly segregated, yet thriving Black community. But following the pattern replicated across the nation, the 1960s brought "urban renewal," which devastated the area. The construction of the Kensington Expressway split East Buffalo in half, leading to economic depression and the loss of manufacturing jobs. Later, in the 1980s, the crack epidemic pushed the neighborhood to the brink. The Black-owned grocers and delis that used to serve the community went out of business, leaving behind corner stores and mini-marts owned by outsiders who peddled subpar food at expensive prices. Some have argued the term *food apartheid* is a more accurate description than food desert.

For years, activists and community leaders fought to bring a grocery store to the neighborhood. Then, in 2003, Tops Friendly Market opened its doors. The store became an important source of food in an otherwise beaten-down neighborhood, where shootings, poverty, and police violence are common. But it also became a place of fellowship, where aunties and neighbors swapped greetings and gossip, where first jobs and last jobs were landed. It became a center point of community life, where you went before a church picnic or family barbecue to buy supplies, and after to thank the butcher for the prime cuts or the baker for the extra goodies slid on the low.

The massacre changed all of that.

Leading up to the reopening on July 15, 2022, there was deep division in the Black community about what should be done with the building. Should it be closed permanently out of respect for those who lost their lives? Should it be turned into a community center or food co-op? Should it be demolished the way that Marjory Stoneman Douglas High School in Parkland, Florida, was after a mass shooting there claimed seventeen? Or should it remain open as a much-needed community resource and testament to East Buffalo's strength and resolve?

Much to the chagrin of some residents who said the community's voices weren't considered, the supermarket chain decided to remain open. On reopening day, when folks made their way back into the store for the first time since the shooting, one woman lamented, "We're pretty much shopping on people's blood . . . I think that this is more about putting people to work rather than letting them heal. Just two months ago, these people were running for their lives."

Another said, "People wouldn't tread over graveyards or cemeteries. This has some of the same perspective for some of our people. On the other hand, we've been traumatized for centuries . . . but our ancestors always rose above it and kept moving forward. That's why I'm here today."

Hours before the store opened its doors, I sat in the passenger seat of Fragrance Harris Stanfield's well-worn Ford Explorer. She was one of those folks who had run for their lives that terrible day. As we drove through the city, we passed row after row of telescope homes, that start with a single room and stretch back with successive additions that sit a bit higher than the one before it, creating a layered effect that gives them their name. They're lasting markers of the city's working class, built with simple materials like wood, brick, and clapboard. They are a common sight in East Buffalo. They reminded me of those long and lanky shotgun houses in New Orleans.

Fragrance was a Tops clerk who'd been working at the grocery store for more than a year. She started off as a cashier and quickly moved up to front-end supervisor, overseeing clerks and other customer-facing employees. When we met, she hadn't been to work for two months. She told me the story of what happened that day, when a white gunman in full body armor and tactical gear opened fire on customers and employees, killing ten and wounding three others. She took cover, cowering with dozens of other people, including her teenage daughter, who worked beside her.

Her fear that day was overwhelming. She recalled, "I literally gave up for a moment." It felt surreal to see a planned attack on her customers and coworkers. "I couldn't believe I was going to die."

In the weeks after the shooting, Fragrance wrestled with the idea of ever stepping foot back inside the store, let alone returning to work there.

"My body memory is just still too strong of what happened," she said.

That the shooter chose the Tops in East Buffalo, an oasis in a food desert, was no coincidence. According to his manifesto, he chose East Buffalo's 14208 zip code because of how Black it was. At 78 percent, it has the highest percentage of Black residents in upstate New York. Armed with an AR-15-style semiautomatic rifle, a shotgun, and rifle, the shooter drove nearly four hours from his overwhelmingly white rural hometown to get to Buffalo. He'd studied previous massacres and visited the store multiple times before the shooting, posting to white supremacist message boards that he was looking to strike at a time when the highest number of Black people would be in the store.

Law enforcement and the media often describe these kinds of perpetrators as lone wolves, but the work of white supremacy is anything but solitary. There's an entire universe of right-wing politicians and pundits who hold their hand and walk them toward murder, seeding their minds with anti-Black and white supremacist ideologies. The shooter's manifesto referenced the "great replacement theory," a baseless and racist belief that there's a plan orchestrated by liberal and Jewish leaders to replace white-majority populations with people of color and Jewish people through immigration, interracial marriage, and eventually violence and a "white genocide." It's a conspiracy theory that's bled from the fringes into the mainstream of Republican and right-wing political thought. A 2022 Associated Press and University of Chicago poll found that up to a third of Americans believe in at least some part of this theory.

Replacement theory isn't benign. It has fueled high-profile mass shootings, such as those in Christchurch, New Zealand, where a gunman killed fifty-one Muslims at a mosque and Islamic center; in El Paso, Texas, where a man shot and killed twenty-three Hispanic people at a Walmart; and in Pittsburgh, where a shooter slaughtered eleven Jewish worshippers at the Tree of Life Congregation. Domestic terrorists have organized around it, plotting and carrying out attacks against those they perceive as "invaders" and individuals they believe are facilitating their so-called replacement. Political violence has also escalated, with threats, harassment, and attacks being directed at politicians and public figures who've advocated for immigrants and championed diversity.

The Buffalo murderer, Payton Gendron, wrote in his manifesto that he was inspired by replacement theory and earlier mass shootings and that he hoped that his violence might spark "revolutionary change" or "civil war." He chose Buffalo as his battlefield and his victims because they were ordinary and Black and he believed they wouldn't put up much of a fight. Defenseless Black people are white supremacists' favorite targets.

As Fragrance and I pulled up to the grocery store, we were greeted by a tall chain-link fence, a reminder of when the place was a giant crime scene peppered with FBI and police investigators. On the inside of the fence was a large invite-only delegation of local, state, and federal officials gathered to celebrate Tops's reopening. Byron Brown, the mayor of Buffalo, was there. So was New York governor Kathy Hochul and US senator Chuck Schumer. Conspicuously missing were many of the local activists and community members who years ago had pushed to get the store opened in the first place. Some, on the other side of the fence, hunkered down in quiet protest. One woman, with a large, curly white Afro, held a huge hot-pink sign that read: "You want us to shop here, yet you have a gate keeping us out now!" Another held one that read, "This is not a win! This is not Justice!" And perhaps the most biting, "Two Months Is Too Soon to Reopen These Wounds."

The lingering trauma of witnessing so many Black folks murdered and maimed hung heavy on Fragrance as she headed inside for a staff-only gathering. Those ten lost lives were each a pillar in East Buffalo. But the dead were only the first line of loss.

"It just seems that there's a forgotten space," Fragrance said. "The workers at the store are also victims. We were there. We're still human beings, and we are still healing."

Black Death, a Spectacle

Black death is often a public spectacle, a centuries-old traveling horror show. Our grief and trauma are communal. When we watched a police officer murder George Floyd in the street over a counterfeit twenty-dollar bill, and another cop shoot Walter Scott in the back in a public field because of a broken taillight, and other cops gun down John Crawford III in a Walmart over a toy gun he picked up on a store shelf, we all carried the weight of their very public killings. When we watched young Tamir Rice shot down outside of a community center and heard Trayvon Martin's final screams at an apartment complex in a 911 call, there wasn't a Black person in America who didn't feel like they could've been any one of our boys. When we watched Ahmaud Arbery chased and shot down by white vigilantes as he jogged through a white neighborhood, we were all stopped by the blast that took his life. When we saw the pictures of the Tops Ten murdered in that grocery store, it was more of the same—a collective public execution.

One of the more disturbing things I heard from witnesses in Buffalo was that when they first heard the gunfire at Tops, they thought it was "normal" gunfire and not the mass-murdering kind. By "normal," they meant the more typical shootings in poorer Black urban communities all across the country. The kind they don't typically even flinch for. The common, everyday kind of gunfire that echoes across street corners and from speeding cars so often it's unremarkable. As devastating as *those* kinds of gunshots can be on a micro level, they just don't register among the general public or even researchers the same way as the high-casualty kind. But they're one and the same. Violence from the hands of white supremacists and the everyday violence from Black hands have become intertwined; bullets ring out the same no matter the intention of the shooter. They function in tandem. How we order and classify American violence is far less important than how we stop it. Be it a second line parade or in the seafood aisle of a grocery store, a house party or a house of worship, there has been no haven.

Daddy's Little Girls

I watched from a perch about twenty yards away as the two little brown girls with white bows pinned in their hair took small, measured steps toward their daddy's casket. And I felt every step in my gut. The younger of the two wore a pink sweater and pink shoes that smiled against the sea of mournful black all around them.

As the girls neared the front row, the choir's songs of Jesus's sweet redemption unfurled high into the far reaches of the arena, where thousands of mourners, filling every seat and every spot along the rafters, stood just a bit taller, seemingly keeping the weight of the world from crumbling in on the girls as they mourned their father's death more publicly than anyone ever should. They sat on either side of their mother and just a few feet from where their father, the Reverend Clementa Pinckney, lay in a mahogany casket as deep and rich as his brown skin. It was a scene eerily reminiscent of another preacher's funeral— that of the Reverend Dr. Martin Luther King Jr., struck down by a white supremacist's bullet nearly fifty years earlier. Images of Dr. King's widow, Coretta, and their children—with her head held high and face beneath a veil, and the children's eyes flooded in tears—have been burned into our collective conscience as a symbol of grace on the heels of great violence. This was heartbreakingly similar.

On that muggy summer afternoon inside the TD Arena in downtown Charleston, South Carolina, I followed the procession of grief and pain and let every hymn and every note from the funeral dirge wash over me like a baptismal cleanse. I was there as a journalist and as a Black man, but having spent my entire career chronicling all manner of gun violence and death, it's often hard to figure which informs the other.

Pinckney's murder was as much a tipping point as it was a tragic verse in the unending elegy of gun violence in America. For years, I'd crisscrossed the states following a trail of gunshots, bloodshed, fire, and rebellion. Trayvon Martin, Rekia Boyd, Michael Brown Jr., Renisha McBride, Jordan Davis, John Crawford III, Tamir Rice were all gunned down. Freddie Gray's neck was snapped in the back of a police van. Eric Garner suffocated in a police choke hold. Then there were the Black victims whose names never made the national news, whose killers were Black like them. These, too, are forms of anti-Black violence, born long before any gun is ever loaded. Community violence is a proxy for a kind of self-destruction seeded by white supremacy, where rage turns inward instead of striking at the systems that bind and oppress. It's more practical to lash out at those close enough to strike.

At Pinckney's funeral, I watched the bullets that took his life ricochet through mourners—each tear, each wince and pained exhale carrying their trajectory. I took notes, panning between the little girls in their bows and the gathering of politicians, clergy, and layfolk, including President Barack Obama, who delivered his eulogy.

Obama spoke of the Black church as a sanctuary in a hostile world.

"Our pain cuts that much deeper because it happened in a church. The church is and always has been the center of African

American life," Obama said, calling the Black church "a place to call our own . . . where children are loved and fed and kept out of harm's way, and told they are beautiful and smart and taught that they matter."

At forty-one, Pinckney was a state senator and the prodigious young pastor of the historic Mother Emanuel AME Church in Charleston. Mother Emanuel is one of the oldest Black congregations south of Baltimore. Throughout its two-hundred-year history, the church has been a safe harbor for Black worship and a target of white hate. In the early 1800s, it defied city and state laws that forbade Black people from worshipping after sunset. The authorities routinely shut the church down. On one such occasion in 1818, 140 "free Negroes and Slaves" were arrested, some whipped, for teaching the enslaved to read and write, a criminal offense. In 1821, Charleston City Council warned its leader at the time, the Reverend Morris Brown, that the council would not tolerate "a school for slaves." In 1822, one of the church founders, the famed abolitionist Denmark Vesey, a former slave who purchased his own freedom, began plotting a revolt for July 14. The enslaved were to take up arms and kill their masters, cutting and blasting their way to the Charleston docks. From there, they'd sail to Haiti, a Black republic that had taken its liberation through a bloody revolution against the French. The rebellion was ultimately thwarted when a couple of enslaved people loyal to their masters detailed Vesey's plans to white authorities. Vesey and thirty-four other coconspirators were rounded up and hanged from the city gallows. Thirty-five others were shipped off to Cuba. The church was torn down and would not be rebuilt until after the Civil War.

Pinckney embodied that history and promise in the face of pressure. He was a faithful servant and fierce advocate for the South Carolina Lowcountry, often called the "Corridor of

Shame" for its entrenched poverty, violence, and failing schools. Preaching by thirteen and ordained at eighteen, he became, at twenty-three, the youngest African American elected to South Carolina's legislature. Pinckney's life was a testament to the fight for justice—and the resilience of Black faith.

On June 17, 2015, almost two hundred years after Vesey's failed revolt, hate and violence once again came knocking at Mother Emanuel. This time, it was armed with a .45-caliber handgun. It was a Wednesday night, and a scraggly young white man named Dylann Roof walked into that old church and joined a group of folks seated around a table preparing for Bible study.

Church member Myra Thompson, fifty-nine, was leading Bible study that night. She had been planning to step down from teaching regular Wednesday-night classes but agreed to stay on for a couple more weeks until the church found a replacement. She spent the week preparing for class, searching for the perfect lesson, the right scripture to teach a group that included Bible-wise pastors and other church leaders, the churchiest of church folks, who were more familiar than most with scripture. She chose Mark 4:14–20, the parable of the sower, which likens the word of God to seed that must fall on good soil to bear fruit:

> Some people are like seed along the path, where the word is sown. As soon as they hear it, Satan comes and takes away the word that was sown in them. Others, like seed sown on rocky places, hear the word and at once receive it with joy. But since they have no root, they last only a short time. When trouble or persecution comes because of the word, they quickly fall away.

Roof blew in like a bad seed.

While their heads were bowed in prayer, Roof lifted his Glock from his fanny pack and fired again and again. Tywanza Sanders, twenty-six, begged him to stop. "You rape our women and you're taking over our country," Roof said. "I have to do what I have to do." Sanders shielded his eighty-seven-year-old great-aunt, Susie Jackson, but Roof kept shooting, reloading five times. Nine people were killed, including Jackson, Sanders, and Rev. Pinckney. Survivors played dead or hid. Before Roof fled, he turned to a woman and asked if she had been shot yet. She said no. "Good. Someone has to live to tell the story, because I'm going to kill myself, too," Roof said. After a sixteen-hour manhunt, Roof was captured by police a few hundred miles away in North Carolina. The sympathetic officers who arrested him took the time to stop at a nearby Burger King on the way back to South Carolina to feed the famished killer.

"[Roof] surely sensed the meaning of his violent act. It was an act that drew on a long history of bombs and arson and shots fired at churches, not random but as a means of control, a way to terrorize and oppress," Obama said. "An act that he imagined would incite fear and recrimination, violence and suspicion. An act that he presumed would deepen divisions that trace back to our nation's original sin."

Roof's .45-caliber Glock was a gift of America's broken gun laws. Despite a drug charge that should have barred him from purchasing a firearm, Roof exploited a loophole in federal background checks—the "three-day rule"—allowing dealers to complete a sale without a finalized FBI review. Lax enforcement and systemic errors turned a blind eye to the danger, a loophole exploited by thousands of prohibited buyers each year. Over the past decade, thousands of prohibited buyers, including criminals, drug users, and the dangerously mentally ill, have exploited the three-day rule. Some of those weapons have been used in violent crimes. In the aftermath, the nation mourned briefly, but grief gave way to inertia. Calls for reform faded as familiar divisions returned. By summer's end, gun sales surged, and Mother Emanuel's victims became another chapter in America's long, unbroken cycle of racialized gun violence.

As I listened to Obama's eulogy, the full weight of the deaths settled squarely on my soul, and I couldn't shake the heartbreak of those two beautiful little Black girls marching toward their father's body. The younger one was just a few years older than Nola, my own precious little Black daughter.

"I know you were shot at the Church and you went to heaven," Malana Pinckney wrote in her father's funeral program.

Healing in Buffalo

I went back to Buffalo to report on the one-year anniversary of the shooting. I'd kept in touch with a few folks like Fragrance, the front-of-store supervisor at Tops.

More than anything, I hoped the city's wounded heart was healing. That word, *healing*, is so hard to define. It's often used as a kind of catchall for approaching normalcy. But real healing requires work; it requires acknowledging the hurt and moving forward.

To some degree, that wound-work was being done in Buffalo. Everyday people doing everything they could for those touched by what happened that day, which meant nearly everyone connected to East Buffalo. After the cameras had gone and the #BuffaloStrong yard signs and promises from politicians faded with the seasons, something beautiful began to flower.

Away from the bright lights of the national media, folks in this tattered community started to mend themselves, one stitch at a time. They ran for office to fight for better public policy. They started food co-ops to offer healthier food options in neighborhoods starved of them. And one group, in a century-old church with an ancient bowling alley in its basement, worked to change the city's tune through music.

"We all know that in this life you have to be able to balance the horrific with the joy," Dawn Martin Berry-Walker, chief executive director of the Pappy Martin Legacy Jazz Collective, told me.

The Love Supreme School of Music was founded in the spirit of Buffalo's legendary jazzman James "Pappy" Martin, Berry-Walker's father. For decades, the school has offered free and low-cost music lessons to young people from the most under-resourced communities in Buffalo. So when Buffalonians were trapped in grief, Love Supreme's students found ways to lift their spirits. They put on shows at venues not far from Tops billed as "the series that heals" featuring young musicians onstage alongside professional concert musicians and international jazz stars.

"If people are going through rough times, someone would play like the trumpet or something for them just to cheer them up," Love Supreme student Genesis Thompson told me one evening after practice. "And then all of a sudden, when this one person does this thing for them, it really lifts their spirit because they make them feel like they're not alone."

The group's work was funded in part by a $1.4 million state grant for mental health programs. "We want the children to understand that this is a form of your own mental health wellness," Berry-Walker said. "You don't have to look outside of yourself, outside of the community. The music has the power to really cleanse you, clean you out, and then fill it with something beautiful."

Then there were folks like Trinetta Alston, also known as Nurse T, who in those early dark days became a bright light and beacon for East Buffalo. Nurse T worked as a licensed practical nurse (LPN) at the Community Health Center of Buffalo, one of just a few Black-owned and -operated health centers in the country. The day after the shooting, her boss dispatched her to a local library where survivors and community members had gathered to mourn. Nurse T isn't a therapist, and she never specialized in trauma response. But at that moment, she knew exactly what her people needed. For some, it was a hug or a shoulder or an ear or a list of resources for city programs and services. She's helped employees facing eviction or who were late on their car payments.

"I can almost feel what it is they feel. And if I can take a little bit of that away from them just for a minute, then I'm going to take a little bit away. Eventually, I'mma chisel it all out," Nurse T told me. Lorraine Baker, affectionately known as Rinny, is a store manager at Tops. And she was there the morning of the shooting, but by the grace of God left shortly before it began. Rinny and Trinetta are both in their fifties with colorfully dyed hair and personalities, and share what feels like a lifelong bond, back then just a year in the making. I listened as these women finished each other's sentences and playfully ribbed each other.

"You fuss at us like a nurse. You tell them to go to the doctor. You say, 'Have you been to the doctor's? I'mma tell your doctor your name!' And I say that because we need that. We need that shoulder," Rinny said, an arm around her buddy Nurse T. "'Cause we a family."

Trinetta Alston has had her own struggles in life. She overcame homelessness and a decade-long crack cocaine addiction.

By the time the shooting happened, she'd been sober for eighteen years and an LPN for a dozen years. Trinetta went into nursing as a way to give back, to genuinely care for people, to help those who aren't used to people being kind without wanting anything in return. A woman in New Orleans, about a decade after Katrina, once scolded me after I said how resilient the people of the city were to have weathered the storm. "Resilience," she told me, "is not a natural state." All the bending and contorting that Black folks have to do to survive is what resilience looks like. Resilience takes us just to the point of snapping over and again, until we no longer bounce back. I'm not sure which word would be more appropriate or more buoyant. But we need a word for people like Trinetta Alston and so many others stung by the most unfair kind of loss who find a way to give to others with no expectation of getting anything at all back.

As part of the redesign of the Tops market, there's a waterfall monument near the front of the store, not far from where the shooter exchanged gunfire with security guard Aaron Salter. The monument features a poem written by Buffalo poet laureate Jillian Hanesworth, where she writes in part:

> Let the hopeful healing waters flow
> Cleansing all pain and fear
> All hurt and regret
> Let the water heal our people

Fight

On the corner of Jefferson Avenue and Landon Street, a memorial had grown to include bundles of flowers and cards. Next to the ten large poster-size portraits of the Tops victims above the corner, I struck up a conversation with Wayne Jones—the only child of Celestine Chaney, who'd survived so much in life to find death in the baking supply aisle at Tops.

I asked Jones the kind of question I'm always pained to ask because there's no elegant way to push into a stranger's heart or spirit.

"It's been a year. Has there been any healing for you and your family?"

"I don't know how you'd be able to heal from something like this. Over a year anyway. I still wake up the same every day, missing my mother," he said.

When I asked him which part of his mother he'd hold closest, he told me:

"How strong she was as a single mother to raise a strong Black man. That's strength. All the days we went without lights or the gas was cut off and we still made it. I'm here today as a testimony to her will and her resiliency," he said. "To have somebody ripped out of your life like that. She had three aneurysms and she had breast cancer, and we defeated all of that. To go shopping and lose your life is sad. For all of us not to sit down and get gun control, that's the worst part of it."

Jones has been trying to put pressure on Congress to do something, but he said his pleas have gone unanswered.

"I don't know what will work," he said. "I'm in disbelief that all the shootings every other week didn't work."

After a gunman in New Zealand armed with a semiautomatic rifle killed fifty-one people in two mosques, the country banned assault weapons.

After a gunman in Norway armed with assault rifles killed seventy-seven people at a youth summer camp, the country banned assault weapons.

After a gunman in Tasmania armed with a semiautomatic rifle killed thirty-five people, Australia banned assault weapons.

After a gunman in Nova Scotia armed with a semiautomatic rifle killed twenty-two people, Canada banned assault weapons.

Since these countries banned weapons of war from private hands, there hasn't been another shooting at their respective scales.

America, meanwhile, has done what it has always done.

Eighteen people were killed in Lewiston, Maine, in 2023; twenty-two people were killed in Uvalde, Texas, in 2022; ten people were killed in Buffalo, New York, in 2022; seventeen people were killed in Parkland, Florida, in 2018; sixty-one people were killed in Las Vegas, Nevada, in 2017.

Nothing.

"How would your mother want you to move forward?" I asked Wayne Jones that day on the corner.

"To fight," he said. "She was a fighter. So tooth and nail, we're going to fight until we get something done."

Postscript

A THOUSAND WAYS TO DIE

My friend Darran Simon, who lost his life to suicide, in a photo I took during my fortieth birthday celebration in Turks and Caicos.

It had been months since my friend Darran ended his life. His death, at forty-three, put me under a miserable spell. I was numb, in a daze. He had just landed his dream job at *The Washington Post* and was working a prime reporting beat at the paper. He was healthy, smart, and classically cool, calm, and collected. He had this way about him that put you at immediate ease.

Then one day, he didn't show up to a city hall press conference he was supposed to cover. And just like that, he was gone. As sad as I was that one of my truly good brothers took an early exit, I was twice as angry. I felt betrayed. Early death under any circumstance can leave you tangling with deeply complicated feelings. But suicide's grief is unlike any other. I felt a constant gnawing of anguish and unearned guilt. Perhaps my anger was selfish, but Darran left without giving me the opportunity to stop him, to say how much I respected him, how I loved him like a brother. He didn't even say goodbye or give me a chance to do the same. I missed my homeboy dearly, but I was also mad as hell at him, stuck in this peculiar kind of selfish hurt.

My daze was broken by a dream. I was being ushered into a big performance hall. There was a warm orange glow that cascaded across the semi-darkened stage, which had a lectern, lit by a bright spotlight. Groups of people were milling through the audience, and the din of their chatter was low and slow. There was a buzz in the air and in my gut. It felt like I was going to get some sort of award or deliver a speech. Up on stage, the Reverend Al Sharpton took his place behind the lectern. Then a tall white woman wearing a pleasant smile and a sensible pantsuit walked up to me just as a small group of strangers gathered around.

"Take these," she said, handing each of us a stack of index cards. "You'll know when you know."

You'll know? The same look of confusion spread across each of our faces as we went off in different directions like mice in a maze. Looking. Searching. For what, I had no idea. But I felt this sense of purpose pulling me through the crowd. As I squeezed past folks—some wrapped in tight hugs or holding one another's faces in tender hands or bowed and weeping on folded knees—the sea of bodies split, and there he was, like Black Moses: Darran, dressed as Darran would be in a perfectly fitted corduroy sport jacket with a scarf draped over his shoulders. My whole chest welled. I didn't speak a single word, but I knew he could hear me.

"Come on, bruh. Why?"

"I just couldn't take it anymore," he said. "I just couldn't."

In that moment, the wall I'd erected in grief began to crumble. My brother was gone, but my brother was hurting. He didn't have the strength or will to carry whatever it was he'd been burdened with. I'll never know why Darran did what he did. I don't know how long he'd struggled with his mental health or what war he'd been losing. But in that moment, hearing his words shook me awake. I still haven't completely forgiven Darran for leaving us, but I do understand what it means to carry too much weight.

Am I Enough?

Being a Black man in America means bearing the yoke of the world on your shoulders. Am I a good enough husband, father, son, or brother? Am I a good enough provider? Am I ambitious and hardworking and smart enough? Can I fight back? Can I protect us or myself? Black men have been portrayed as hypermasculine and hypersexual, both feared and fetishized. We've been told to dance, to sing, to rap, to tell jokes, to run fast and jump high. Shut up and dribble. Man up. "Run, nigger, run!" We're told a lot of things but rarely told that we're enough. We've been both caricatured as brutes and emasculated for laughs. There have been boundaries placed around the imagination of what Black manhood can be.

These burdens we carry are a specific kind of weight, accumulated over generations and passed from parent to son. We give our boys the *talk*, where we initiate them with the same *burden* that threatened to buckle our granddaddies and their granddaddies and their daddies before them: You are not safe. Your teachers, your neighbors, the police, they'll never see you as they see their own boys. Your shoulders, your back, your hue, your bop. Boy, they see you as a *man*. And they might hurt you because they're scared of you. They'll see you as a thief even with spending money in your pocket. They'll see you as a criminal with that hood on your head even when there's a chill in the air.

They'll see you jogging in the suburbs and think you're running from a break-in. They'll see your gun permit and your gun and shoot you just in case. They'll see you as a violent threat as you march for peace. Hands up, Don't Shoot! And sometimes, lots of times, boys who look just like you will see you as a threat, too, because they've been taught to despise themselves. In you, they'll see their reflection. You might even feel so unsafe that you'll think about getting a gun yourself. Know that a gun offers as much destruction as it does protection. Guns bring you closer to death either way.

It's not fair, we tell Black boys, but the world is as it is and not as we want it to be. The stereotypes. The low expectations. The red lines drawn around our neighborhoods. The wealth of land and homes stripped from us. The applications rejected because of the phonetics in your name. The unfair public policies that bankrupt our schools, poison the water we drink and the air we breathe, and keep quality food outside of our reach. The way police are trained to treat us, to shoot us. The way white America is trained to treat us, to shoot us.

Black men are sidelined in the political process that make the country go round, then blamed when they don't show up and the "allies" lose. Black men are the most feared, pathologized, and targeted people in America, a reality that leaves so many with deep emotional and psychological welts. We have to fight to live at every turn. A lot of Black men will win. But too many won't. All the fighting, all the physical and emotional labor in trying to break free from the forces yanking at our humanity, is exhausting. And it's killing us. This country is Black America's greatest comorbidity. The average Black man in the United States will die six years sooner than a white man. Six years is what it takes to earn a bachelor's *and* master's degree. Six years is a full term in the US Senate and the time it would take to watch your daughter enter seventh grade and then graduate from high school. Six years might as well be a lifetime.

Slow Death

There are a thousand ways to die; a bullet is just one. Long before the violence of a gun ever tears into us, a universe of systems pushes us toward early death. *Our* American death often comes in dramatic, violent bursts, a staccato of gunfire. But it also comes in the slow legato of social, emotional, and economic suffocation.

For every one hundred dollars in wealth that a white man's family has, a Black man's family has just fifteen dollars. The Black homeownership rate is 41 percent compared to 71 percent for whites. And Black people with college degrees, even those solidly in the middle class, are more likely to live in segregated communities with higher levels of environmental toxins and lower access to quality schools, health care, and jobs compared to white people who make less money and never made it through college. Black men face an incarceration rate that's six times that of white men and face longer prison sentences for conviction on the same crimes.

The disparities in the way we live and die in this country even penetrate our dreams and nightmares. Daily stress has Black people and Black men in particular getting fewer hours of sleep and less quality sleep than their white counterparts, which health experts correlate to a slew of deadly health outcomes like cardiovascular disease and high blood pressure, which disproportionately kill Black people: Black men have a 70 percent higher chance of a heart attack than white men. "There's never been a time, not a single year, where the US population of African descent hasn't been sicker or died younger than whites," writes Mary Bassett, professor of the Practice of Health and Human Rights at Harvard T. H. Chan School of Public Health.

There's such great violence in the systemic and structural racism that guides us from life to death that a growing number of cities, including Chicago, LA, and New York and smaller ones like Indianapolis and San Antonio, have joined states including Michigan, Ohio, and Wisconsin, in declaring racism a public health crisis.

If you were to take a sheet of transparency film, like the ones our middle school math teachers used to slide onto an overhead projector during geometry lessons back in the day, and draw a map of our poorest zip codes on it, then do the same with our sickest, our hungriest, our most toxic, and the ones with the weakest infrastructure, you'd find the zip codes experiencing the most gun deaths would fit neatly on top of one another like a grim puzzle, connecting the dots of the inescapable lethality of systemized racism in America.

The slivers of life between those puzzle pieces is where my friend Darran shone the brightest light as a reporter. Like me, Darran was a journalist who chronicled life and death in America. Police killings. Car crashes. Racial massacres. Gang shootings. He told the kinds of stories that rattled police and politicians, and he did so with deftness and grace and humility. Here's how he once described his *WHY*: "I am drawn to writing about suffering and trauma because I am in awe of the human spirit's ability to persevere."

Black Man Missing

When Darran left us, he joined the millions of Black men who are among "the missing," a term coined by *The New York*

Times in a jarring, decade-old report on Black men who've essentially disappeared from society. For every one hundred Black women not in jail, they found there are only eighty-three Black men. The remaining 1.5 million back in 2015, are "in a sense, missing."

By their estimation, more than one out of every six Black men who should be between twenty-five and fifty-four years old today have disappeared from daily life. These missing men, now surely numbering in the millions, have been removed from our families, our communities, and public spaces all together. New York: 120,000. Chicago: 45,000. Philadelphia: 30,000. There are more missing Black men nationwide than there are Black men who reside in New York City, or Boston, Detroit, Houston, Los Angeles, Philadelphia, and Washington combined.

These men are both living and dead. Some have disappeared into the abyss of the US carceral system, caged in prison cells at a rate higher than anywhere else in the world. Others have been lost to early death, from myriad health maladies and gun violence—blood clots and bullets. But among those gone from life and society are a growing number of Black boys who are taking their own lives. The Centers for Disease Control and Prevention has listed suicide as the third-leading cause of death for young Black men. In 2022, for the first time, the suicide rate among Black youth between ten and nineteen passed that of their white peers, jumping 54 percent since 2018. The suicide rate among Black youth increased faster than any other racial group in the country. Between 2007 and 2020, the suicide rate for Black ten-to-seventeen-year-olds spiked. Black men and boys make up 81 percent of all Black suicides.

I see little coincidence in the rise of Black suicides and the rise of Black youth homicides. Our children are in pain and lashing out at themselves and one another. But the young aren't the only ones suffering. There's a quiet suffering that's ending Black men's lives. We are suffering from a silent mental health crisis of loneliness and disconnection that we mask with our vices or jobs or the roles that we assume. We've been taught that acknowledging our pain is a sign of weakness, of surrender. And for some, who suffer mental illness, there's even more of a stigma. Black men are ailing, and too many don't know where to turn. So we dap and head nod and "I'm good" ourselves into a dissonance, until we burn ourselves down.

We Laughed, then We Cried

Darran and I became fast friends on the heels of my tenure at *The Times-Picayune*. I wanted to make sure that someone Black had a shot at my old position, or at least got introduced to the hiring managers. So I posted a note to the National Association of Black Journalists' LISTSERV for young Black journalists, and Darran was the first to respond. He introduced himself as a reporter for the *Miami Herald* and an admirer of my work. Darran didn't get my open police-reporting job at *The TP*, but he ended up getting hired as an education reporter.

From that first email, we became fast friends. Our friendship would stretch across many years, cities, relationships, jobs, marriages, a divorce, a child, deployments to uprisings, and riots and racial massacres, and the birth of the Black Lives Matter movement. Darran was a reporter's reporter. He was dogged. He was determined. He was crafty. He was smooth, slender with a runner's build, a clean-shaven head and face, with rich brown skin. I always teased him that he looked like a "fake-ass Taye Diggs," the equally smooth actor. We shared a love for poetry and jazz and journalism. My brother loved a good lede.

Over the years, he'd send me an email when he hit one out of the park or to applaud one of mine. We'd spent hours over whiskey or wine, talking about race, women, and journalism. He was a journeyman, with stints at the *Miami Herald*, *The Times-Picayune*, *The Philadelphia Inquirer*, *Newsday*, and CNN. His dream was to one day work at *The Times* or *The Post*. When he landed at the latter, I cheered him on. Yessir. He finally did it.

Darran was among a group of my closest friends who joined me at a villa in Turks and Caicos to celebrate my fortieth birthday. We laughed. We drank. We hit the beach. We partied. It ranks among my life's greatest memories. For a handful of days, we managed to mute all the noise and stress of our lives and just *be*. One night, as folks faded into their own little pockets in the villa, I stepped onto the balcony, where I found Darran alone. He was sitting reclined deep in a chair, his head cocked back, his eyes closed. In that moment, he looked to be at perfect, supreme peace. I was struck by the way the overhead light shone down on him, carving him out of the Caribbean night sky behind him like an eclipse. I captured the moment in a photo. I look back now and wonder if what I saw that night was peace at all.

Several months later, the COVID pandemic swept the globe and left a path of death and panic. Darran was in the thick of it in DC, covering the worst of what the plague left behind. Then one day that April, I got *the* call. It was a good friend and fellow journalist, John, breaking the news to me. Darran was dead. The way his words landed over the phone struck a familiar register, like the call I got twenty-five years earlier telling me that Latoya had drowned. The gut punch of early death is a blow that never gets easier, no matter how many times you've felt it.

Epilogue

On a recent summer evening in Martha's Vineyard, after wrapping up a panel discussion on Black voters ahead of the 2024 presidential election, I made my way to a small reception at the lovely home of a Black couple in Oak Bluffs, the heart of the island's historic Black community. The house is a former inn now owned by Danroy and Angella Henry, who occasionally open up the place for salon dinners and small receptions like this one. Between glasses of wine and small bites, the couple told the history of their house and what it means to them. They call it the Dragonfly House, and it was once a Black-owned and -operated inn listed in the *Negro Motorist Green Book*, a Jim Crow–era guide of safe places for Black travelers. Before that, it had been owned by John Ritchie, a white man who served as the quartermaster for the famed Fifty-Fourth Massachusetts Regiment, the valiant Black Civil War infantrymen made famous by the movie *Glory* starring Denzel Washington. The film was based in part on Ritchie's diaries. The Henrys purchased the house in 2017. They said during negotiations they sat at a familiar bench not far from the property, overlooking the water, when a swarm of dragonflies settled around them. They'd sat on this bench many times before. It had become a place of reflection in the years after the tragic death of their son in New York. The dragonfly, they learned, is considered a messenger by the Indigenous people of the island. Those dragonflies were a sign from their boy.

As they told their story that evening, I began to feel a chill ripple up the back of my neck. I looked into Angella's eyes, then across the room to Dan's. And like a bolt, it hit me. I knew them. Back in 2010, when I was a reporter with *The New York Times*, I'd spent a number of months working a rewrite shift. Several times a day, I'd make my way through a long list of local and regional police, fire, and emergency departments, calling to see if there was any news to report. On one of these calls, I learned that a police officer had shot and killed a young man in Thornwood, New York, not far from Pace University. The young man was a Pace student and a member of the university's football team. His name was Danroy Henry Jr. He was twenty years old, unarmed, and shot under extremely questionable circumstances. Danroy, known as DJ, was Dan and Angella's son.

Early on the morning of October 17, 2010, several hours after playing in Pace's homecoming football game, DJ joined friends at a local bar and restaurant. At some point, a fight broke out, which spilled outside as the owner of the place cut the music and kicked everyone out. DJ wasn't involved, but as police arrived, they found him sitting with a friend inside his Nissan Altima parked in a fire lane. An officer banged on DJ's window to get his attention, motioning for him to move out of the fire lane. As DJ pulled off and headed toward the exit, another officer, Aaron Hess, jumped in front of the car, eventually ending up on the hood. Hess fired several shots inside the car, fatally shooting young DJ through the windshield. In the days that followed, police published several false accounts of what happened. Hess claimed he fired in self-defense and that DJ tried to mow him down. However, eyewitness accounts contradicted Hess's version, leading to widespread outrage, legal battles, and a federal investigation. Still, no criminal charges were ever filed against the officer.

After years of fighting in their son's name, the Henrys

ultimately settled the case for $6 million and what they say is most valuable—a public apology from the city. In an interview on the tenth anniversary of his son's death, Danroy described the settlement as "blood money" and the "least significant thing to us." At that time, the family hadn't touched the money. "It's in a trust," he said back then. "That is the pattern, though, of these cases. We'd hold it there and give it back gladly with interest if they gave DJ back to us."

Two years before I helped break the story of Trayvon Martin in Sanford, Florida, and four years before I was among the first national reporters on the scene of Michael Brown's killing in Ferguson, Missouri, I was early on the case of DJ Henry. DJ's killing lit something inside of me that I still haven't extinguished. It challenged me inside the newsroom and inside my head.

There's a certain kind of insecurity that comes with trying to tell stories about Black people in white newsrooms, especially when those stories involve white cops killing them. Even when there's ample evidence suggesting something's amiss, the default position is to give the benefit of the doubt to law enforcement and the officials who cape for them. But I did my best to push, to illuminate DJ's story. I canvassed the area where he was killed, looking for witnesses. I went to campus and talked with his friends and classmates. And I went to his funeral, where he was memorialized before hundreds of loved ones on what would have been his twenty-first birthday.

I'll never forget the first time I met with Angella and Dan Sr. When I looked into Angella's eyes, I saw something in them that would later become awfully familiar: the unquenchable pain of a mother who has lost a child to police or vigilante violence. Sybrina Fulton. Lesley McSpadden. Gwen Carr. Samaria Rice. It's never been easy to look into a grieving mother's eyes. Each time, it felt like I was absorbing just a small piece of their anguish, and even that was almost too much to bear. So I've always gravitated toward the fathers. Some stoic. Some deeply saddened. But as Black men, we've learned to bury—or at least mask—our pain.

When Angella finished speaking, I went over, reintroduced myself, and gave her a hug. Then made a beeline to Dan.

"I'm not sure if you remember me. Trymaine Lee."

"I know who you are," he said. "I saw your name on the list. I was waiting for you."

I wrapped him in a bear hug, and though it might've been forgiven under the circumstances, I did my best to keep one of those strong Denzel-from-*Glory* tears from tumbling down my cheek.

It was a full-circle moment. When I first met the Henrys, I was still a reporter in progress. In the years to come, that flame in my belly, kindled by their son's story, would turn into a blaze. I'd become more than just a reporter; I became a journalist, a modern-day griot. From telling the tales of America's daily bloodletting to beginning to understand the complexity and nuance of the systems that ripen that violence, I kept pushing.

Through the harrowing years of American uprisings in the wake of police killings all across the country, I began to shift from writing in print and on digital to doing broadcast news. There's something so much more immediate about reporting on television. Though I'd never imagined myself in front of a camera, it felt surprisingly natural. The more TV I did, the more TV brass and audiences wanted me on. While I've never considered myself especially polished on television, I've always been myself.

While I still use my platform to amplify the experiences of Black folks in America, I've developed a disdain for the way Black pain has become commercialized and commodified. I've stopped sharing every video or gruesome detail of the latest police killing of a Black person. At times, I opt to let younger up-and-coming journalists cut their teeth on the day-to-day violence. Instead, I explore the violent collision of race, power, and politics and how it shapes our understanding of America and ourselves. As the media continues to evolve, so has my storytelling. These days, you're as likely to see me reporting from inside the Democratic National Convention in Chicago as you are from outside a community center in Miami. I've done numerous one-hour specials and documentaries, and my podcast, *Into America*, has earned me and my team a shelfful of awards. But I'm still as committed as ever to telling authentic stories from Black America.

On this journey, following the ricochet of bullets in Black lives and my own, it's never been more clear that something has to be done. Our country's gun insanity is too costly and too damning to continue to push to the next generation. I don't have the answers, but there's little doubt that comprehensive gun reform shouldn't be just some liberal fantasy. Restrictions on guns save lives. States with looser gun laws have higher gun death rates. Nations that have banned assault rifles have all but eliminated mass shootings. Even if you don't care about individual gun deaths, all Americans are still paying a price for them. While the rate of gun violence has fallen across the country over the last twenty years, the resulting micro and macro costs remain staggering—and unsustainable. These figures are not isolated to the communities that suffer from violence most. They are costs shouldered by our society as a whole, billions including both the immediate and more long-term care costs: emergency room visits, hospital and trauma care, police investigations, court costs, funerals, lost wages, and so on. These costs begin accruing right after someone is shot, and if they survive, those costs bleed from their lives into our own. The gun lobby and gun manufacturers must have their ambitions curbed for all our sakes.

We must save America's future generations. In recent years, firearms have become the leading cause of death among young people. The US now holds the grim distinction of having the highest rate of child and teen firearm mortality among similar nations. For every young life lost, many more survive to endure the long trauma of gun violence. As recently as 2022, the firearm death rate among Black youth was an alarming 12.2 per 100,000—the highest of any other group and six times higher than the gun death rate for white youth. Between 2018 and 2022, the gun death rate for Black youth doubled, while Hispanic youth saw a 73 percent increase.

The gun itself needs stricter regulation, perhaps limitations on how many can be produced by manufacturers each year, how they're sold to the public and between private citizens, as well as bans on the deadliest firearms. But none of those things will matter if the ecosystems in which they land remain so deeply stratified by race and class. Nothing stops a bullet like a paycheck, job opportunities, and a quality education. America will never fully untether itself from the violence of its past. But it can begin to ease the current pain that so many Black Americans endure through unfair public policy and the unraveling of past civil rights gains. An unequal America is inherently violent. The gun is just the most lethal manifestation of that inequality.

As my life and career have evolved, so have some of my ideas on gun ownership in Black America. While I think the federal government and states should do everything in their power to protect citizens by tightening gun laws, I also think historic efforts to disarm Black Americans have left Black people vulnerable to state and white supremacist violence. My closest friends, who I consider brothers, have talked a lot about what we can do to protect our people. It's a complicated conversation to have as Black folks are dying by the gun every single day. But it's an important one to have. Should Black people legally adopt the very means used to suppress them for generations to defend itself? Is the Second Amendment the last right for Black Americans to claim? In my daily life, I'm much more concerned about a racist with a gun than a Black man, though I'm much more likely to die from the latter than the former.

After the reception that night at the Henrys' in Martha's Vineyard, I had to call my mother. I was amazed to have run into the Henrys the way that I did. I'd never told them how much their story impacted my life and career. And what was I, this working-class kid from South Jersey, even doing in Martha's Vineyard, the mecca of the so-called Black Bourgeoisie? It was my first extended trip to the Vineyard, and despite the preconceived notion of this being a place for the Black elite, being in Oak Bluffs felt as much like home as anywhere else. Perhaps more so. It's part family reunion, part Black Ivy, part HBCU homecoming, and all love. How did I get here? Truth is, the place has been a safe space for all kinds of Black people going back a century.

In a spiritual way, that trip reminded me of just how far I've come. There was a time when I wasn't sure if I'd ever finish college—it took me six years and a stint at community college to earn my bachelor's degree. And times when I didn't have enough money to fill my gas tank—I shudder at how many times I pumped two gallons of two-dollar regular in my tank. Times that almost broke me. The haunting memories of addiction, murder, and dysfunction that were never too far away. But here I was in Martha's Vineyard, wearing a fancy summer suit, an esteemed guest whose words people traveled to hear. Eating finger foods and drinking wines that I could barely pronounce.

My mother laughed the way she does, literally to the point of almost passing out. And I smiled through the phone. I told her all about the Black men's luncheon I attended and the panel with esteemed colleagues and the fancy dinners I'd been invited to. She was proud but not surprised. My mother is part of what got me here. One of my earliest memories is of her telling me that I was the *one*. And later, before in elementary school, we had a morning ritual. My mother would pull me close and get down on a knee. She'd say, "I am," and I'd say, "Somebody." I Am. Somebody. I Am. Somebody. I AM SOMEBODY! I believed her then, and I believe her now. There's not a room I've entered since that I haven't felt that I am worthy, I am valued, that I am *SOMEBODY*.

But self-confidence was never what I was fighting through. It was something much heavier. It took almost dying to realize that I'd been carrying way too much for my heart to bear. And thank god I survived to put in the work to heal physically and spiritually. For a long time after my heart attack, I couldn't write. Whatever muscles help you draw words from your head, emotions from your soul, and skills from your hands were paralyzed. I was also scared. I didn't know how much time I might have left, and I didn't want to spend any of it stressed out over paragraphs and prose.

Looking back, I was subconsciously connecting almost dying to the act of writing. Just a few weeks before it happened, I sent more than ninety thousand super-rough words to my editor, Elisabeth. It was a mess, a purging of reporting, ideas, and characters that I'd strung together hoping they might reveal something close to an early draft of a book. I was more stressed than I'd ever been, which is saying something considering the life I've lived. With the heart attack came a writing paralysis that froze any action on the page and years of complete abstention from touching this book. There were stops and starts and lots of come-to-Jesus moments. Yet all these years later, here we are. Won't HE do it!

I like to joke that this book almost killed me. But in reality, it's given me new life. Tangoing with death, seeing my own mortality up close, I was able to face the constancy of death throughout my family line and the many other deaths that have shaped my worldview, and my sense of self, with deep honesty. I've been given the gift of reflection from whence I came, and I'm thankful and proud to have made it this far. Who you are seeing today is Trymaine 4.0, the best version of myself yet. I've become a runner. I meditate. I've returned to one of my favorite childhood pastimes—fishing. I bought a summer house and fish every chance I get. Spend any time around me and I'll inevitably bring up the importance of sleep hygiene. I put my family and my mental and physical health first. I've reckoned with the past by taking it head-on, unpacking our history and shining light on the shadows that have stalked us. It's been therapeutic. I've also had to just slow down and breathe and be intentional about breaking down stress as it comes and not try to pack pieces of it here and there. The stories I've told in this book, and those I've left out, will always sit in me. But I've learned to unpack them to lighten my load.

A week or so before my trip to Martha's Vineyard, Nola and her mother joined some friends of ours there while I was on a fishing trip with some of my old Milton Hershey School buddies in Florida. They sent back photos of Nola being the most beautiful carefree Black girl I'd ever seen, her hoodie up, ice cream cone in hand, cell phone in the other, bouncing from the arcade to the Inkwell, the traditional Black beach on the Vineyard. I couldn't help but think about myself at her age and the trouble I'd already seen by then. Or to see her swimming in the pool and think about my friend Latoya, who died because she couldn't. As I've grown in these post–heart attack years, so has Nola. She'll be in high school soon, and I'm so proud of the young lady she's becoming. She's smart and curious and has a deep well of gumption. She is *somebody*, and she knows it.

I want Nola to inherit a world without the incessant snatching of Black life, unburdened by the weight of the past and the role the gun has played in our deaths. As much as this story has been my own to tell, I know that my not-so-little girl will find a way to write her own postscript. She wants to be a journalist one day, to tell stories that matter, just like her dad. These days, when she asks about life and how it ends, I tell her there are a thousand ways to die, and even more ways to live.

Acknowledgments

I've told the story of my mother looking me in the eyes and telling me, "I Am Somebody," more times than I can count. And there's no doubt I'll tell it again. It's amazing what believing her has done for me. It gave me confidence, purpose, and a deep belief that I am worthy of every good thing that has ever happened or will ever happen to me. Her words put a shield around my spirit, a suit of armor around my self-worth, and a sword of ambition in my hand. All these years later, I still believe I Am Somebody.

But now, in these grown-man years, I know it's true not just because my mother said so. I know it because of the village—family, friends, believers—who never once let me think I was anything less than somebody. I AM because WE ARE. I am the result of every prayer spoken over my name, every ounce of hope and pride poured into me, and every opportunity I was gifted. I owe an unpayable debt to every person who believed in me when there was no hard proof that my dreams were worth investing in.

That unshakable belief in me, and in the dream of becoming a writer, made this moment—this book—possible.

To my mother, Wanda Taylor, thank you for giving me the confidence to show up as I am, and for trusting me to tell our family's story with honesty, respect, and dignity. I owe a spiritual debt to my great-uncles Cornelius and MacClinton Woods, and to my grandfather Horace Worthington Sr., whose spirits guided me every step of the way. Grandmom Ida, your faith made all of this, and all of us, possible.

To my wife, Gabrielle Maple Lee, and my daughter, Nola Lee, thank you for your grace, space, and patience when I needed them most. Nola, baby girl, you have been my greatest inspiration. Know that there is power in telling OUR stories. Never forget that ours is a beautiful struggle. Don't be afraid to fight!

To my agent, Jennifer Gates, you were the first to believe in this book, back when it was just a seed called *Million Dollar Bullets*. You always said whatever I wrote would be special, and you manifested that seed's growth. Thank you for helping me trust the process and trust myself.

To my editor at St. Martin's Press, Elisabeth Dyssegaard, thank you for your patience, your commitment, and your steadiness. You stood by me year after year, even after I nearly lost my life and during the long road back when I sat the project down. This book could have died then, but you refused to let it.

Professor Blair L. M. Kelley, when I found myself tangled in the weeds of this story, you helped me cut free to the heart and soul of the work. My sister, you reminded me that everything I needed was already inside me (and in the mountain of words I'd written over the past decade). Thank you for helping me carve it out.

Thank you to New America and Emerson Collective for supporting this project in its earliest stages. Your support helped put a battery in my back.

To the many people I interviewed for this book and throughout the course of my career—those whose stories made it to the page and those whose didn't—and to the loved ones lost and those still with us, I will forever carry pieces of you in my heart. But I want to offer a special thank-you to the late Kevin Johnson and his mother Janice Jackson-Burke. Thank you, Kevin, for showing me that the light of love and hope cannot be dimmed, no matter how dark the circumstance. I will never forget you. And Janice, thank you for allowing me the privilege of revealing a bit of your family's incredibly tough journey. We shared but a moment, but it changed me in ways I cannot fully articulate. Without you and Kevin, this book would never be.

To my big sister Erica Jones and big brother Oliver Lee, I know you've always had my back, no matter how far your baby brother has gone to make his own way in life.

Thank you to my best friends—my brothers from other mothers—who I've known since I was twelve and who keep me rooted: Omokhape "Martin" Agbuigui, Bernard Adams, and Rasheed Muse. Your friendship has buoyed me through the most challenging times while I was writing this book. The celebrations. The fishing trips. The concerts. The running. The accountability. The hundreds of games of *Madden* that kept me distracted from the stress of it all. (Marty Mar, your reign on top was short like leprechauns. The champ is here!) The conversations, and even the stretches of silence. All of it was necessary and appreciated as I embarked on this Herculean effort that tested me in ways I never showed the world.

Finally, I must thank all those younger versions of myself. There were times when it wasn't clear how we'd make it or if we'd make it at all. There were so many setbacks, heartbreaks, and disappointments—but you took them all in stride. You were never defeated, despite all the challenges. Then came the wins. And they've never stopped. It's only because of you that this book is seeing the light of day. I am so very proud of what we've accomplished.

Say it with me. I Am . . .

About the Author

Wayne Lawrence

TRYMAINE LEE is a Pulitzer Prize- and Emmy Award-winning journalist and MSNBC contributor. He's the host of the *Into America* podcast, where he covers the intersection of Blackness, power, and politics. A contributing author to the 1619 Project, he has reported for *The New York Times, HuffPost,* and *The Times-Picayune/The New Orleans Advocate. A Thousand Ways to Die* is his first book.